A Touchstone Book

PAPERS ON THE WAR

BY

Daniel Ellsberg

SIMON AND SCHUSTER
New York

For permission to reprint certain material in this book, grateful acknowledgment is extended to:

Harper & Row, Publishers, for "The American Way of War," from *No More Vietnams? The War and the Future of American Foreign Policy*, edited by Richard M. Pfeffer, copyright © 1968 by the Adlai Stevenson Institute of International Affairs.

Holt, Rinehart and Winston, Inc., for "On War Crimes" and "On My Lai," from *War Crimes and the American Conscience*, edited by Erwin Knoll and Judith Nies McFadden, copyright © 1970 by *Congressional Forum*.

The Macmillan Company, for material from Albert Speer's *Inside the Third Reich*, copyright © 1969 by Verlag Ullstein GmbH.; copyright © 1970 by The Macmillan Company.

The New York Review of Books, for "Murder in Laos," originally published as "Laos: What Nixon Is Up To," in Vol. XVI, No. 4, March 11, 1971; copyright © 1971 by Daniel Ellsberg.

Washington Post, for "The Lost Counterrevolution," originally published as a review of Robert Shaplen's *The Road to War* in the *Washington Post*, November 4, 1970; copyright © 1970 by the *Washington Post*.

First Printing

SBN 671-21185-4 Casebound edition
SBN 671-21186-2 Touchstone paperback edition
Library of Congress Catalog Card Number: 72-81350
Designed by Irving Perkins
Manufactured in the United States of America
By The Book Press, Inc., Brattleboro, Vermont

*For the children of Indochina
and for our own children*

ACKNOWLEDGMENTS

Obviously a book that spans as much of my experience as this one places me in the debt of many people for their instruction and inspiration. There are some who would be embarrassed in their careers or even subpoenaed if their contribution to my work were acknowledged. Many of those, however, to whom I owe most have already paid this price and can be mentioned here. Some have already been through the courts or in prison for their resistance to the war: Tran Ngoc Chau, Randy Kehler, Burt Wallrich, Vinnie McGee, Frank Kroncke, Eqbal Ahmad, Dave Hawk, Noam Chomsky, Howard Zinn. Others are among the former colleagues who have taught me most with respect to the content of this book, although we may have come to disagree on various matters: Harry Rowen, the late John T. McNaughton, Edward G. Lansdale, John Vann, Frank Scotton, Dick Moorsteen, Vu Van Thai, Konrad Kellen, Hoang Van Chi, Jim Thomson, Mort Halperin, and Les Gelb. Also I want to thank Everett Hagen and the Center for International Studies at M.I.T., who encouraged and supported this work; Joan Hawk and Bob Silvers for their helpful advice; and Ted Solotaroff, for his patient and painstaking editing under difficult circumstances. And these others: my father and brother; Robert and Mary; Janaki; my comrade, Tony Russo; our defense team; and my partner, lover and closest friend, Patricia.

CONTENTS

INTRODUCTION

For over seven years, like many other Americans I have been pre-occupied with our involvement in Vietnam. In that time I have seen it first as a problem; then as a stalemate; then as a crime.

Each of these perspectives called for a different mode of personal commitment: a problem, to help solve it; a stalemate, to help extricate ourselves with grace; a crime, to expose and resist it, to try to stop it immediately, to seek moral and political change.

None of these aims—mine or, I would suppose, anyone else's—has met with success. It may be that five individuals, our Presidents from Truman to Nixon, should be excepted from this generalization, if I am right in concluding that each of them aimed mainly to avoid a definitive failure, "losing Indochina to Communism" during his tenure, so that renewed stalemate has been for them a kind of success. For the rest of us, efforts to *end* the conflict—whether it is seen as failed test, quagmire, or moral disaster—have been no more rewarded than efforts to win it. We fail or tire, it persists.

There are some who have been resisting for years, by a variety of means, what they saw clearly as an unjust war, a brutal fraud, a lawless imperial adventure. I deeply respect their courage, their insight, and commitment; I have, belatedly, joined them in spirit and action; indeed, although most Americans do not admire "antiwar activists," polls now indicate that a majority agree with them that the war is morally wrong. But the war persists. Why?

9

Is it simply because the forces maintaining the war are too strong? Too strong, say, to be defeated "quickly": i.e., by seven years of teach-ins and demonstrations, five years of large-scale draft resistance and emigration, four years of universal disillusionment (the Tet offensive took place four years ago this spring!); by an electoral drive in the primaries that unseated an incumbent President (again, four years ago), the creation of a mood among voters that defeated his designated successor and produced a Presidential mandate to "end the war"; by another year, 1969-70, that saw the largest demonstrations yet, two years of unprecedented legislative challenges in the Senate (though not yet to defense appropriations), the largest action of nonviolent civil disobedience in U.S. history (producing 13,000 arrests in May, 1971, mostly illegal); by the draft board raids of the Catholic Left, small mutinies in Vietnam, the My Lai prosecutions; by twenty-five years of continuous resistance by the Vietnamese, making even the largest, most violent phase—from 1965 to the present—our longest war? Is more of just this opposition what is called for; is it simply too soon to expect an end?

Perhaps. In any case, without each of these forms of protest and resistance (except of the Vietnamese), the war might well be even larger and more murderous than it has been. Yet perhaps the failure to end the war reflects not only the undoubtedly great strength of the forces sustaining it, but reflects, as well, the limits and defects of the best current understanding of those forces and of the overall system in which they operate: an inadequate grasp of all the motives and institutions that matter, and of their vulnerabilities to change. That is not so necessarily; but I believe that it is the case. As the war goes on, the meaning of its nature and of its continuance becomes more and more challenging.

In my opinion this war, even at this late stage, needs not only to be resisted; it remains to be understood.

I am speaking of the limitations not only of public awareness but of the best analyses by "experts"—former officials, radical critics, journalists, or academic specialists. No one known to me—and that includes myself—seems to possess as yet an adequate comprehension of the forces, institutions, motives, beliefs, and decisions that have led us as a nation to do what we have done to the people of Indochina as long as we have. No one seems to have an understanding fully adequate, that is, either to wage successful opposition against the process or effectively change it; or even adequate to the intellectual challenge of resolving the major puzzles and controversies about the way the process works today and has worked for at least the past quarter-century.

Each failure of political opposition to the war has challenged the adequacy of earlier explanations. Each has suggested the need for a broader, deeper, in this sense more radical, appreciation of the "stalemate machine": the system of factors that support the war process and each other. Indeed, so-called "radical" analysts have had less backtracking to do in recent years than most others, having seen and reported the nature of the war with an uncommon clarity. The writing of Noam Chomsky and Gabriel Kolko, and of the "revisionist" historians of the Cold War following the lead of William Appleman Williams' *The Tragedy of American Diplomacy* (New York, 1962), powerfully illuminates the economic and corporate motives underlying our defense budget and our militarized, imperialist foreign policy.[1] Yet these works seem least enlightening about the causes of our specific intervention in Vietnam, and its continuation. ("The war is essentially over," one radical critic from the West Coast told me in the fall of 1970, "because both Wall Street and the generals have turned against it." I agreed with him on the shifts in the factors he described. Yet it did not seem to me to be over.)

If these studies, too, seem far from satisfactory, perhaps the main reason is that they tend to neglect the roles both of the bureaucracy and, more importantly it seems to me, of the U.S. domestic political system, including the special role of the President. It is these last factors that are emphasized in two of the principal essays here, "The Quagmire Myth and the Stalemate Machine" and "Murder in Laos." I recognize, however, that both essays leave unanswered important questions concerning broader social and economic interests that

[1] Two good overall accounts from this point of view of the period since World War II are Walter Lafeber's *America, Russia, and the Cold War 1945-1967* (New York, 1967) and Stephen Ambrose's recent *Rise to Globalism* (Baltimore, 1971). Also see the concluding essay in *Cold War Essays* (New York, 1969) by Gar Alperowitz, and Carl Oglesby's "Vietnam Crucible" in *Containment and Change* by Oglesby and Richard Shaull (Toronto, 1967). For a useful critique of this approach, see Robert Tucker, *The Radical Left and American Foreign Policy* (Baltimore, 1971).

may influence the political and bureaucratic fears that seem to me directly to drive policy.[2]

One problem is that few analysts personally command experience or data concerning more than a few of the many dimensions of this process. Another is the relative lack of specialized studies in some of these areas, e.g., on the domestic politics of U.S. foreign policy. Above all, crucial data on the bureaucratic decision process have been closely guarded, limited to a few analysts—I was one—and publicly lied about.

I repeat the premise: efforts at better understanding cannot be put off till the triumph of resistance, the end of the war (any more than continued resistance can await a perfect understanding).

It was in this belief that I undertook, beginning in the fall of 1969, to reveal to Congress and the American people the documents and analyses that came to be known as the Pentagon Papers. That was, of course, itself an act of resistance, but of a particular sort, aimed at a broader and ultimately better understanding of the war process. And it is in that same spirit that I offer these essays.

Like the Pentagon Papers themselves, they are limited, incomplete, at most a useful contribution to a discussion that must occupy many different voices for many years. Far from purporting to be the last word, they are not my own last words on any subject, or even, in many cases, my most recent thinking. The greater part of my research since the fall of 1970 has gone toward deepening my historical understanding of some critical subjects touched upon in the principal essay included here, "The Quagmire Myth and the Stalemate Machine": in particular, the origins, development, and politics of the Cold War, China policy, and McCarthyism. None of this study has invalidated any of the conjectures presented in that essay —on the contrary, I am now more confident of them, so far as

---

[2] To be specific: I am increasingly convinced of the direct influence on officials' behavior—as argued in these essays—of fears of a McCarthyite "right-wing backlash" if they should be associated with "losing Indochina." But how realistic have those fears been over the last decade? Why do those officials act on them still without testing their reality? And why do they so often act, in addressing the public, to give them greater reality? Whose interests, finally, are served by a policy adapted to those fears and a society organized around them? My recent research has made these further questions seem highly cogent; my answers are yet very tentative, and in any case they will have to await further research.

they go—but it has enabled me to see our Vietnam involvement in a much broader context of Cold War policy and of U.S. interventions in the Third World. Having arrived at some tentative conclusions on these matters over the last year, it is frustrating to contemplate releasing a book—based on papers done earlier—that reflects this later work only in small part and that does not fully exploit the general accessibility, at last, of the documents in the Pentagon Papers.

But it is this book or nothing for quite a long time, as I have at last come to acknowledge. Events in my life since June, 1971, have not been conducive to the production of new, finished essays, though I spent most of the fall in the effort, filling files with notes and drafts. Meanwhile the indictment against me is not winding down any more than the bombing is winding down; the most recent set of legal charges, increasing the original two counts to a dozen, resolved my dilemma for the immediate future. For the next six months my further contributions to public understanding of the issues of the war must be through the medium of the trial, or trials, rather than by extending these writings.

But these are merely an author's private misgivings. Had I time to present here my latest conjectures, the results would still have been tentative, incomplete, transitional. If my thinking on the Cold War and other matters is not what it was last year, when the last of these essays was written, it is not what it will be next year either. Meanwhile, the war goes on and demands to be understood: and there is no doubt in my mind that these pieces have their contribution to make to that evolving understanding.

This, then, is a book about U.S. policy in the war: not about me, or how I revealed the Pentagon Papers, or even about the Pentagon Papers themselves.

I have added prefaces that indicate the original circumstances of my writing each piece, and the remainder of this Introduction presents more general background. But the pieces—except for those, written in Vietnam, grouped together as "Background: Vietnam, 1965-1967"—have not been chosen to illustrate any major development in my thinking; for that, much more would have to be included from the preceding five years, as well as a number of other public statements or memoranda written between 1969 and 1971, most of it of very narrow interest today.

These recent papers stand on their own as separate, complementary discussions of various aspects of current policy, each one in my opinion still valid within its own terms. Together they comprise a fairly coherent viewpoint at which I arrived between the late summer of 1969 and the fall of 1970 and have not changed substantially since.

All of these papers were written prior to June 13, 1971, when the *New York Times* began publishing documents from the McNamara Study; none of them, regrettably, was written on the assumption that readers would have these documents available for reference. But except for the "Background" section, all of the pieces were written after the fall of 1969, when I completed reading the Pentagon Papers.[3] Thus, they all reflect and draw directly, though tacitly, upon my knowledge of that entire study (including parts not yet made public).

The interpretations and hypotheses in these essays also reflect my research and governmental experience over the decade prior to the Pentagon Papers. This includes studies of "decision-making under uncertainty";[4] of Presidential "command and control";[5] and of

---

[3] Hereafter the phrase "the Pentagon Papers," not in italics, will be used to refer to the documents and analyses, whether yet made public or not, that comprised the output of the McNamara study group (discussed in the following). Citations to my main source of references, *The Senator Gravel Edition: The Pentagon Papers,* 4 vols., Beacon Press (Boston, 1971), will be abbreviated as follows: *PP,* followed by volume and page numbers. Citations of the Government Printing Office version, declassified for the House Armed Services Committee by the Department of Defense, entitled *U.S.-Vietnam Relations, 1945-1967,* 12 vols., will be abbreviated *GPO,* followed by volume and page numbers. The *New York Times* account, *The Pentagon Papers,* Bantam Books (New York, 1971), with far fewer documents than either of these editions, will not be used here as a reference.

[4] This was the subject of my Harvard honors thesis in 1952 and of my Ph.D. thesis in 1962 (both in economics). My Ph.D. thesis on subjective probability and statistical inference—entitled "Risk, Ambiguity, and Decision" (Harvard University, June, 1962)—begins: "To act reasonably one must judge actions by their consequences. But what if their consequences are uncertain? One must still, no doubt, act reasonably: the problem is to decide what this may mean." The summary opens: "How is it reasonable to choose among alternative actions when information bearing on their possible consequences is highly ambiguous: scanty, marked by gaps, or obscure and vague, of dubious relevance or contradictory import?"

These conditions, of course, characterize virtually all major defense fields. It was in part this very interest of mine that led the Rand Corporation to invite me, while a Junior Fellow at Harvard, to spend the summer of 1958 as a consultant, and in 1959 to join the Economics Department full-time. Over the next ten years, a recurrent theme of my consulting to officials was to be: "The future is even

Presidential decision-making in specific crises.[6] It also includes my actual experience in the Pentagon as Special Assistant to the Assistant Secretary of Defense (International Security Affairs), in the election-and-escalation period 1964-65; and in my two years in Vietnam, 1965-67, as a State Department volunteer on General Edward Lansdale's senior liaison team, and then as Special Assistant to the Deputy Ambassador, William Porter.

All of this experience made it natural for me on my return from Vietnam to be urged, and to agree, to participate from the outset in the McNamara task force studying "the history of United States involvement in Vietnam from World War II to the present."[7] At a later period I was, in fact, the only researcher in the country with authorized access to the completed McNamara Study. Indeed, it was these earlier interests in studying the decision-making process that had brought me to join the Defense Department full-time in 1964 and were among my motives in going to Vietnam in 1965.

A letter which I wrote from Saigon in June, 1966, to Secretary McNamara (with whom I had worked closely on several occasions since 1961) expresses my long-time concern to understand policy-making. It begins:

One of my main motivations in leaving John McNaughton's office to come to Vietnam last August was a feeling that a year of reading official cables from that country had not satisfied my "need to know" about the nature of the problems there. Too many events came—to me, and, it seemed, to others

---

more uncertain than you think: and so is the present, and the past. Now, what is it useful to do in face of that?"

[5] For Rand, and as a member of the CINCPAC Command and Controls Study, 1959-60, and of the [General] Partridge Task Force on Presidential Command and Control in 1961, among others. These all dealt with protecting and assuring the President's control of nuclear forces, and the prevention of "unauthorized actions" (the "Strangelove/Fail-Safe" problem).

[6] My background on problems of nuclear posture and control led to my participation in both the Defense and State staff working groups serving the Executive Committee of the National Security Council during the Cuban missile crisis of 1962. In 1964 I was sole researcher on a project sponsored by Walt Rostow, then Chairman of the Policy Planning Council of the State Department, to study patterns in high-level decision-making in crises, with unprecedented access to data and studies in all agencies on past episodes such as the missile crisis, Suez, the Skybolt decision, Berlin, and the U-2 incident. My work on general war problems had first focused my attention on the transcendent role of the President, further confirmed by this study of major crises.

[7] See the "Letter of Transmittal of the Study" (*PP*, I, XV) for a brief account of the project by the official in charge of it, Leslie H. Gelb.

in the building—as surprises, too much behavior seemed puzzling and un-motivated, the reasons for our persistent failures and setbacks there seemed too uncertain. At the end of a year's work on Vietnam affairs I felt scarcely more educated on the situation than at the beginning. I took the chance to come to Vietnam with General Lansdale as, in large part, an opportunity to reduce that ignorance.

After only a few months I was fully convinced of what I had suspected before: that official reporting (including Nodis and Eyes Only, Back Channel and what-have-you[8]) is grossly inadequate to the job of educating high-level decision-makers to the nature of the essential problems here. It did not tell them what they needed to know. Nor did official, high-level visits to Vietnam (though somewhat better) in practice fill that lack. Nor are there reports to be read in Saigon that answer the questions; to rely entirely on the official reporting to Saigon from the field (as many high officials in Saigon do) is to remain untutored on many critical problems of Vietnam, as I felt, and was, in Washington.

The purpose of the letter was to urge him to supplement his read-ing and visits by private, frank talks with knowledgeable "Vietnam hands" on their occasional returns to the States: I gave him a list of those from whom I had learned the most (headed by John Paul Vann; see the pieces under "Background: Vietnam 1965-1967").

What I had learned, by June, 1966, or before it, was that the war was stalemated. By the next year I knew it would remain so. Two years of field work had discredited, in my eyes, any hopes of suc-cess, in almost any terms, in Vietnam, given the courses we were following and the increasingly obvious unlikelihood of our changing them. The prospect I saw was one of continued conflict, at increas-

---

[8] These are designators on cables and memoranda—separate from "classifica-tion," though usually associated with Top Secret or Secret classification—indicat-ing the highest degree of "sensitivity," demanding that the document must be "closely held": in principle, seen only by the addressee. Thus, the first signifies No Distribution (in contrast, say, to "Limdis," or Limited Distribution, to be seen by a designated, narrow group of officials); the second, "For the eyes only of the addressee." "Back Channel" means "sent over intelligence circuits," which ensures specially "secure" handling for sensitive messages: e.g., for messages between the Chairman of the Joint Chiefs and the Commander in Vietnam that the Secretary of Defense was meant definitely not to see. (Examples would be the messages reproduced or paraphrased by Marvin Kalb and Elie Abel, in their book *Vietnam: The Roots of Intervention,* between Generals Wheeler and West-moreland after Tet, 1968; these are not to be found in the Pentagon Papers be-cause they were never available to the Office of the Secretary of Defense.) During one period while I was a Special Assistant in the Pentagon, I directed the Message Center of ISA (International Security Affairs) to limit the "traffic" sent to me daily to Top Secret, Nodis/Limdis, and Eyes Only messages on Southeast Asia; this cut my daily reading load to two piles of paper about two and a half feet high.

ing levels of violence, followed some day—probably later rather than sooner, and after more and more deaths, costs, destruction, and dissension at home—by U.S. withdrawal and NLF dominance.

It was not to find this—or to find out the shortcomings of American officials, practices and policies that seemed heavily at fault—that I had come to Vietnam two years earlier. The process of reaching these conclusions was, quite simply, the most frustrating, disappointing, disillusioning period of my life. I had come to Vietnam to learn, but also to help us succeed; and the learning was as bitter as the failure.

Yet my observations in Vietnam did not, in themselves, discredit the intentions of the policy-makers or the legitimacy of our original involvement, despite our evident "mistakes." The explanation that inadequate, misguided policies in Washington had been based on "bad information" from Vietnam seemed almost inescapable, watching the cable traffic from the transmitting end of the channel. It is easy for most Americans to guess that the President receives misleadingly optimistic reports from the field; in Vietnam, it is easy to *know* this is so.

I came to spend much of my time driving the roads on personal field trips—and on some occasions, accompanying, in order to observe, Vietnamese or U.S. troops operating in jungles and rice paddies—simply because there was no other reliable way to get at realities screened out by successive "progress"-hungry headquarters as field reports flowed upward.

In April, 1967, writing suggestions to an old associate, Robert Komer, who was coming to Vietnam to take charge of all civil field operations, I emphasized this problem:

One of the things that most need changing is the state of *ignorance* of Vietnam and the nature of our problems here that has managed to perpetuate itself over the years at the Mission Council level. . . .

. . . In addition to absorbing information from all of these sources, you should do something that no other high-level American administrator connected with Vietnam has ever done, to discourage the bureaucratic practices that poison this flow of information. You should take stringent steps to *punish lying,* evasion, and the concealing of information. You should make no apologies whatever for exploiting to the fullest informal channels of information, to check official reporting; bypassing layers of command and utilizing special representatives as fact-finders; responding in a harsh and discouraging way to every instance, military and civilian, of (a) lying to you and the President, or (b) encouraging or requiring subordinates to lie to you and the President.

The urgent need to circumvent the lying and the self-deception was, for me, one of the "lessons of Vietnam"; a broader one was that there were situations—Vietnam was an example—in which the U.S. Government, starting ignorant, did not, would not, *learn*. There was a whole set of what amounted to institutional "anti-learning" mechanisms working to preserve and guarantee unadaptive and unsuccessful behavior: the fast turnover in personnel; the lack of institutional memory at any level; the failure to study history, to analyze or even record operational experience or mistakes; the effective pressures for optimistically false reporting at every level, for describing "progress" rather than problems or failure, thus concealing the very need for change in approach or for learning. Well, helping the U.S. Government learn—in this case, learn how to learn —was something, perhaps, I could do; that had been my business. Meanwhile I had gotten hepatitis in late March and was confined to bed until June. Although Komer and other new officials who came out to take over the pacification program in mid-1967 asked me to stay on, the need to recuperate would keep me out of the field for at least six months; in those circumstances, I decided to return to research in the States.

As I prepared to leave Saigon at the end of May, 1967, I wrote to a high official in the Defense Department, a close friend, suggesting among other things that he propose to Secretary McNamara personally two sorts of studies: a set of case histories of field projects in Vietnam; and a high-level study of U.S. decision-making in Vietnam "on the model of Dick Neustadt's study of the Skybolt crisis," a pioneering study for President Kennedy (to which I had contributed informally in 1963). I said that I would be willing to consult on the first, and to participate in or head the second, if my health permitted. A few weeks later, Secretary McNamara himself proposed his historical study, mentioning the Neustadt Skybolt study as a guideline. I spent the late summer "debriefing" to high officials in Washington, and in effect lobbying—unsuccessfully—to change our support for Thieu in the upcoming Vietnamese presidential election toward a policy of extrication. By fall, once again employed by Rand, I was at work on the McNamara Study.

My own intellectual interests have always been analytical, rather than directed toward "telling the story," an historical narrative of events and decisions. But analysis needs detailed narratives to work with, case studies to compare and from which to generalize, and these did not yet exist for Vietnam. For reasons of health, as well as interest, I would have preferred to enter the project at a later, analytical stage; but Leslie Gelb, given the task of producing the studies and being shorthanded in researchers, warned me that access to the final reports for further analysis would be limited to those who had worked on them.

To all the anti-learning mechanisms operating at the field level, the high-level decision-making process adds the barrier of extreme secrecy. My earlier study of crisis decisions had reflected and confirmed my conviction that a prerequisite to improving the government's performance was that it become self-aware, that it begin systematically to discover and analyze its own "hidden history." Openings to that secret past came rarely. Now suddenly a disillusioned Secretary, six years into a lost war that had once been labeled his, had pulled together cables and papers of a generation of officials from all parts of the government into file-safes in a single room near his office, to be read for weeks or months—no one knew how long—and then destroyed or scattered back to their sources. Despite some misgivings among Rand officials about lending my efforts to a study to which Rand as an institution would never have access, and despite my frustratingly slow recuperation, I felt that the "price" of drafting a volume of the study had to be met. I chose the Kennedy commitments of 1961 to study, and I started by sifting through the Pentagon files of the 1950's.

The 1961 period was one of which I knew little and wanted to know more. My first visit to Saigon had been in the fall of 1961, shortly before the Taylor-Rostow mission, described at length in "The Quagmire Myth and the Stalemate Machine," for an intensive week of discussions as part of a Department of Defense "Task Force on Limited War Research and Development." What we neard then about the regime of President Ngo Dinh Diem seemed so unpromising as a basis for any additional U.S. involvement that—after

writing an internal memo at Rand on my return about the "dilemmas" of counterinsurgency—I paid almost no further attention either
to counterinsurgency or to Vietnam in the next few years, while I
worked on problems of general war, international crisis, and NATO
policy. (I did not even follow Vietnam events closely in the newspapers, until that became part of the full-time preoccupation with
Vietnam to which I was assigned by Assistant Secretary McNaughton
when I became his Special Assistant in mid-1964.) When President
Kennedy, after the Taylor-Rostow mission, decided to increase our
commitment by sending U.S. advisors[9] and support elements, I assumed he must have received far more encouraging reports about
the situation and the adequacy of such measures from Taylor and
Rostow than our visiting team had heard at the staff working level.
That would hardly have been unusual; and it was this interpretation
of Kennedy's decisions that appeared in virtually all later journalistic
accounts.

Thus, the hypothesis I brought to the data on 1961 was the familiar one, in line with my own field experience in 1965-67. This
was essentially the "quagmire" model: that optimistic operational
reporting plus ill-founded assurances from advisers in Washington
had confirmed for President Kennedy, mistakenly, the adequacy of
the course recommended to him, which was the one he chose.

I knew from journalistic accounts that reassuring operational reporting and optimistic military proposals of the sort I had witnessed
in 1966-67 had likewise been characteristics of 1962-63, the late
1950's, and the period just before Dien Bien Phu. Like many others,
I assumed this to be true, as well, of our critical years of commitment: to the French effort in 1950; to Diem in 1954; and in 1961.
I knew from my own year in the Pentagon that it was not true for
1964-65, but I imagined this to have been an exceptional crisis of
pessimism. I was wrong.

What I found, instead, in the cables and memos in the file-safes
is essentially described in "The Quagmire Myth and the Stalemate
Machine." The starting point for its analytical speculation is what
I described in a working paper written for Gelb in late November,
1967, as one of the major findings of my research: "the ultimate dis-

---

[9] Here and throughout, "advisor" refers specifically to American military serving with Vietnamese, "adviser" to all other customary uses of the term.

crepancies between the Presidential policy emerging in November and December, 1961, and the policies recommended by high-level advisers either in the State or Defense Departments." I continued:

In effect, the President reasserted U.S. commitment to preexisting aims, and considerably increased U.S. involvement by increasing advisors and combat support, while forgoing *every one* of the elements urged by one or another high-level adviser as *essential* to adequate chances of success: e.g., *U.S. combat forces in Vietnam;* Vietnamese political and administrative reforms; changes in ARVN command organization; strengthened U.S. leverage or partnership in decision-making; or U.S. combat forces in Laos.

One need not find such Presidential decisions paradoxical or perverse, as though his subordinates' judgments must be accepted as a matter of course. On the contrary, to have followed their advice on combat troops then would probably have led even sooner to the costly failures that they correctly predicted to be the result of continuing our involvement *without* following their advice. One cannot, then, infer that the President's judgment was worse or better than that of his advisers; but it was clearly *different*.

What is evident is that the President's role was not passive, "inadvertent," nonresponsible; it did not merely reflect bureaucratic pressures, or optimistic reporting, or assurances of the adequacy of his chosen course. Contrary to most public accounts, the last two elements simply were not present in 1961. Nor were they—I found to my surprise as I looked through past intelligence estimates—present in 1950 or 1954-55. I knew already that neither optimism nor assurances had existed in late 1964 or early 1965; that year turned out to be not so exceptional after all, as a year of crisis and escalation. In each of these years of decision, what stood out from among the internal documents was the President's personal responsibility for the particular policy chosen. And in each case, as in 1961, this fact of his responsibility was concealed from the public by misleading accounts of the internal matrix of advice and predictions on which he supposedly based his decision.[10]

---

[10] Most recently, this was again the nature and import of the Nixon Administration's deception exposed by the "Anderson Papers" on the President's position with respect to the India-Pakistan war. The public had been misled not so much about what the President was doing as about why he was doing it, the purposes he pursued, and on what advice—in particular, the discrepancy between his views and values and those of most advisers. Hence, the electorate was misled about what was to be expected from him in the future and how his judgments and those of his advisers were to be judged.

Whatever it was each President thought privately he might achieve from what he had decided to do, it must have differed from the written estimates and much of the advice he was receiving in those years; it could not simply be the product of bureaucratic euphoria or deception. Indeed, in each of those crisis years—in contrast to the years in-between—there had been enough realistic intelligence analyses and even operational reporting available to the President that it was hard to imagine that *more* truth-telling or even pessimism would have made any difference to his choices.

Could it be, then, that none of the lying to the Presidents had mattered? Or that it had mainly mirrored and supported their own deception of Congress and the public? If each President had been told at the point of escalation—as it appeared from the record— that what he was ordering would probably not solve the problem, what then was he up to? Why did he not do more—or less? And why did each President mislead the public and Congress about what he was doing and what he had been told?

In any one of these years, one could find specific, *ad hoc* reasons that seemed sufficient to explain the President's choice in that particular case. Thus, my draft[11] on the 1961 decisions emphasized among other things Kennedy's desire in the fall of 1961 not to discredit the ongoing Laos negotiations either in Hanoi (by putting U.S. combat troops into Vietnam) or in the Pentagon (by not increasing our involvement in Vietnam at all). Yet working through additional volumes of the Pentagon Papers as they became available, what came to need explaining was the recurrence of similar crises, of similar sets of alternatives, and of similar patterns of Presidential choice, responsibility, and deception, across the administrations of four Presidents. A coherent explanation seemed called for. I puzzled over what it might be at Rand in 1968 and 1969, on a project funded by the Defense Department to draw general "lessons of Vietnam" that could enlighten Executive policy-makers in future times, future places. I had not yet drawn the lesson that it was the power and practices of the Executive branch itself and the interests sustaining

[11] Completed by early 1968 and considerably rewritten, like most of the volumes, by a second analyst for the final report: see *PP*, II, "The Kennedy Commitments and Programs, 1961," pp. 1-127.

these—rather than any shortage of information or insight within the Executive—that was perpetuating the war.

Once I had concluded, in 1967, that we were not going to succeed in Vietnam, I worked actively toward ending our involvement. I did so as a private citizen, but all my background led me to work behind the scenes and almost exclusively with actual and prospective Executive officials and their staffs; these included a number of Presidential candidates and their advisers, and finally, at the end of 1968, the National Security Council staff of the new President-elect.

Indeed, on Christmas Day, 1968, two colleagues from Rand and I flew to New York for discussions with Henry Kissinger, at the President-elect's office at the Hotel Pierre. Kissinger had requested in early December that Rand present the incoming President with a range of policy "options" on Vietnam, and I had been in charge of defining these and coordinating the work.

In January, a second version of the "options" paper, edited by a Rand colleague, was the basis for the first discussion of Vietnam policy at the opening meeting of the National Security Council in the new Administration. In retrospect, the one substantive change between the two drafts, made at Kissinger's request, takes on some significance. Five Rand colleagues had previously expounded and proposed a policy of "extrication"—a U.S. commitment to total, unilateral withdrawal by a fixed date—to the preceding Administration. I did not myself favor adopting such a policy before the onset of negotiations. I preferred first to test the possibilities in Paris of a negotiated mutual withdrawal of U.S. and North Vietnamese forces; but I included their draft of its pros and cons among the options presented, despite some misgivings expressed by Kissinger. His misgivings were intensified when a military adviser to the President-elect disdained even to comment on this one option, and at Kissinger's request it was omitted entirely from the second, edited draft that went to the National Security Council. Thus, all of the "complete range of options"—as the study was described to the press—considered formally by the new Administration in January made U.S. extrication contingent upon decisions in Hanoi and Saigon, omitting mention of any policy that guaranteed withdrawal: which was to be the approach endorsed, within twenty months, by 73 percent of the electorate.

Meanwhile, also in January, 1969, a set of questions I had proposed and drafted in order to elicit major uncertainties and controversies among the agencies dealing with Vietnam was sent to
each of them by Kissinger as "National Security Study Memorandum
No. 1" (NSSM-1: the first of a series of studies for the President that
by now numbers more than a hundred). I spent February in the
Executive Office Building reading and helping to summarize the
answers, which ran over a thousand pages, for the President.

This period of late 1968 and early 1969 was one of enemy quiescence, and thus—following the "Phase B" pattern described in
"The Quagmire Myth and the Stalemate Machine"—a period of
relative optimism at high levels in Defense and State. But as always,
there were more pessimistic—or more realistic, as I and others saw
it—assessments at lower levels or in agencies that did not have
primary operational responsibility and thus were not "writing their
own report cards" when they evaluated "progress." The device of
asking all of the agencies to answer separately the same questions
brought out these negative views that would otherwise have been
submerged.

No previous President dealing with Vietnam had been exposed
to such comprehensive evidence of the contradictory and uncertain
positions, and the limits and frailty of knowledge and hopes within
his bureaucracy. "We found out how ignorant we were," Kissinger
has recently been quoted, recalling NSSM-1.[12] That was precisely
the effect intended. Whatever misgivings I might have had about
working for Richard Nixon—which were not strong with respect
to Vietnam, where I hoped he might use a freer hand than a Democrat could to repudiate past policy—I had none about this contribution. Helping the President to be better informed—if only to be
less certain about some matters—seemed, simply, the most effective
service one could perform as an applied researcher working for
one's country: no less so when the problem was how to get out
of Vietnam than when it was how to succeed there.

The "lessons of Vietnam" study, to which I returned in the spring
of 1969, addressed among other things "criteria for noninterven-
tion"—warning indications of involvements we should avoid or

[12] *Newsweek*, February 7, 1972, p. 15.

terminate. Yet as late as that summer, the question "How *could* we have won in Vietnam?" still held an intellectual attraction for me, along with its counterparts: "What might the U.S. have done to improve the odds of success? When would it have had to begin? If certain goals were infeasible—at least, after some point—to what lesser aims might the Presidents reasonably have aspired?"

These are among the questions I find addressed in a working paper that I wrote in July and August of 1969, entitled "Infeasible Aims and the Politics of Stalemate." They still reveal, at that date, what Richard Barnet has described as an especially American preoccupation; in his strong words, "The American national purpose is to win." My perspective was just about to change drastically— one among several reasons being that I was soon to finish reading the Pentagon Papers—so the concerns reflected in this draft paper mark the end of a period for me.

This memo began in novelistic form, with an exchange I had had with the French General André Beaufre (at a conference of fellow Cold War strategists, members of the Institute of Strategic Studies) at Oxford in September, 1968.

The general is of a Western army whose cause was defeated by Asian Communists, a decade and a half ago. The same Asian Communists that are defeating U.S. aims in the same country, in a war the American has just left behind him. So the American listens with curiosity.

"In 1950, De Lattre de Tassigny asked me to go with him to Indochina as his deputy. I refused. He asked what I thought of his assignment. I said: 'Mon Général, you should not go there. You will lose your reputation there, and you will lose your health.'"

"And?"

"He went. I went with him. He did not lose his reputation there; but he died."

So the general is an officer who tells unwelcome truths to his superior; one who can imagine and foretell a lost war. Rare qualities, no more appreciated, surely, in the French army than in the American. ("Oh no, my views were not popular among the staff," the general says.) But how was he so wise? What had informed him?

"But I was there in 1947. At first, of course, I did not see it; but before long, before 1950, I saw that it was too late for us. The Vietnamese we might have allied with, to rally the people and confront the Communists, were dead by then. The Communist apparatus had grown too large, it penetrated too deeply. . . . It was no longer to be defeated by us."

"When, then, was your last chance? When did it become too late?"
"1947. At the latest. Perhaps 1946."
1946? It was the end of that year that the French began fighting. They fought for seven more years.

Now the American thinks of his war, the Americans' war, that started—depending on how you counted—four or five years, or a decade, from 1954.

"What year then, did it become too late—if it ever did—for the Americans?"
"1947."

I went on to comment in the memo:

In 1961 most American officials, myself included, would have known how to interpret that remark: that is, how to dismiss it. It would have meant, to us, another Frenchman telling us that what the French couldn't do, the Americans could hardly do. . . . But in 1968, his proposition demanded more attention: even from a French general, especially one who was evidently right in 1950. Eighteen years later it appeared that our differences from the French had not, after all, made that much difference.

Indeed, my memo went on to argue that the long-run goal four Presidents had chosen to pursue in Indochina—the permanent exclusion of the Indochinese Communist party from open politics, and ultimately its destruction as an organization—had always been beyond their reach. What was always likely to result from their efforts was what had happened: defeat in the North, stalemate in the South.[13] It was also likely, I was later to conclude, that each President would make this effort, nevertheless, in spite of forewarning of its dim prospects, for reasons conjectured in the essays that follow. Thus, I come later to see the two components that made up the "stalemate machine": in Vietnam, a conflict that promised to American intervention the possibility of stalemate, but almost surely noth-

[13] As an analytical conclusion, this reflects more than reasoning after the fact, though there is no counterpart piece in this book to the research memo cited above. Thus, I argued: There are historic, cultural, and political differences between the southern and northern regions of Vietnam that "permitted" the French and Americans to achieve prolonged stalemate in the South at bearable costs, while the different dynamics of the conflict in the North tended strongly to much higher, "excessive" costs for them, and to defeat: and would have done so in the North, it seems clear, even if the U.S. had entered the conflict in 1954 with troops or planes, as Nixon and Dulles urged, or with nuclear weapons, as Admiral Radford proposed.

Those differences would still operate today, to make an invasion into North Vietnam—as was considered, evidently, for the spring of 1968 and perhaps again for the spring of 1971—a catastrophe incomparably greater than even the present conflict.

ing better; in Washington, a disposition by each President in turn to choose stalemate rather than failure.

This is not to say that the four Presidents, now joined by a fifth, foresaw all this, when they looked beyond the immediate future. They did not, probably, fully comprehend or accept the long-term logic of the "stalemate machine," even though all its elements were —in a reasonable sense, reflecting documentary evidence—accessible to them,[14] and though there were, at various times, advisers who did foresee the process in much these terms.

At the time of writing that memo I still could not end without asking if some more moderate "success"—that of *containing* Communist influence in the South alone, without a U.S. troop presence —might not have been won. Even on this point the paper ended with a discouraging dialogue similar to the opening one; surprisingly, this one was with my former team leader, General Lansdale, to whom I had put this modified goal, in late 1968, after describing my exchange with Beaufre:

> The general is American . . . His views are not those of many American generals, or policy-makers. He knows more about Vietnam than any of them.
> "No, it wasn't too late for that, I don't think, in 1956. By 1958 and 1959 it was getting very late: maybe as I see it now, too late. But even in 1961, I thought then that there was a chance . . . At the same time, I can't be sure anymore; your Frenchman just may be right, even for the South. I can't say for sure he's not."
> "When, if it has, did it finally become too late for us to meet such a goal?"
> "In January, 1964: with the Khanh coup. The Minh government had some possibilities. Khanh's coup finished them. And when the Americans began to shell the villages, as they were almost bound to do, about June of '65, that confirmed it. I knew there wasn't any real hope after that."
> As in the Frenchman's memory, dates overlap for this American, and for me, with harsh irony. A "last chance" for a favorable outcome expires at least one year *before* the Americans launch their combat commitment . . . "confirmed" a few months before the American general is called, and goes, back to Vietnam. Taking me with him.

I wrote that in August, 1969: five years to the month from the Tonkin Gulf incidents, when I had joined the Defense Department;

---

[14] This is the point underlying much of Arthur Schlesinger, Jr.'s critical comments on "The Quagmire Myth" in "Eyeless in Indochina," *New York Review of Books,* October 21, 1971. I accept it as valid; I have amended my exposition correspondingly (pp. 123-25).

four years from the month I had gone with General Lansdale to Vietnam; two years since I'd come back, to work on the McNamara Study. August, 1969, was the month—Rand's affidavit to a Los Angeles grand jury reminds me—when I brought back to Santa Monica the remaining volumes of the Pentagon Papers, and the month I read what I had left until last to read: the earliest volumes, dealing with the period 1945-54—the First Indochina War, General Beaufre's war. It was to be the last month that my writings expressed a concern with how we might have won in Vietnam.

As I reread now my analyses written before mid-1969—and the writings of other strategic analysts, as well as official statements —I am struck by their tacit, unquestioned belief that we had had a *right* to "win," in ways defined by us (i.e., by the President)[15]; or, at least, a right to prolong a war, to "avoid defeat"; or at very worst, to lose only gracefully, covertly, slowly: all these, even the last, at the cost of an uncounted number of Asian lives, a toll to which our policy set no real limit.

That belief ended for me in August and September, 1969, when I had finished reading of the origins of the war: not only in the Pentagon Papers, but in books that Beaufre's comments had finally provoked me to read.[16]

---

[15] It was Noam Chomsky's *American Power and the New Mandarins* (New York, 1970), I believe, that first brought me face to face with this moral axiom of U.S. officials, which I had shared.

[16] In particular, John T. McAlister Jr., *Vietnam: The Origins of Revolution* (Princeton, 1969) and *The End of a War* by Jean Lacouture and Philippe Devillers (New York, 1969); also see Donald Lancaster, *The Emancipation of French Indochina* (London, 1961). It is noteworthy that the Devillers-Lacouture book on the Geneva negotiations of 1954, first published in French in 1960, did not become available in English for over nine years, well into the Paris talks. It took twice as long for one-third of Paul Mus' classic, *Viet Nam: sociologie d'une guerre*, first published in 1952, to appear in English in *The Vietnamese and their Revolution* by John T. McAlister, Jr., and Paul Mus (New York, 1970). To this day, Philippe Devillers' key work, *Histoire du Viet-Nam de 1940 à 1952* (Paris, 1952) has not been translated, nor have *most* of the works cited in that or in the bibliography of Devillers and Lacouture. It is fair to say that Americans in office read very few books, and none in French; and that there has never been an official of Deputy Assistant Secretary rank or higher (including myself) who could have passed in office a midterm freshman exam in modern Vietnamese history, if such a course existed in this country. (Until recently, there were two tenured professors in America who spoke Vietnamese; now, I believe, there are three.) Is this failure to translate or learn from the French to be seen as the root or the symptom of American officials' near-total ignorance of the "First Indochina War"—or one more phenomenon of their "need not to know"?

For one thing, reflection on these beginnings of our direct aid in 1950—in the context of other world events and U.S. domestic politics at the time—led to my sense of recurrent motives and patterns of policy-making, which underlies all the later essays in this book. As in later years, intelligence analysts from 1946 to 1950 portrayed with striking clarity the probable indecisiveness of French and American intervention to high officials of the Truman Administration; as later, these estimates were never conveyed to the public. Thus the President, especially after the decision to support the war directly in May, 1950, must—like each of his four successors, in similar situations—take heavy responsibility for the ensuing bloody stalemate and subsequent "crisis." Why each President exercised responsibility as he did, all in such similar fashion, is the question that occupies much of this book. But it was not only on my conceptual understanding of the process that these early volumes had a major impact. The moral implications of our Presidents' choices can hardly stand out more clearly, or in a harsher light, than in the documents of the earliest period, from 1945-1948, when the Vietnamese had just begun their struggle to retain their newly proclaimed independence.

Hoang Van Chi—a Vietnamese friend, consulting at Rand[17]—had told me in the spring of 1969, "You must understand that in the eyes of all Vietnamese, we gained our independence in March, 1945, and the French set out to *reconquer* us in the North almost two years later." I scarcely knew, then, what he was talking about; nor would, I suspect, almost any U.S. official I had worked with. (The Japanese had interned the French occupying force on March 9, 1945, and the Emperor Bao Dai proclaimed independence five months later, abdicating formally to Ho Chi Minh.) By the end of the summer I knew this story. I urgently recommend it to American readers, as told in the works I have cited.

In that reading, two quotations stand out as epigraphs to the whole of the Pentagon Papers. The first is that of Ho Chi Minh's somber plea to Jean Sainteny in the fall of 1946 in France, at the close of negotiations in which Ho had received full honors as a head of state

[17] Author of *From Colonialism to Communism* (New York, 1964), a major source on the Communist takeover in North Vietnam. Hoang Van Chi had been a Viet Minh official in the North until 1954, then served Diem, then worked for USIA.

but no assurances that the French would honor their written accords, signed on March 6 (by Sainteny, for France), promising to abide by a referendum. "Don't let me leave this way; arm me against those who seek to surpass me. You will not regret it. . . . If we must fight, we will fight. You will kill ten of our men, but we will kill one of yours. And in the end it is you that will tire."[18]

Thus, our soon-to-be adopted "enemy," in September, 1946. But in one of our internal memoranda at the end of that year, official foresight is no less chilling. On December 19, 1946, a month after an "incident" in which French warships, planes, and artillery had shelled and bombed civilian quarters of Haiphong, killing over six thousand civilians,[19] fighting had broken out in Hanoi. The French then began their military attempt—almost unique in the postwar world—to reconquer their former colony. Four days later, on December 23, 1946, John Carter Vincent, Director of the Bureau of Far Eastern Affairs, sent a memo to Under Secretary of State Dean Acheson, which made this assessment:

Although the French in Indochina have made far-reaching paper-concessions to the Vietnamese desire for autonomy, French actions on the scene have been directed toward whittling down the powers and the territorial extent of the Vietnam "free state." This process the Vietnamese have continued to resist. At the same time, the French themselves admit that they lack the military strength to reconquer the country. In brief, with inadequate forces, with public opinion sharply at odds, with a government rendered largely ineffective through internal division, the French have tried to accomplish in Indochina what a strong and united Britain has found it unwise to attempt in Burma. Given the present elements in the situation, *guerrilla warfare may continue indefinitely.* [*PP*, I, 29; italics added]

A quarter-century later, the week before Christmas, 1971, an article

[18] Jean Sainteny, *Historie d'une Paix Manquee: Indochine 1945-1947* (Paris, 1953), p. 210.

[19] See McAlister, *op. cit.*, p. 287. The portion of an official cable—of December 17, 1946, then classified "secret"—commenting on this French "incident" has been withheld from the declassified version of the McNamara Study: See *GPO*, 8, 88. That white space on the page—followed by the broken sentence beginning page 89, "clear that with a different French commander at Haiphong than Colonel Debes, who is notorious for graft and brutality and who has admitted that he cannot control his own troops, the trouble might have been confined to the original incidents"—is eloquent of the pains our security officers still take to protect American consciousness from unpleasant realities of twenty-five years ago, when our war was beginning.

on the Op-Ed page of the *New York Times*[20] described what Fred
Branfman has elsewhere called "the Third Indochina War": the war
of sensors, air-dropped mines and bombers, the "automated, elec-
tronic battlefield" *above* Indochina that has largely replaced the war
of American ground offensives and American casualties at the old
rate of one to ten. But on the front page of that same issue, there
was an ominous note: a story headed "Hanoi Challenges Air Power
of U.S.," which began: "The American air war in Indochina has
entered a new phase, with direct confrontations between American
and North Vietnamese planes." (In the previous two days, four U.S.
planes had been downed over Laos and North Vietnam; later, starting
the day after Christmas, the President launched a thousand U.S.
bombers during five days against North Vietnam, in the heaviest raids
since 1968.[21]) The lengthy *Times* report on this "new phase" concluded: "One young pilot in Danang summed up his experience this
way: 'We keep on bombing and we keep underestimating how
ingenious an enemy we're up against. When we try something, he
develops counter-tactics, and it just never ends.' " The dateline of
this story is Saigon, December 19, 1971: the twenty-fifth anniversary
day of the Indochina War.

A few more quotes from the Pentagon Papers, Truman period.
These are from the Department of State Policy Statement on Indochina, September 27, 1948,[22] a year and a half before we took up—
for the next generation—what it calls the "onus of intervention":

> . . . Since V-J day, the majority people of the area, the Vietnamese, have
> stubbornly resisted the reestablishment of French authority, a struggle in

---

[20] "Sensors Don't Bleed" by Herbert Mitgang, *New York Times*, December 20,
1971, p. 35.

[21] I was reminded of Christmas Eve, 1964, when I was called by a duty officer
in the Pentagon with the news that the Brinks Officers' Quarters had been blown
up in Saigon "by persons unknown." Ambassador Taylor, CINCPAC, and the
JCS all recommended a one-day mission in "reprisal" by forty strike aircraft
against the Vit Thu Lu Army barracks (see *PP*, III, 263); but that year the President
decided, so my boss told me, not to present the American public with that
surprise on Christmas morning. Therefore, the sustained bombing program
against the North, the opening campaign of "the Third Indochina War," did not
start for another six weeks.

[22] *GPO*, 8, 143-49; italics added. This extremely illuminating discussion should
be read in full. Regrettably, it is not included in either the Beacon or Bantam editions; Books 8, 9 and 10 of the *GPO* edition remain essential for many documents
of the 1945-60 period such as this one.

which we have tried to maintain insofar as possible a position of non-support of either party.

While the nationalist movement in Vietnam (Cochina, Annam, and Tonkin) is strong, and though the great majority of the Vietnamese are not fundamentally Communist, the most active element in the resistance of the local peoples to the French has been a Communist group headed by Ho Chi Minh. This group has successfully extended its influence to include practically all armed forces now fighting the French, thus in effect capturing control of the nationalist movement.

. . . We have not urged the French to negotiate with Ho Chi Minh, *even though he probably is now supported by a considerable majority of the Vietnamese people,* because of his record as a Communist and the Communist background of many of the influential figures in and about his government.

. . . Our greatest difficulty in talking with the French and in stressing what should and what should not be done has been our inability to suggest *any practicable solution* of the Indochina problem, as we are all too well aware of the unpleasant fact that Communist Ho Chi Minh is the strongest and perhaps the ablest figure in Indochina and any suggested solution which excludes him is an expedient of uncertain outcome. We are naturally hesitant to press the French too strongly or to become deeply involved so long as we are not in a position to suggest a solution or until we are prepared to accept the onus of intervention.

Sixteen years later, relationships reversed, the French were pressing *us* to allow self-determination to the Indochinese. In response to De Gaulle's proposal to negotiate on the basis of "neutralization," Secretary McNamara in March 1964 summed up for President Johnson a decade of the "Second Indochina War":

While De Gaulle has not been clear on what he means by this—and is probably deliberately keeping it vague as he did in working toward an Algerian settlement—he clearly means not only a South Vietnam that would not be a Western base or part of an alliance structure (both of which we could accept) but also withdrawal of all external military assistance and specifically total U.S. withdrawal. To negotiate on this basis—indeed without specifically rejecting it—would simply mean a Communist takeover in South Vietnam. *Only the U.S. presence after 1954 held the South together under far more favorable circumstances, and enabled Diem to refuse to go through with the 1954 provision calling for nationwide "free" elections in 1956.* Even talking about a U.S. withdrawal would undermine any chance of keeping a non-Communist government in South Vietnam, and the rug would probably be pulled before the negotiations had gone far. [*PP*, III, 502-3]

And as a postscript, some words from the State Department Assistant Secretary, William P. Bundy, in November, 1964—on the "atypical
features" that have made South Vietnam and Laos "so difficult":

A bad colonial heritage of long standing, totally inadequate preparation for
self-government by the colonial power, a colonialist war fought in half-baked
fashion and lost, a nationalist movement taken over by Communists ruling
in the other half of an ethnically and historically united country, the Communist side inheriting much the better military force and far more than its
share of the talent—these are the facts that dog us to this day.[23] [PP, III, 625]

Here are some things I understood when I had finished reading
the Pentagon Papers.

There have been no First and Second Indochina Wars, no Third
War: just one war, continuously for a quarter of a century. In practical terms, it has been an American war almost from its beginning:
a war of Vietnamese—not all of them but enough to persist—against
American policy and American financing, proxies, technicians, firepower, and finally, troops and pilots. Since at least the late 1940's
there has probably never been a year when political violence in
Vietnam would have reached or stayed at the scale of a "war," had
not the U.S. President, Congress, and citizens fueled it with money,
weapons, and ultimately, manpower: first through the French, then
wholly owned client regimes, and at last directly.

The popular critique that we have "interfered" in what is "really
a civil war"—a notion long held privately by many of my former
colleagues as a pledge to themselves of their secret realism—is as
much a myth as the earlier official one of "aggression from the North."
To call a conflict in which one army is financed and equipped entirely
by foreigners a "civil war" simply screens a more painful reality: that
the war is, after all, a foreign aggression. Our aggression.

Our role has defied the U.N. Charter and every principle of self-
determination from the beginning, and violated our international
assurances at Geneva since 1954. In the technical language of
Nuremberg—American language ratified by the U.N. in 1951—it is a
"crime against peace."[24] It persists as such: a wholly illegitimate uni-

---

[23] The Joint Chiefs of Staff commented on this paragraph of Bundy's draft: "This
seems mainly to be more in the sour grapes vein."

[24] "Crimes against peace: namely, planning, preparation, initiation, or waging
of a war of aggression, or a war in violation of international treaties, agree-
ments, or assurances, or participation in a common plan or conspiracy for the

lateral intervention, desperately unwanted by most of those of another nation and culture, designed to determine who should govern them, how they should live, and which of them should die.

I had, of course, heard all these arguments before: and dismissed them, as my coileagues had, as overblown rhetoric. It was what "extreme" critics—and most international lawyers—had been saying about the nature of our involvement for years. I had not believed them. Now I had to.

A reader still hesitant to accept these propositions as precise and accurate, rather than "emotional," will not find them demonstrated in the essays that follow. This book is not a substitute for reading the Pentagon Papers themselves (with respect to origins and justification, see Volume I of the Beacon Press edition and the documents in Books 8, 9, and 10 of the GPO edition) or the other historical works cited above; there is scarcely any other reading I could recommend more highly for its bearing on the current controversy over "reasonable negotiating positions" versus the urgency of terminating American violence in Indochina.

For myself, to read, through our own official documents, about the origins of the conflict and of our participation in it, is to see our involvement—and the killing we do—naked of any shred of legitimacy. That applies just as strongly to our deliberately prolonging it by a single additional day, or bomb, or death. Can it ever be precipitate to end a policy of murder?

Along with their implications of the illegitimacy of our policy and thus the urgency of changing it, the Pentagon Papers revealed to me that *the President was part of the problem.* This was clearly a matter of his role, not of his personality or party. The concentration of power

---

accomplishment of any of the foregoing," Charter of the Nuremberg Tribunal, 1945; see Quincy Wright, *The Role of International Law* (New York, 1961), p. 108, and see *Vietnam and International Law,* ed. Richard Falk, 2 vols. (Princeton, 1967, 1969). For example, the air attacks on North Vietnam from early 1965 to the present appear to meet every legal test of "aggression," or illegal use of armed force in international relations (Wright, pp. 59-65). Moreover, the U.S. Government gave a unilateral "international assurance"—in binding fashion—that it would "refrain from the threat or use of force to disturb" the Geneva Accords of July 21, 1954, which called for nationwide elections—i.e., throughout Vietnam, which was regarded by all as one nation—in July, 1956 (*PP,* I, 570-72). As the Pentagon Papers reveal unequivocally, we proceeded to supply arms and pay an army and police force devoted to repressing by force every element in "South Vietnam" that favored the honoring of the Accords, from 1954 to the present; while a regime totally dependent on our arms and money refused even to discuss the implementation of the Accords.

within the Executive branch since World War II, I speculated, had focused nearly all responsibility for "failure" upon one man, the President; and at the same time, it gave him enormous capability to avert or postpone or conceal such personal failure by means of force and fraud. Confronted by resolute resistance, as in Vietnam, that power could not fail to corrupt the human who held it.

Such conclusions challenged most of the premises that had guided my professional career. To read the continuous record of intelligence assessments and orecasts for Vietnam from 1946 on was finally to lose the delusion that informing the President better is the key to ending the war—or to fulfilling one's responsibilities as a citizen. It appeared that only if *power* were brought to bear upon the Executive branch from outside it—with the important secondary effect of sharing responsibility for later events more broadly—then might the Executive preference for endless, escalating stalemate rather than "failure" be overruled. "Inside" consulting, as in the normal Rand pattern, withheld from Congress and the public the facts and authoritative judgments needed for the self-confident exercise of such a power; and by that very silence—no matter what was said "privately" —it supported and participated in the structure of inordinate, unchallenged Executive power that led directly to its rigid, desperate, outlaw behavior.

Indeed, it was during the same time that I read these early documents in August and September of 1969 that friends in the Administration, both in Washington and Vietnam, revealed to me the outlines of future policy. President Nixon, I was informed, had in effect made his choice from among the "options" that I and others at Rand had helped draft at the end of 1968; and his choice was *not* the formally "suppressed" option of extrication, a definite end to our involvement. Once more an Administration planned to postpone failure: to buy time by maintaining indefinitely American troops at reduced levels in Vietnam, and by continuing to impose American bombing, Indochinese casualties, and the threat of worse.

So this was what the "options exercise" and NSSM-1 had come to. Indeed, the very answers to NSSM-1 had implicitly told the President early in 1969 that there was *no other way reliably* to postpone throughout one term, let alone two, what he saw as national "humiliation" in Vietnam. One of the questions asked had been, in substance, "When could the South Vietnamese armed forces be made capable of handling a sizable challenge by North Vietnamese forces without both U.S. ground forces and U.S. combat support?" (In other words, when would "*total* Vietnamization," as the American public was later led to understand it, be feasible?) The answer from the Pentagon in February, 1969—never revealed to the public—was clear-cut: *Never*. And the Pentagon's *private* plans for the subsequently announced "Vietnamization" program—which allowed for very gradual reduction to a large residual U.S. force, indefinitely maintained along with air support—were adapted realistically to this conclusion.

But that was not what the public was meant to comprehend. Once again, the true nature of internal predictions given to the President was concealed, misleading the public as to Presidential values and intentions. By exploiting verbal ambiguities between "reduction" and "withdrawal," and among "ending U.S. ground combat," "ending our involvement," and "ending the war," the Administration would encourage the public to hear, wrongly, what they wished to believe: that Nixon's public announcement of unachievable "conditions" for the total withdrawal of U.S. troops, and his consistent refusal to name a deadline or reveal a schedule, were mere window-dressing, concealing what was no more than a tactical difference from his dove critics. Indeed, after "backgrounders" given by a persuasive, unnamed White House source over subsequent months, most editorialists and columnists assured readers that Nixon intended and expected—no matter what he said—to withdraw all U.S. combat involvement, land and air, in a fairly short time.[25]

The ultimate aim was what I have since called an "Invisible War." Nixon's plan was to reduce those dimensions of the war that were most salient to U.S. media and the public—U.S. casualties, U.S. ground presence, draft calls, and costs—and transfer the greater part of the combat to the Indochinese and to areas where reporters could less easily follow—to the air, and to Laos, Cambodia, and North Vietnam. He was gambling that the indefinite prolongation of the

---

[25] By this point in our history—someone at the White House seems to have surmised—the Credibility Gap can work *for* a President who wants to mislead the public without lying. He can be perfectly straightforward about his plans, while the contrary impression can be effectively conveyed by an assistant, who merely suggests—again, without saying so—by allusions and tone of voice in "background" sessions, that the President is, as usual, only kidding.

war would then cease to be a matter of concern or even of awareness to most Americans. The war would become invisible to them. With the human burden of the war falling almost exclusively upon the Indochinese, statements that "we are getting out of the war" or "the war is ending" would meet no challenge, even while U.S. bombing continued and expanded in area coverage, and Indochinese died in combat or became homeless at increasing rates. If the strategy were successful in these terms (and it has since come close enough for Nixon still to bank on it), Orwell's slogan "War Is Peace" would be political currency in the U.S. a dozen years ahead of 1984.

What stood between the Indochinese people and three to seven more years of what would soon be "Nixon's War," it seemed to me in the fall of 1969, was the possibility that a new President might instead be persuaded, or forced, to shift the burden of blame for national failure onto his predecessors in the opposing party—where, indeed, it still belonged—and take up the option of extrication that he had excluded at the outset of the year. In practical terms, that path might not be open much longer, as the end of Nixon's first year approached. Mutual withdrawal had been rejected by Hanoi in the spring; I now agreed with the five heretics at Rand who had long been saying that total unilateral withdrawal remained as the only path out of the quagmire. Yet no major public figure had yet even suggested such a course. (Senator Goodell first announced his proposed bill to this end in early October, and he could find no cosponsors.) And my hopes were soon disappointed that former officials could be found to share, and thus reduce, the President's political risks in choosing extrication by publicly urging that course. Their own risks, and their party's, they seemed to feel, were great enough already. There were even some Democrats, I came to suspect, who were not unhappy to see bloody stalemate becoming "Nixon's War" in a few more months, even though—it seemed clear enough to me —that almost surely meant prolonging it by another three years at least.

Among the dozen or so former officials who at this time possessed copies of the Pentagon Papers, and were thus physically in a position to draw public conclusions based on them or even to reveal them to Congress and the people, there were at least two differences in myself that sharpened my sense of personal responsibility. Only two of us—

I became the second that September, and a year later there were still only three—had actually read the whole of the McNamara Study, or even any substantial part of it; only the two, then three, of us knew the story the Pentagon Papers told and had been changed by it. And of the whole dozen—the rest of whom had served at higher levels than these three—only one, myself, had ever lived in Vietnam, or had Vietnamese friends, had worked in the countryside and seen the war close at hand. In the words of a poster I saw recently, "There came a time when the people of Vietnam were as real to me as my own hands." The months between 1965 and 1967 had changed me in ways that the previous year of reading high-level cables in Washington could not; and many of those memories changed character abruptly when the Pentagon Papers stripped away all legitimate rationales for what we were doing.

Within a few weeks or months from September the President would probably be committing himself publicly to the course of indefinite involvement I had heard privately described. Only Congress and the public—newly informed by "authoritative" warnings and, perhaps, by documentary evidence on the illegitimate origins and hopeless prospects of the war—might act to dissuade or prevent the President from pursuing the American war in Vietnam carried on by his four predecessors.

To ask myself, a man who had spent the last decade serving four of those five Presidents, to act on such perceptions was asking me to jump out of my skin. Something harder than risking it: that I had done already, along with some three million, mostly younger Americans who had gone to Vietnam. Most of us had seen our going as the response of loyal Americans to our President; until recently, few had supposed that might conflict with serving the legitimate interests of our country. What was needed now, to go beyond that reflex response, was the inspiration to find in oneself loyalties long unconsulted, deeper and broader than loyalty to the President: loyalties to America's founding concepts, to our Constitutional system, to countrymen, to one's own humanity—and to our "allies," the people we were bombing.

At this point it was other young Americans who helped me by their example. That same month of August, 1969, that I began to read the origins of the war and to learn the President's plans, I met for the first time, face-to-face, Americans who were on their way to prison for refusing to collaborate in an unjust war. I found them to be sober, intelligent, principled; they showed, in fact, the dedication I had respected in many officials I had known in Vietnam, but they were acting on different premises, which I now shared. These personal acts of "witness" gave me what reading alone could not.

In October, I joined my five colleagues at Rand in the first critical statement on Vietnam policy addressed to the public that any of us had ever signed: a letter to the *New York Times* calling for U.S. unilateral withdrawal within one year.[26] At the same time, without the knowledge of anyone at Rand, I acted privately to reveal the information in the Pentagon Papers, beginning with the Senate Foreign Relations Committee.

As it worked out, nearly twenty months went by before the information finally reached the public and the rest of Congress (or, for that matter, the Executive, which till then had neglected totally to unlock and study its own copies of the McNamara Study). Meanwhile, as warned, two more invasions had taken place; another million tons of bombs had fallen; nearly ten thousand more Americans had died, as well as hundreds of thousands of Indochinese. It had become painfully clear that much of Congress, too, was part of the problem; so I acted, as well, to inform the sovereign public through the "fourth branch of government," the press.

Almost a year later now, the war goes on: still endlessly "ending," while bombing persists at the steady rate of World War II and heavy daily raids are again made over the North. The cumulative total tonnage dropped on Indochina is now three times that dropped in all theaters of World War II. In four years under Lyndon Johnson the U.S. dropped more bombs (three million tons) than in World War II and Korea combined; in little more than three years, President Nixon, while "winding down the war," has dropped more bombs than Johnson: more than any other ruler in history.

"I've just been reading John McAlister's book," Cyrus Vance told me in early 1971, as we went in to hear a private "backgrounder" by Henry Kissinger at a meeting outside Cambridge. "If only we had had it in the mid-sixties!" I knew what he meant. I would like to

---

[26] *New York Times,* October 9, 1969; for full text, see the *Washington Post,* October 12, 1969.

believe that such a book could have made a difference to us in the Executive then—to what we did, as well as what we might have felt about it. But it *was* available now, say, to Henry Kissinger (along with a White House copy of the McNamara Study, which in September, 1970, I had urged him, unsuccessfully, to scan or to assign to some assistant to study for him. "Is there really much to be learned from that?" he asked. "After all, we make decisions very differently now.") Yet it was while we heard Kissinger tell us that evening, "We are ending the war . . . the war is trending down, and I assure you that it will continue to trend down," that we learned the next morning, the pre-invasion bombing of Laos had begun.

Will the Pentagon Papers in the hands of the public eventually do more? Or is it possible that the American people, too, are part of the problem; that our passivity, fears, obedience weld us, unresisting, into the stalemate machine: that *we* are the problem for much of the rest of the world?

It is too soon to conclude that. There is too much information to be absorbed from the Pentagon Papers and the disclosures and analyses that are beginning to follow; too many myths and lies to be unlearned; habits too strong to be changed so quickly in a public that has let its sovereignty in foreign affairs atrophy for thirty years.

Still, one cannot be sure. There are times when I suspect that current efforts to end the war are as quixotic as my early efforts to help win it. Have I, then, simply moved my own pressures from one side to the other of an immovable, inevitable stalemate? Have I, recently, only imagined an America that "could"—short of radical change in its own society and politics—change itself to abandon counterrevolution in Vietnam and elsewhere, as once I imagined American and Saigon governments that could master it?

That is one position on the Left. It could be correct; yet it is a counsel of despair—which I am not ready to accept—with respect to the fate of the people of Indochina, whose remaining social structures could be destroyed before another Presidential term is over. Their hope of survival as a people must rest on the possibility of a different sort of radical change, in the behavior of individuals *within* our existing, highly imperfect institutions: however urgent it is, on a longer time scale, that those institutions themselves be changed.

To be radical is to go to roots; and in Dwight Macdonald's phrase "the root is man." The stalemated killing "machine," so far as there is one, is made of men and women, of human habits and relationships that they have made or maintained, and that can be unmade by them. In releasing the Pentagon Papers I acted in hope I still hold: that truths that changed me could help Americans free themselves and other victims from our longest war.

THE QUAGMIRE MYTH
AND THE
STALEMATE MACHINE

An expert—I once heard—is a man who has read a book that no one else has read. At the time an earlier version of this paper was first delivered—at a panel of the American Political Science Association's annual meeting, Los Angeles, September, 1970—there were just two people who had read the seven thousand pages of a study entitled "United States Decision-making in Vietnam, 1945-67." Leslie H. Gelb was one, I was the other. As it happened, both of us were speaking at the same panel, presenting analyses on that subject which showed (naturally) some strong similarities in assertions of fact along with (inevitably) some differences on speculative matters.[1]

I can't speak for my friend Leslie Gelb, but I know that I was feeling very uncomfortable in the position of "expert" in this sense; and frustrated, since I had taken steps to end that lonely role nine months earlier, when I first revealed parts of the McNamara Study to the Senate Foreign Relations Committee in expectation of immediate public hearings. At the time the panel met—a few months after the

[1] My paper, "Escalating in a Quagmire," appeared in abridged form with the present title in *Public Policy,* Spring 1971, pp. 217-74; my essay that follows is considerably revised from both of these earlier versions. Gelb's paper, also abridged, has been published in *Foreign Policy,* Summer, 1971, pp. 140-67, with the title "Vietnam: The System Worked."

Cambodian invasion, a few months before the Laotian invasion—
I was still urging such hearings. If only for purposes of a deeper understanding of this mass of material, it needed to be approached from
a great many different perspectives, not just by a few government-
approved analysts; but more importantly, the larger issues it raised
were not matters for "experts" at all. They were the deepest concerns
of all American citizens, who urgently needed to know truths improp-
erly concealed from them—some for almost a quarter-century—
about a war in which they had been led to participate during that
whole period: a war that was, and is, still going on.

My paper, in any case, was purely analytical, meant to reveal to the
public at least some generalizations drawn from the McNamara Study,
as well as speculations on the motives underlying the patterns revealed there. Even these limited revelations seemed too pertinent to
current policy debate for me to weaken their meaning and authority by
obeying the tradition among former officials of omitting any reference
to the fact that these inferences had been drawn in part from classified sources. Though I was requested by former associates to forgo
even oblique mention of the McNamara Study—whose existence, as
Secretary McNamara was understood to have wished, had received
no newspaper attention at all—I suggested the limits and bases of
the analysis in the following statement:

> For one critical decision period, at least—the fall of 1961—information
> now publicly available is sufficient to test, and indeed to establish, certain
> propositions. This is possible mainly because of the revelation by the "Ken-
> nedy historians" of much previously concealed data relating to the decisions.
> For few other periods are the public data comparably adequate. Thus, until
> more of these materials are made public, readers who have not had official
> access to them can only regard most of the propositions presented here with
> respect to periods other than 1961 as hypotheses. Even so, their implications,
> at least, can be analyzed; and they can be tested to some extent against the
> judgments of others who have had relevant governmental experience, as well
> as against past and current events.
>
> The assertions and speculations below on U.S. decision-making reflect the
> writer's experience as a government official and his research since that time,
> in part as a consultant, with official access. All of these functions posed the
> responsibility and opportunity to learn data on earlier decision-making. Un-
> satisfactory as it is to present generalizations and assertions without specific
> citation, it seems less so than either to rely entirely on the public record or
> to pretend to do so, to forgo generalizations or to subscribe to wrong ones.

By now, of course, the Senator Gravel Edition of the Pentagon Papers (Beacon Press) and the Government Printing Office version (somewhat expurgated by the Department of Defense for purposes of "declassification"), entitled "United States-Vietnam Relations, 1947-1967," have transformed the base of public data available. The two versions tend to complement each other, with Books 8, 9, and 10 of the twelve-volume GPO edition comprising an indispensable collection of documents on the 1945-60 period, omitted from the Beacon edition, which in turn presents far more documentation on the 1964-65 period. (It should be noted that *The Pentagon Papers,* published by the *New York Times* and Bantam Books, does not include enough official documents—in particular, it omits National Intelligence Estimates—for an adequate test of hypotheses on patterns of official decision-making for periods other than late 1961; but for that period, it does include many of the references used in the following paper.)

None of the published versions include material directly from the four volumes of the McNamara Study dealing with negotiating contacts, which were made available by me only to the Senate Foreign Relations Committee.[2] Except for these volumes, the entire Study is now substantially available.

The timing when any of this material might become accessible to readers was unforeseen when the earlier versions of this essay were written, so they were limited in their citations to public sources. To some extent, this limited the subject matter as well, for I have arrived at a number of generalizations and interpretations regarding Vietnam policy over the last eight years whose plausibility and significance seemed too hard to establish without being able to refer directly to data previously classified. With a few exceptions,[3] I have not tried to remedy this last limitation in the present book; neither this essay nor the book as a whole comes close to being a compre-

[2] The rationale for restricting these volumes to Congress and the Executive seems to have disappeared after President Nixon's own recent precedent of releasing the details of secret current negotiations by unilateral decision. No further harm could be done to future contacts, it would seem, by releasing the history of past negotiating efforts to the public, and I believe that Congress should now arrange to do so.

[3] For example, the new discussion of the "good doctor" theme among rationales for bombing the North in 1964, pages 86-93.

hensive analysis of the McNamara Study as a whole; nor have I, in revising these essays and adding citations to and quotations from the published versions of the Pentagon Papers, even fully exploited their availability. Thus, the relative focus on the 1961 decisions still reflects in part the fact that the disclosures by Schlesinger, Sorensen, and Hilsman about that period made it possible to address certain hypotheses adequately—in particular, to refute the quagmire thesis—on the basis of published sources, though I have now substituted citations of the actual documents instead of paraphrases or quotations of them made by these authors.

Some caveats are needed about the Pentagon Papers as a basis for speculations about the motives and perspectives of individual officials; these are discussed at some length in the text (pages 74-79).

This paper (including its earlier versions) was written while I was a Senior Research Associate of the Center for International Studies at M.I.T. That is also true of the other papers in this book, with the exception of those grouped under "Background: Vietnam 1965-1967" and "Bombing and Other Crimes." Much of the research —drawing upon authorized access to the Pentagon Papers and other studies and upon my own experience—had, of course, been done earlier. But quite apart from any questions of classified or official source material, very few of these papers, in my judgment, could appear at this time if I were still in any official relationship to the U.S. Government, as employee, consultant, or contract researcher, requiring me to submit work intended for publication for "policy" clearance (i.e., for censorship of material possibly embarrassing to the Administration or its policies). The repeated refusals by Secretary Laird to make available the McNamara Study to the Senate Foreign Relations Committee—even on a classified basis—in response to four formal requests from the chairman of the committee between November, 1969, and June, 1971, seem to confirm that guess. As much past experience of colleagues has shown, comments as critical as mine, even of past policy, on a subject so "sensitive" as Vietnam, could not be expected to pass the policy review process, at least for some years.[4]

---

[4] A transcript of spontaneous remarks at a seminar need not be "cleared" in this fashion; that is how the comments in "Bombing and Other Crimes" came to be published while I was still at Rand.

This is a good point, therefore, at which to express my gratitude to the Center for International Studies, and especially to Everett Hagen, its Acting Director from the time I was invited to join the Center until recently, for offering me a position where "no one would have to read what I wrote until it was published" and where at the same time I could count on useful criticism when I asked for it. I could not have wished for greater freedom or better support than I have received, which allowed me to write these essays and to make them available while they may still be useful.

———————————————

It sometimes happens, on certain coasts of Brittany or Scotland, that a man, traveler or fisherman, walking on the beach at low tide far from the bank, suddenly notices that for several minutes he has been walking with some difficulty. The strand beneath his feet is like pitch; his soles stick to it; it is sand no longer, it is glue. The beach is perfectly dry, but at every step he takes, as soon as he lifts his foot, the print which it leaves fills with water. The eye, however, has noticed no change; the immense strand is smooth and tranquil, all the sand has the same appearance, nothing distinguishes the surface which is solid from the surface which is no longer so; the joyous little cloud of sand fleas continues to leap tumultuously over the wayfarer's feet. The man pursues his way, goes forward, inclines toward the land, endeavors to get nearer the upland. He is not anxious. Anxious about what? Only, he feels somehow as if the weight of his feet increases with every step which he takes. Suddenly he sinks in. He sinks in two or three inches. Decidedly he is not on the right road; he stops to take his bearings. All at once, he looks at his feet. His feet have disappeared. The sand covers them. He draws his feet out of the sand, he will retrace his steps, he turns back, he sinks in deeper. The sand comes up to his ankles, he pulls himself out and throws himself to the left, the sand is a half-leg deep, he throws himself to the right, the sand comes up to his shins. Then he recognizes with unspeakable terror that he is caught in the quicksand, and that he has beneath him the fearful medium in which man can no more walk than the fish can swim. He throws off his load if he has one, he lightens himself like a ship in distress; it is already too late, the sand is above his knees. . . .

VICTOR HUGO, Les Miserables

"In South Vietnam, the U.S. had stumbled into a bog. It would be mired down there a long time." So Nikita Khrushchev remarked, in July, 1962, to an American official,[5] who reported it in a cable soon forgotten in the hurly-burly of rescuing Khrushchev from miring down in Cuba.

The image was more familiar, then, to our other opponents of

[5] Ambassador Llewellyn Thompson; his cable, not publicly available, recounted a private *tour d'horizon* by the Soviet Premier, who neglected to mention that Soviet medium- and intermediate-range missiles were being loaded that month for shipment to the Caribbean.

that period, the French. By the middle of the "First Indochina War," a dozen years earlier, French journalists, contradicting French generals, were telling their readers that the war in Indochina was a bog. Thus the title of Lucien Bodard's partly prophetic account of the French experience in Indochina in 1946-50: *L'Enlisement* ("The Bogging Down"), or in its American version, *The Quicksand War.*[6] George Ball, one of the few U.S. officials who could imagine that American experience could be like French, was warned by De Gaulle that Vietnam was *"pays pourri,"* a "rotten country," not suitable for tanks or Western politics, not, it was hinted delicately, white man's country [*PP*, II, 23].

But the metaphor began, about the same time, to be heard from some Americans. In early 1962, writing to the President to argue against sending American combat units to Vietnam or otherwise deepening our involvement, John Kenneth Galbraith spoke of his fears of the bright promise of the New Frontier "being sunk under the rice fields" [*PP*, II, 124]. (This did not fail to happen, though the promise had come to be renamed the Great Society.) By late 1964 and early 1965, David Halberstam could find no better title for his memoir than the somewhat awkward *The Making of a Quagmire.*

"Many people thought the title was too harsh, more pessimistic than was warranted," Halberstam recalls. But the real buildup of American ground forces and airpower was just beginning; within two years many of the same people had come to find his title just right. These included some former officials—Arthur Schlesinger, Jr., for one, and Richard Goodwin and Townsend Hoopes—who now saw the war, with its greatly increased human and material costs, as reflecting good intentions but unfounded hopes that had drawn our leaders on disastrously.

For a great many, perhaps most Americans, visions of "quagmire . . . morass . . . quicksand . . . bog," along with the notion of "stumbling in," have come to dominate their perceptions of America's position in the "Second Indochina War." More than

---

[6] *The Quicksand War: Prelude to Vietnam* (Boston, 1967); this combines, somewhat abridged, translations of *L'Enlisement* (Paris, 1963) and its sequel, *L'Humiliation* (Paris, 1965).

image, more than attitude, these metaphors convey a rather precise, widely shared understanding of the process of decision-making that has yielded a steadily expanding American military involvement in Indochina.

To spell out the process of becoming enmired, as in Hugo's description above, is to reveal at once the power of the analogy; to many Americans, surely, no more than this evocation is needed to prove the case. So many of the gross, observable features of our involvement are encompassed: the gradualness; the publicly expressed, sometimes clearly genuine optimism; the evidently surprising setbacks, followed by new commitments; above all, the presumption of Presidential *unawareness,* attenuating his responsibility for crises, partial failures, and stalemate.

It is a conception of which the implications—overoptimism, lack of foresight, awareness, or calculation—are not highly flattering to past Presidents but are at least extenuating, if correct; ignorance *is,* after all, an excuse. And it suggests specific answers to the by now agonized questions: How did "Vietnam" happen to us? How did we get so deeply into this war? What did our Presidents think they were doing? What was aimed at, what was hoped; what were they told to expect from various courses?

But are these answers valid? If they are not, the "quagmire" notion will yield poor predictions of future decisions and events, and poor advice on how to bring about change. Does the analogy really fit the evolution of American intervention in Vietnam, or does it mainly mislead?

The Schlesinger "Quagmire Model"

The precise implications of the "quagmire" notion for an understanding of the policy process have been spelled out by Arthur Schlesinger, Jr., in two much-quoted passages, the first referring to the increases in the level of military advisors in Vietnam under President Kennedy, in November, 1961:

This was the policy of "one more step"—each new step always promising the success which the previous *last step* had also *promised* but had unaccountably failed to deliver . . .[7]

[7] *The Bitter Heritage: Vietnam and American Democracy, 1941-1966* (New York, 1968), page 39. Italics added.

And so the policy of "one more step" lured the United States deeper
and deeper into the morass. In retrospect, Vietnam is a triumph of the
politics of inadvertence. We have achieved our present entanglement,
not after due and deliberate consideration, but through a series of
small decisions. It is not only idle but unfair to seek out guilty men.
President Eisenhower, after rejecting the American military intervention in 1954, set in motion the policy of support for Saigon which
resulted, two Presidents later, in American military intervention in
1965. Each step in the deepening of the American commitment was
reasonably regarded at the time as the last that would be necessary.
Yet, in retrospect, each step led only to the next, until we find ourselves
entrapped in that nightmare of American strategists, a land war in
Asia.[8]

By this dynamic model, step by step, each one promising
success, Schlesinger purports to explain the whole process that
led from Eisenhower's offer of support to Diem in 1954 to American military intervention in 1965. The generalization could be
tested as well over the whole period from our first direct military
grants to the French in 1950 under Truman—Schlesinger neglects
these Democratic roots—to the present. Many would find it
equally persuasive, perhaps compellingly so, for the longer period.

It is an unusually satisfying explanation. It is simple, even
elegant. It sums up coherently a long series of decisions to explain a baffling outcome. It is unquestionably plausible: almost
surely more so than any simple alternative drawing upon evidence publicly available (prior to the Pentagon Papers). And
it accords with the major, widespread presumption that the
"nightmare" outcome *must* have been unforeseen even as a
strong possibility by those who made the decisions leading
toward it; or else they would have drawn back, or at least warned
the public of the demands ahead.

As a generalized account of the important decisions, and the
considerations that led to them, which increased American involvement in Indochina, this explanation is marred only by being

[8] Ibid., page 47, italics added. It is only because this statement—of a familiar
point of view—is so explicit, and because his own factual testimony is crucial
to refuting it, that Arthur Schlesinger, Jr., is so often cited critically in this paper.
In other respects he has elsewhere said many cogent and useful things about
our Vietnam involvement. (Since the earlier publication of this essay, and of the
Pentagon Papers, Schlesinger has recanted the particular assertions cited; see
page 73 and footnote 30.

totally wrong for each one of those decisions over the last twenty years.

This is not to deny that there were months and years in those two decades when ill-founded optimism actually ruled the minds of most insiders, including the President. For example, during most of 1962;[9] and in parts of 1953, 1957, and 1967. And obviously, our cumulative investment of dollars, rhetoric, and manpower continued to increase, and chances to cut losses or lessen our commitment were passed by, during these periods when the "inside" mood actually matched the optimism that officials expressed to the public almost continuously.

But in none of these periods were significant new U.S. commitments, in any qualitative sense,[10] determined or begun. Indeed, what needs explaining is not how optimism led regularly to decisions to escalate—there is no such pattern, nor even a major instance through 1968—but how bureaucratic optimism developed after, and out of, decisions to expand the nature of U.S. involvement. Those decisions, as revealed in internal documents, reflected more desperation than hope.

The specific years in which these new involvements and new programs were chosen and begun were without exception periods of crisis and pessimism, generally far darker than ever admitted to the public. Nor, in retrospect, do the grave assessments during these periods appear nearly so distorted or unfounded as do the moods of optimism that regularly came later. Ignorance and foolish proposals abounded throughout the two decades. Yet in the actual years of decision, the gap between estimates and reality concerning the current situation and the prospects of the specific option actually chosen was relatively small: small

[9] See Schlesinger's accurate description of the exuberant mood in that year, going into 1963: *The Bitter Heritage*, pages 41, 42.

[10] For a list of proposed actions that were seen by all Administrations as significant political thresholds that would change the *nature* ot our involvement in ways that increased domestic and/or external risks, see page 105. For actions actually taken that were seen in these terms, both within the Administration and outside it, see page 71. (Certain later decisions in the air war, such as the bombing of the oil system in 1966, might deserve to be added to this list.) In contrast, such increases in the magnitude of our involvement as the buildup of advisors in 1962-63 and of ground troops in 1966-67 were seen from within the bureaucracy as "purely quantitative," requiring no great policy debate, representing essentially the *implementing* of previous Presidential policy choices.

enough that it is hard to argue that more realism or pessimism would have changed the decision.

Not one of these decision points, in fact—1950, 1954, 1961, 1963, 1964, 1965 (see the discussion below)—fits Schlesinger's generalization to the slightest degree. Indeed, for each one of them, viewed from the inside, his description is radically misleading.[11]

That is strikingly true of the very decision that Schlesinger characterizes as typifying the "policy of 'one more step'": President Kennedy's decision to break openly through the 1954 Geneva ceiling on U.S. military personnel in South Vietnam, starting the climb from under a thousand to over fifteen thousand American "advisors" and support personnel at the time of his death.

To be sure, newspaper accounts at the time of this episode of policy-making—whose public aspects began with Kennedy's sending General Maxwell Taylor and Walt W. Rostow on a mission to Saigon—fully support, in retrospect, the "quagmire" interpretation. But those accounts were mistaken, based partly on official lies. Ironically, it is Schlesinger's own account that reveals the facts that contradict both these earlier, "managed" inferences and his own generalization. Because the phenomenon of deception is part of what needs to be explained, let us look first at the newspaper versions, then at Schlesinger's report.

The November 1961 Decisions

The day that General Taylor and his mission left Washington for South Vietnam, the *New York Times* headlined a story by Lloyd Garrison: "Taylor Cautious on GI's for Asia"; "Departs for South Vietnam—Hints U.S. Reluctance to Commit Troops."[12]

---

[11] The same is true of a more recent formulation by Schlesinger, which places the burden of responsibility on the military: "At every stage of our descent into the quagmire, the military have played the dominant role . . . At each point along the ghastly way, the generals promised that just one more step of military escalation would bring the victory so long sought and so steadily denied." See *Partisan Review*, XXXVII (No. 4, 1970), page 517.

[12] *New York Times*, October 16, 1961; story datelined October 15. All newspaper stories cited in this section are from the *New York Times*; dates are dates of publication of stories (generally datelined a day earlier). All italics added.

The story noted:

Last week President Kennedy announced that he was sending General Taylor and an eleven-man mission to South Vietnam to make "an educated guess" about whether the United States would be required to send troops to stop Communist advances in Southeast Asia. . . .

Before he departed aboard a military jet airliner, General Taylor, who is the President's special military adviser, was asked to comment on reports that President Kennedy was becoming increasingly reluctant to commit United States forces to a fighting role in South Vietnam. . . .

General Taylor declined to speak for the President, but declared: "Any American would be reluctant to use troops unless absolutely necessary."

His remarks appeared to reflect a tendency on the part of high Administration sources to pull back from earlier warnings of the possible use of United States troops in the fighting.

James Reston, in a column from Washington dated October 19, declared that reports aroused by the Taylor mission that "the United States is about to plunge into the guerrilla warfare of Southeast Asia . . . should be taken with considerable skepticism, at least for the time being."

General Taylor is not only a soldier but a philosopher with a soldier's respect for power and geography, and a philosopher's sense of perspective. Accordingly he is not likely to favor plunging blithely into a jungle war 7,000 miles from home where the landscape and the logistics favor the enemy. . . .

President Kennedy is not eager to add to his problems in Germany by mounting an adventure in Southeast Asia, and while additional troops may be sent there to help train and direct the defenders, General Taylor has certainly not gone there to organize an invasion.

Over the next week, speculation continued to focus on Taylor's conclusion as to whether or not U.S. combat troops would be needed in South Vietnam. Speaking at the airport as he left Saigon, Taylor agreed that this issue was "one of the principal things I have been asked to look at," but kept his opinions for the President.

"I am going back with my own impressions of what might be done. . . . Obviously I cannot discuss what these recommendations will be as they are primarily the property of my President and he will have to decide what to do about it," General Taylor declared.

"I have great confidence in the military capability of South Vietnam to cope with anything within its border," he went on, and to "defend the country against conventional attack." [October 26, 1961]

On November 3, General Taylor returned to Washington, spoke to reporters at the airport, then saw President Kennedy for two hours at the White House. The lead story in the *New York Times* on November 4, by E. W. Kenworthy, reported:

On his return from a three-week mission to Southeast Asia, General Taylor said that President Ngo Dinh Diem had the "assets" available to prevail against the Communist threat.

The General declined to comment directly on whether he would recommend sending United States combat troops to stiffen the Vietnamese forces in their fight against the Viet Cong (Communist) guerrillas.

However, when General Taylor was reminded at the airport that his remarks before leaving Saigon had been interpreted as meaning that President Ngo Dinh Diem's problem was not manpower, the General replied: "That is correct. It is a populous country."

Officials said it was correct to infer from this that General Taylor did not look favorably on the sending of United States combat troops at this time. . . .

Although some officials in the White House and the State and Defense Departments are known to favor the dispatch of American forces, there would be considerable surprise here if General Taylor recommended such a move.[13]

Furthermore, the President is known to be opposed to sending troops except as a last resort. . . .

While opposing the sending of American combat forces, General Taylor is understood to favor the dispatch of necessary military technicians and to propose intensified training of South Vietnamese elite troops in anti-guerrilla warfare by United States Rangers.

On November 16, Kenworthy reported:

President Kennedy has decided on the measures that the United States is prepared to take to strengthen South Vietnam against attack by Communists.

The measures, which received final approval yesterday at a meeting of the National Security Council, closely follow the recommendations made by General Maxwell D. Taylor, the President's military adviser. . . .

[13] As we shall see, he had recommended it formally by cable two days earlier, to no one's very great surprise.

The United States' plans do not include the dispatching of combat units at this time. . . .

Officials emphasized that President Kennedy and the National Security Council had not foreclosed the possibility of sending ground and air combat units if the situation deteriorated drastically. The President, it was said, does not wish to bind himself to a "never-position."

However, the President and General Taylor are agreed, according to reliable information here, that the South Vietnamese Government is capable of meeting and turning back the Communists' threat provided it speeds the training of its regular forces, solves the problem of mobility, develops a reliable intelligence system and adopts reforms in its military staff structure to free it from political interference.

From this series of articles, based on "reliable, official" sources, uncontradicted by any official, readers of the *New York Times* could only conclude that Taylor and Rostow had recommended against sending combat forces and had assured the President that the lesser measures he adopted, which did not include combat units and which allegedly encompassed their recommendations, were adequate to meet U.S. objectives.

This was the opposite of the truth.

What Taylor and Rostow actually recommended was first exposed to the public by Schlesinger's own account, half a decade later:

The Taylor-Rostow report recommended an enlargement of the American role, essentially through the penetration of the South Vietnamese army and government by American "advisors," attached to Vietnamese military units or government offices and designed to improve the level of local performance. Taylor and Rostow *also recommended* that an American military task force—perhaps 10,000 men—go to Vietnam, commissioned to conduct combat operations for self-defense and perimeter security and, if the Vietnamese army were hard pressed, to act as an emergency reserve. The report concluded by saying that this program would work only if infiltration from the North were stopped and that, therefore, should this infiltration continue, the United States should consider a contingency policy of retaliation against the North, graduated to match the intensity of Hanoi's aid to the Viet Cong.

Kennedy rejected both the northern strategy and the use of combat soldiers . . . He increased the number of military advisors.[14]

[14] *The Bitter Heritage*, page 39; italics added.

Schlesinger does not seem to have noticed the damage this account does to his generalization on the "policy of 'one more step'—each new step always promising . . . success."

He reports, after all, no promises of success concerning the set of programs Kennedy actually adopted, which omitted both of the critical elements mentioned, the northern strategy and the use of combat soldiers. And in fact, for the programs that remained, no promises of adequacy were made by Taylor and Rostow, or by anyone else.

The implications of this discrepancy are obscured by Schlesinger's rather offhand comment that Taylor and Rostow "also" recommended—or as he put it elsewhere, "even envisaged"[15]— sending an American combat task force. Such phrases hint that this proposal was presented as merely one among many, perhaps an optional element that could be rejected without affecting essentially the prospects of an otherwise adequate strategy.

The fact is that Taylor, in a personal message "Eyes Only,"[16] described the sending of U.S. ground combat units as *essential:* "an essential action if we are to reverse the current downward trend of events." "In fact," he reported, "I do not believe that our program to save South Vietnam will succeed without it." As Theodore Sorensen reports, "Many believed that American troops were needed less for their numerical strength than for the morale and will they could provide to Diem's forces and for the warning they could provide to the Communists."[17] But if these were, as Sorensen describes them, "speculative psychological reasons," Taylor did not put them forward lightly. In a separate Eyes Only cable to the President, he wrote that the immediate problem he found in Vietnam (and Southeast Asia) was:

a double crisis of confidence: doubt that [the] U.S. is determined to save Southeast Asia; doubt that Diem's methods can frustrate and defeat Communist purposes and methods. The Vietnamese (and

[15] Arthur Schlesinger, Jr., *A Thousand Days* (New York, 1965), page 504.
[16] I.e., "to be read only by" the addressee, in this case the President. Unlike some Eyes Only messages, this particular cable was, in fact, extraordinarily closely held at the time and later. See *PP*, II, 90-92. See also *The Pentagon Papers*, Bantam edition, pages 141-43. Unless otherwise noted, all quotes by Taylor in this passage are from this message, which deserves to be read in full.
[17] Theodore Sorensen, *Kennedy* (New York, 1965), page 653.

Southeast Asians) will undoubtedly draw—rightly or wrongly—definitive conclusions in coming weeks and months concerning the probable outcome and will adjust their behavior accordingly. What the U.S. does or fails to do will be decisive to the end result. [*PP*, II, 88]

And no alternative action, Taylor maintained, could be "so convincing of U.S. seriousness of purpose and hence so reassuring to the people and Government of South Vietnam and to our other friends and allies in Southeast Asia as the introduction of U.S. forces into South Vietnam."

A force large enough to have the psychological effects required, Taylor suggested, must be more than "a bare token" —Taylor suggested an "initial size" of about eight thousand— and must be capable of performing tasks of significant value, including (following Schlesinger's account) "conducting combat operations for self-defense and perimeter security and, if the Vietnamese army were hard pressed, of providing an emergency reserve."

Taylor underlined the urgency by making explicit his "full recognition" of an impressive list of disadvantages of the proposed move. These included:

a. The strategic reserve of U.S. forces is presently so weak that we can ill afford any detachment of forces to a peripheral area of the Communist bloc where they will be pinned down for an uncertain duration.

b. Although U.S. prestige is already engaged in SVN, it will become more so by the sending of troops.

c. If the first contingent is not enough to accomplish the necessary results, it will be difficult to resist the pressure to reinforce. If the ultimate result sought is the closing of the frontiers and the clean-up of the insurgents within SVN, there is no limit to our possible commitment (unless we attack the source in Hanoi).

d. The introduction of U.S. forces may increase tensions and risk escalation into a major war in Asia. [*PP*, II, 90]

It was in the face of all these possible drawbacks that he made his recommendation to introduce a task force without delay—made it on the grounds that a U.S. program to save South Vietnam simply would not succeed without it.

Thus, the initial task force was presented as *necessary* to success. Would it also be sufficient? Certainly not in case of any invasion from the North, which it might possibly provoke: in that case, it was made clear, the initial eight thousand troops would be no more than an advance guard. But even short of that contingency, the report emphasized that continued infiltration—which was more likely than not—would require not only larger U.S. forces, but the bombing of North Vietnam. In Schlesinger's words:

Taylor and Rostow *hoped* that this program [i.e., including the Task Force] would suffice to win the civil war—and were sure it would *if only* the infiltration from the North could be stopped. But if it continued, then they could see no end to the war. They therefore raised the question of how long Saigon and the United States could be expected to play by the existing ground rules, which permitted North Vietnam to train and supply guerrillas from across the border and denied South Vietnam [sic] the right to strike back at the source of aggression. Rostow argued so forcibly for a contingency policy of retaliation against the North, graduated to match the intensity of Hanoi's support of the Viet Cong, that "Rostow Plan 6" became jocularly established in the contingency planning somewhere after SEATO Plan 5.[18]

In the spring of 1961, speaking at the Fort Bragg Special Forces School, Rostow had characterized "the sending of men and arms across international boundaries and the direction of guerrilla war from outside a sovereign nation" as a new form of aggression, calling for unilateral retaliation against the "ultimate source of aggression" in the absence of international action.[19] (Apparently the major lesson Rostow had learned from the Bay of Pigs operation, which took place shortly before his speech, was that Castro, or Khrushchev, had had the right to bomb Florida and Washington.)

As Taylor put it in his letter of transmittal to his report:

While we feel that the program recommended represents those measures which should be taken in our present knowledge of the situation in Southeast Asia, I would not suggest that it is the final word. . . . It is clear to me that the time may come in our relations to Southeast Asia when we must declare our intention to attack the source of guerrilla aggression in North Vietnam and impose on the Hanoi Govern-

---

[18] *A Thousand Days,* page 505; italics added.
[19] W. W. Rostow, "Guerrilla Warfare in Underdeveloped Areas," in T. N. Greene (ed.), *The Guerrilla—And How to Fight Him* (New York, 1962), page 60.

ment a price for participating in the current war which is commensurate with the damage being inflicted on its neighbors to the south. [*PP*, II, 97-98]

Such were the views of President Kennedy's most trusted military adviser, whom he had brought out of retirement and later named Chairman of the Joint Chiefs of Staff. Sent to Vietnam precisely to evaluate which, if any, of several proposed schemes of U.S. combat deployment would be appropriate, Taylor came back to tell the President that the situation was "serious but not hopeless": i.e., not hopeless if and only if the President promptly dispatched sizable U.S. combat units, with the understanding that more troops, and bombing of the North, would probably be required as later steps.

With the task force, the initial program was presented as adequate for the short run, but probably inadequate for the long run, requiring major additional measures. Without the vital element of the task force, for which there was no convincing substitute, the remaining measures were almost surely inadequate for both long-term and short-term aims. President Kennedy bought the program minus the task force.

Evidently the President disbelieved his emissaries, Taylor and Rostow. Yet they were far from alone, either in their proposals or their priorities. The Joint Chiefs of Staff had advocated a commitment of U.S. ground troops to Vietnam (and/or Laos) as early as May, 1961 [*PP*, II, 49]. After Taylor's return, they reiterated this recommendation. They also subscribed to Taylor's emphasis on its urgency and, among the whole shopping list of proposals, its critical priority. Moreover, in the first week in November, 1961, Secretary of Defense Robert McNamara and his Deputy, Roswell Gilpatric, strongly associated themselves with the judgments and recommendations of Taylor and the Joint Chiefs. Both in the unusual explicitness of its logic and in the content and urgency of its judgments, this memorandum is remarkably revealing. I cite it in full:

MEMORANDUM FOR THE PRESIDENT   November 8, 1961

The basic issue framed by the Taylor Report is whether the U.S. shall:

a. Commit itself to the clear objective of preventing the fall of South Vietnam to Communism, and

b. Support this commitment by necessary immediate military actions and preparations for possible later actions.

The Joint Chiefs, Mr. Gilpatric, and I have reached the following conclusions:

1. The fall of South Vietnam to Communism would lead to the fairly rapid extension of Communist control, or complete accommodation to Communism, in the rest of mainland Southeast Asia, and in Indonesia. The strategic implications worldwide, particularly in the Orient, would be extremely serious.

2. The chances are against, probably sharply against, preventing that fall by any measures short of the introduction of U.S. forces on a substantial scale. We accept General Taylor's judgment that the various measures proposed by him short of this are useful but will not in themselves do the job of restoring confidence and setting Diem on the way to winning his fight.

3. The introduction of a U.S. force of the magnitude of an initial 8,000 men in a flood relief context will be of great help to Diem. However, it will not convince the other side (whether the shots are called from Moscow, Peiping, or Hanoi) that we mean business. Moreover, it probably will not tip the scale decisively. We would be almost certain to get increasingly mired down in an inconclusive struggle.

4. The other side can be convinced we mean business only if we accompany the initial force introduction by a clear commitment to the full objective stated above, accompanied by a warning through some channel to Hanoi that continued support of the Viet Cong will lead to punitive retaliation against North Vietnam.

5. If we act in this way, the ultimate possible extent of our military commitment must be faced. The struggle may be prolonged and Hanoi and Peiping may intervene overtly. In view of the logistic difficulties faced by the other side, I believe we can assume that the maximum U.S. forces required on the ground in Southeast Asia will not exceed 6 divisions, or about 205,000 men (CINCPAC Plan 32-59, Phase IV). Our military posture is, or with the addition of more National Guard or regular Army divisions, can be made, adequate to furnish these forces without serious interference with our present Berlin plans.

6. To accept the stated objective is of course a most serious decision. Military force is not the only element of what must be a most carefully coordinated set of actions. Success will depend on factors many of which are not within our control—notably the conduct of Diem himself and other leaders in the area. Laos will remain a major problem. The domestic political implications of accepting the objective are also grave, although it is our feeling that the country will respond better to a firm

initial position than to courses of action that lead us in only gradually, and that in the meantime are sure to involve casualties. The overall effect on Moscow and Peiping will need careful weighing and may well be mixed; however, permitting South Vietnam to fall can only strengthen and encourage them greatly.

7. In sum:

a. We do not believe major units of U.S. forces should be introduced in South Vietnam unless we are willing to make an affirmative decision on the issue stated at the start of this memorandum.

b. We are inclined to recommend that we do commit the U.S. to the clear objective of preventing the fall of South Vietnam to Communism and that we support this commitment by the necessary military actions.

c. If such a commitment is agreed upon, we support the recommendations of General Taylor as the first steps toward its fulfillment.

Signed: Robert S. McNamara

[*PP*, II, 108-09]

It is easy to spot judgments here that seem ludicrous in the light of the next ten years: in particular, the estimate by the Joint Chiefs that the "maximum" U.S. ground forces required would "not exceed" 205,000 men even if China, as well as North Vietnam, intervened overtly. (Seven years later, without facing any Chinese, General Westmoreland was requesting almost that identical force—206,000 troops—as an *addition* to the 520,000 already under his command.) Indeed, neither here nor in any other Department of Defense document of the time is there a hint that later years might possibly find us—after four years of steady bombing of North Vietnam—with over a half-million men engaged in an inconclusive struggle in South Vietnam. Nor does any military estimate or analysis seem to have imagined the contingency of large-scale covert infiltration of regular units, impossible to interdict by airpower.

As General Taylor put it in his message cited earlier:

The risks of backing into a major Asian war by way of SVN are present but are not impressive. NVN is extremely vulnerable to conventional bombing, a weakness which should be exploited diplomatically in convincing Hanoi to lay off SVN. Both the DRV and the Chicoms would face severe logistical difficulties in trying to maintain strong forces in the field in SEA, difficulties which we share but by no means to the same degree. There is no case for fearing a mass onslaught of

Communist manpower into SVN and its neighboring states, particularly if our airpower is allowed a free hand against logistical targets. [*PP*, II, 92][20]

Yet it would surely be a misreading of these proposals to suppose that their "optimism" could have been thought reassuring to the President, biasing him toward the proposed ground task force (which he rejected, anyway). On the contrary, the McNamara memo is almost unique in presenting any estimate at all of the "total ultimate involvement" that might be required, and its forecasted ceiling can be assumed to have been a shocker, hardly less daunting than one—more realistic, in retrospect—two or three times as high.

For McNamara and the Joint Chiefs to endorse a course of action and at the same time to expose with such unwonted frankness potential costs, risks, and uncertainties as sobering as these could only underscore the importance of the goals and their contention that lesser measures could simply not "do the job." Indeed, in defiance of the quagmire model, it would be hard to conceive of counsel more uncompromising and explicit in its judgment (paragraph 2 of the memo) that an alternative course—the one shortly to be chosen by the President!—would be inadequate.

Nor was there any lack of emphasis on the need for speed in sending combat units. The phrase "immediate military actions" in the McNamara memo followed Taylor's mention of "coming weeks or months [being] decisive," and the proposition in the Taylor report:

It is evident that morale in Vietnam will *rapidly* crumble—and in

[20] Likewise, the Taylor-Rostow report, in a passage probably drafted by Rostow, pointed out in contrasting the current war to the one the French lost: "Finally, the Communists now not only have something to gain—the South—but a base to lose—the North—if war should come" [*PP*, II, 97]. These cheerful views were never supported by the intelligence community. A Special National Intelligence Estimate (SNIE), issued just three days before the McNamara memo, is summarized by the Pentagon Papers analyst: "The gist of the SNIE was that North Vietnamese would respond to an increased U.S. commitment with an offsetting increase in infiltrated support for the Viet Cong . . . On the prospects for bombing the North, the SNIE implies that threats to bomb would not cause Hanoi to stop its support for the Viet Cong, and that actual attacks on the North would bring a strong response from Moscow and Peiping, who would 'regard the defense of North Vietnam against such an attack as imperative.' " [*PP*, II, 107-08]

Southeast Asia only slightly less quickly—if the sequence of expectations set in motion by Vice President Johnson's visit and climaxed by General Taylor's mission are not *soon* followed by a hard U.S. commitment to the ground in Vietnam. [*PP*, II, 93; italics added]

On the eve of Taylor's mission, one of the most experienced and influential sub-Cabinet officials, William P. Bundy, who had spent a decade in the CIA and was then the Deputy Assistant Secretary of Defense (ISA), later Assistant Secretary of State for Far East Affairs, had emphasized "the element of time" in a personal note for McNamara, commenting on proposals to put in twenty to forty thousand U.S. combat troops:

Even if the decision at tomorrow's meeting is only preliminary—to explore with Diem and the British, Australians, and New Zealanders would be my guess—it is clearly of the greatest possible importance. Above all, action must proceed fast.

For what one man's feel is worth, mine—based on very close touch with Indochina in the 1954 war and civil war afterwards till Diem took hold—is that it *is* really now or never if we are to arrest the gains being made by the Viet Cong. . . .

An early and hard-hitting operation has a good chance (70 percent would be my guess) of *arresting* things and giving Diem a chance to do better and clean up. Even if we follow up hard, on the lines the JCS are working out after yesterday's meeting, however, the chances are not much better that we will in fact be able to *clean up* the situation. It all depends on Diem's effectiveness, which is very problematical. The 30 percent chance is that we would wind up like the French in 1954; white men can't win this kind of fight.

On a 70-30 basis, I would myself favor going in. But if we let, say, a month go by before we move, the odds will slide (both short-term shock effect and long-term chance) down to 60-40, 50-50, and so on. Laos under a Souvanna Phouma deal is more likely than not to go sour, and will more and more make things difficult in South Vietnam, which again underscores the element of time. [*PP*, II, 79][21]

Thus, even a decision by the President to *postpone* by several months or more a decision to send in troops represented a major departure from the advice he was receiving from civilian and military advisers in the Pentagon and the White House.

It should be obvious from the passages cited that there was

---

[21] This is one of the few memos in the Pentagon Papers that mentions as a significant possibility that we might "wind up like the French."

no haziness in internal discussion about the distinction between U.S. ground combat units, on the one hand, and the mixed bag of advisors, logistics, and combat support troops, including intelligence, communications, and helicopter personnel, on the other. These two categories were regarded by all as posing very different risks and benefits; and by October, 1961, even prior to Taylor's trip, it was regarded as almost a foregone conclusion that the latter would be supplied, in any case.

Thus it seems likely that the President himself and his high-level officials regarded his *rejection* of the proposal to send combat units immediately as his most, perhaps *only*, significant decision of the period concerning Vietnam (although, as such, it was successfully concealed from the public). As Sorensen puts it: "All his principal advisers on Vietnam favored it,[22] calling it the touchstone of our good faith, a symbol of our determination. But the President in effect voted 'no'—and only his vote counted."[23] Yet at the same time the President voted "yes" to a set of other programs which every one of his advisers described as almost surely inadequate by themselves: inadequate not only to achieve long-run success but to avoid further deterioration in the mid-term.

That the President so "voted," against advice from Pentagon and White House officials, is surely no sign that his own judgment or decisions were mistaken. Why he did so is a subject for later and more speculative discussion, as are the consequences, and a critical evaluation of his choices. But what is indisputable about this description of the alternatives and forecasts presented to Kennedy, and of his decisions, is that it is in flat contradiction to Schlesinger's "quagmire" model.

There is no basis whatever for describing the President in this instance as taking a "small step" because he was promised success with it, or because it was "reasonably regarded as the last that would be necessary." What he was told was the contrary, and that from virtually every source. His decisions, he was assured, held out the almost certain prospect that new, larger

---

[22] This may not be true for State: see the Rusk cable and Rusk-McNamara memo cited below.
[23] *Kennedy,* page 653.

steps, or else retreat, would present themselves as hard choices in the not-distant future.

The "promise" of inadequacy of the chosen measures was not limited to the Pentagon, nor did it relate merely to the omission of combat forces. Each agency had its own top candidates for changes in U.S. policy which were "essential" to success in Vietnam. Before the year was out, however, the policy had given up pretensions, at least temporarily, to achieving *any* of these features.

In Saigon, the Military Assistance Advisory Group continued to emphasize administrative, intelligence, and command changes as "essential" to long-run success. (Taylor also emphasized these; he did not—contrary to many journalistic accounts—mention any requirement for Vietnamese political or social change among his personal recommendations to the President.)

Meanwhile, the State Department pressed political reforms and "broadening" of the Saigon regime to include divergent non-Communist elements as "essential." Without these changes, it was judged, even the full military commitment recommended by the Pentagon would probably fail. One of the most striking exhibits in the Pentagon Papers—considering the source, rarely heard in his own voice in the documents available—is Dean Rusk's cable from a conference in Japan on November 1, 1961:

Since General Taylor may give first full report prior my return, believe special attention should be given to critical question whether Diem is prepared take necessary measures to give us something worth supporting. If Diem unwilling trust military commanders to get job done and take steps to consolidate non-Communist elements into serious national effort, difficult to see how handful American troops can have decisive influence. While attaching greatest possible importance to security in SEA, *I would be reluctant to see U.S. make major additional commitment American prestige to a losing horse.*

Suggest Department carefully review all Southeast Asia measures we expect from Diem if our assistance forces us to assume de facto direction South Vietnamese affairs. [*PP*, II, 105; italics added][24]

[24] Both Schlesinger and Roger Hilsman in his *To Move a Nation* (New York, 1967) comment on Secretary Rusk's failure to send along anyone from State of comparable rank to Taylor or Rostow on their mission to Vietnam, and—neither being an admirer of Rusk—each one explains his reasons in almost identical, rather patronizing terms. Hilsman: "He did not want the State Department to play a prominent role in the upcoming decisions on Vietnam. For he regarded

This same tone is heard in a joint Rusk-McNamara memorandum to the President of November 11. Probably reflecting the President's personal views, as well as those of Secretary Rusk, who had returned from Japan, this memo omits combat units from its proposals for immediate action—in sharp contrast to Taylor's views and to McNamara's own memo written just three days earlier—deferring the decision on ground troops but proposing that the Pentagon prepare plans for sending them "if that should become necessary for success." If there were not a "strong South Vietnamese effort," the November 11 memo asserted, agreeing with Rusk's personal cable from Japan, "United States forces could not accomplish their mission in the midst of an apathetic or hostile population."

Thus, even the immediate actions recommended, which did not include combat units, were to be offered to the Saigon regime only conditionally. Applying "leverage," the U.S. would demand in return "expression from the GVN of the undertakings it is prepared to make to insure the success of this joint effort," such as:

(a) Prompt and appropriate legislative and administrative action to put the nation on a wartime footing to mobilize its entire resources. (This would include a decentralization and broadening of the Government so as to realize the full potential of all non-Communist elements in the country willing to contribute to the common struggle.)

(b) The establishment of appropriate Governmental wartime agencies with adequate authority to perform their functions effectively.

(c) Overhaul of the military establishment and command structure so as to create an effective military organization for the prosecution of the war. [PP, II, 115]

Vietnam as essentially a military problem . . ." (To Move a Nation, page 421). Schlesinger: "It expressed a conscious decision of the Secretary of State to turn the Vietnam problem over to the Secretary of Defense. Rusk doubtless decided to do this because the military aspects seemed to him the most urgent . . ." (A Thousand Days, page 504). The cable above belies their answer, and suggests a more interesting one. Rusk seems to have had an excellent sense of just what it was he was generously turning over to his Cabinet colleague; the subsequent total failure to get any of the "necessary [political] measures to give us something worth supporting" can scarcely have been a surprise to him, or encouraged him to take the problem back. Rusk's sensitivity here to the perils of betting on a losing horse—and his dexterity in detaching his own prestige from the gamble—throws a new light on the supposedly obtuse and simplistic quality of his thinking. In a bureaucratic endurance race, a man who had survived the test of being Assistant Secretary of State for the Far East during the loss of China and the outbreak of the Korean War was never one to bet against.

As to the importance of the stakes, the Rusk-McNamara memo agrees with Taylor and with McNamara's earlier statements. Indeed, to the familiar forecast of "domino" effects abroad, an unusual warning of dangers at home was added, one of the few occasions in the entire McNamara Study when the bureaucratic taboo against mentioning domestic political considerations in writing is breached:

The loss of South Vietnam to Communism would not only destroy SEATO but would undermine the credibility of American commitments elsewhere. Further, loss of South Vietnam would stimulate bitter domestic controversies in the United States and would be seized upon by extreme elements to divide the country and harass the Administration. [PP, II, 111]

Taylor and Rostow, the Joint Chiefs, and McNamara had all earlier described a formal commitment as being in itself essential to success, along with combat units. Likewise, the first of the Rusk-McNamara recommendations is that:

1. We now take the decision to commit ourselves to the objective of preventing the fall of South Vietnam to Communism and that, in doing so, we recognize that the introduction of United States and other SEATO forces may be necessary to achieve this objective. [PP, II, 113]

But in adopting essentially the Rusk-McNamara recommendations of November 11—which omitted immediate deployment of troops—as his action program in mid-November, President Kennedy likewise omitted their initial proposal for a commitment. He did, however, include the provisions for "leverage" to get the reforms regarded as essential by officials in State. His cable of instructions to Ambassador Nolting asserted:

A crucial element in USG willingness to move forward is concrete demonstration by Diem that he is now prepared to work in an orderly way on his subordinates and broaden the political base of his regime. [PP, II, 118]

By December and January, U.S. insistence on "essential" political and administrative reforms had gone the way of the "assurances" of performance Eisenhower had announced as provisions for U.S. aid in 1954, once again in the face of Diem's open resistance to these attempted interventions. This time, Diem's intransigence and the demonstration of the *lack* of effective U.S. "leverage" were even more marked than usual, reflecting embarrassment on both sides that Diem was getting neither the bilateral defense treaty for which he had privately asked nor the U.S. troop deployment for which Taylor had led him to hope.

Since the White House had deliberately concealed both of these latter considerations, it was impossible for outsiders— i.e., Congress and the public, along with journalists—to interpret U.S. policy or the results of our negotiations accurately. Thus, the account of this episode in *The Lost Revolution* by Robert Shaplen, long an advocate both of leverage and reforms, concludes: "By January, 1962, after prolonged discussion, a communiqué was issued, and it became apparent that Diem and Nhu had *obtained everything they had sought* in the way of additional military and economic support without any clear indication that they would really carry out any reform measures."[25]

To the contrary, of course, the President was well aware that he was offering Diem much less than he had been led to expect, and at the same time asking for a *quid pro quo* that Taylor and Rostow had not mentioned at all. Ambassador Nolting reported, "As anticipated"—in the President's earlier cable of instructions —Diem's "first question was re[:] introduction U.S. combat troops. . . ." A week later, Nolting reported a conversation with Thuan, Diem's Defense Minister:

Thuan said that Diem had not yet discussed fully with him U.S. proposals presented last Friday; but had given him impression of being "very sad and very disappointed." Thuan said Diem had said he now hesitates to put proposals before even his cabinet ministers, fearing that they would be disappointed and lose heart. He had intended to

[25] Robert Shaplen, *The Lost Revolution* (New York, 1966), p. 154; italics added. Although the Schlesinger and Sorensen revelations had appeared by this time, the earlier public impression of Diem's requests and Taylor's advice was so firmly fixed in the minds of Vietnam-watchers—reflecting White House deception—that Shaplen was far from alone in continuing to believe that these were fully reflected in the President's program. Likewise, Shaplen supposed, with many others, that Taylor "also felt strongly" about the need for political reforms and freeing of non-Communist political prisoners, matters on which he was actually silent in his personal recommendations.

discuss U.S. proposals with both cabinet and selected members of assembly who had been consulted re[:] advisability of U.S. forces at time of Taylor mission, but now thought contrast between his earlier question and our proposals too striking. Thuan conveyed impression that Diem is brooding over U.S. proposals and has made no move yet to develop specific ideas on actions GVN expected to take. Thuan said President's attitude seemed to be that U.S. asking great concessions of GVN in realm its sovereignty, in exchange for little additional help; that this is great disappointment after discussions with General Taylor involving, in particular, concept of Delta Task Force; that Diem seemed to wonder whether U.S. was getting ready to back out on Vietnam as, he suggested, we had done in Laos. [PP, II, 121]

So the net result of the Taylor visit seemed to be a *worsening* of the "crisis of confidence" resulting from the Laos negotiations that Taylor had reported as the major problem. The fact is that with the eventual abandonment of "leverage" for reforms, broadening, or changes in ARVN command—after the rejection of a bilateral defense treaty, a formal commitment to Vietnam, or U.S. combat troops in Vietnam or Laos—the Presidential program for Vietnam preserved the peculiar character of omitting every feature advocated by any U.S. agency, or by the Diem regime, as "essential" to long-term success.

The President, of course, had his reasons for his decisions. Many of them were good enough reasons, even in retrospect. But they had little to do either with optimism or inattention. For one thing, it was those ongoing Laos negotiations that provided one tactical reason for postponing the deployment of combat troops which Taylor had prescribed as the solution.

As the President pointed out in a cable to Ambassador Nolting accompanying his decisions:

Introduction of U.S. or SEATO forces into SVN before Laotian settlement might wreck chances for agreement, lead to break up of Geneva conference, break Laos cease fire by Communists with resumption of hostilities.[PP, II, 119]

Moreover, John F. Kennedy, who had first visited Indochina in 1951 and had criticized the French effort both in the House and Senate, was one of the few officials—George Ball was another—who both knew the French experience and could perceive it as a warning to Americans. "If it were ever converted into a white man's war," he told Schlesinger in November, "we would lose as the French had lost a decade earlier."[26]

In addition, by November, 1961, President Kennedy—"his skepticism deepened by the Bay of Pigs experience and the holes in the Laos report"[27]—had bureaucratic lessons of his own to draw upon, warning him not to rely on the optimism of military advisers concerning their preferred courses. Both bodies of experience pointed to the same moral: the threat of quicksand. Or, to use Kennedy's own metaphor in a pithy remark to Schlesinger relating to Taylor's request, the risk of addiction:

They want a force of American troops . . . They say it's necessary in order to restore confidence and maintain morale. But it will be just like Berlin. The troops will march in; the bands will play; the crowds will cheer; and in four days everyone will have forgotten. Then we will be told we have to send in more troops. It's like taking a drink. The effect wears off, and you take another.

"Yet"—the sympathetic historian is forced to record—"he felt obliged to offer a small drink himself, and he increased the number of advisors."

More drinks were still to come. At the end of 1961 there were 1,364 American military personnel in South Vietnam; and the end of 1962, 9,865; at the time of Kennedy's death in November, 1963, about 15,000. This was the policy of "one more step." . . .[28]

Why? Why that small drink? Ignorance of the risks of addiction is belied by Schlesinger's own anecdote of his conversation with the President; belief that one small drink was all that the doctor ordered, as Schlesinger's generalization implies, is belied by his whole account, as it is by the fuller account in the Pentagon Papers. If Kennedy had learned from Cuba and Laos to distrust military optimism about proposed escalations, had he also learned—if so, where?—that military pessimism about lesser courses was equally to be mistrusted?

[26] *A Thousand Days*, page 505.

[27] *Kennedy*, page 652. And see also Schlesinger, *A Thousand Days*, page 316: "When I returned from my post-Bay of Pigs trip to Europe on May 3, the President said, 'If it hadn't been for Cuba, we might be about to intervene in Laos.' Waving a sheaf of cables from Lemnitzer, he added, 'I might have taken this advice seriously.' "

[28] *The Bitter Heritage*, page 505.

At the same time as he rejected—or at least postponed—what he was told by a variety of advisers were minimally adequate immediate measures for success, President Kennedy increased the U.S. involvement and suggested important stakes and ambitious goals for the U.S. in the conflict: while refraining from revealing any of the recommendations above, or their rejection, to the public. If the President was not willing to do more than he did, why did he not do much less? Why court both commitment and costly failure, while risking charges of deception?

Two Decades of Choosing Stalemate

In the light of the internal documentation in the Pentagon Papers, it appears that the pattern of Presidential choice described above for 1961—and the questions it raises—apply virtually across-the-board to major Presidential initiatives on Vietnam over the last two decades. (This paper, however, addresses decisions only up to 1968.) No more than in 1961 were any of the measures of increased involvement that a President actually adopted described previously to him by officials as being adequate "last steps" or, indeed, as anything but holding actions, adequate to avoid defeat in the short run but long shots so far as ultimate success was concerned. This is true of each of the major years of escalating decision over that generation:

1. 1950, when the first $10 million in credits were granted by the Truman Administration to the French and Vietnamese efforts against the Viet Minh (in May, a month before the Korean invasion);

2. 1954, when direct entry into the war was considered and rejected by Eisenhower, followed by a gradually hardening commitment to the support of Diem;

3. late 1961 (discussed above);

4. 1963, the Kennedy decision to encourage the overthrow of Diem;

5. 1964, the decision in the fall to bomb North Vietnam thereafter in "retaliation" for "provocations"—as after the supposed August 4 attack on a Navy intelligence patrol in the Tonkin Gulf; implemented after VC attacks on Pleiku and Qui Nhon, February, 1965; and

6. 1965, the Johnson decisions to bomb North Vietnam steadily; then to deploy U.S. troops in limited numbers to South Vietnam and employ U.S. air support; then after mid-July, to accept open-ended ground force commitment.

In not one of these years—any more than in 1961—had officials described, previous to the President's decision, the specific measures of increased involvement that he actually chose as being adequate to success, "the last that would be necessary." To be sure, in nearly every case, there are optimistic claims to be found in the Pentagon Papers for these very approaches; yet on closer inspection, these appeared *after* the course had been adopted, in what I call below the "Phase B" periods of implementation in between the "Phase A" periods of crisis and decision listed above.

Even in the Phase A years of decision, analyses were not devoid of optimism; on the contrary, it was typical that certain approaches were presented by their proponents as winning strategies: but *these were never the options chosen.* Nor should they have been, in most cases; the claims, particularly military ones, were implausible—nearly always controverted by civilian intelligence estimates at the time—and in retrospect almost surely invalid. The point here is that such claims of adequate effectiveness were *not* made—by anyone, civilian or military, intelligence analyst or commander—before the decision, for the measures actually chosen. Neither of these sorts of optimism, in other words, can account for the President's actual choices.[29]

And if the mood at this one moment of escalation was optimistic for the long-term prospects of the chosen course, that mood did not last long. For McNamara, it had clearly dulled by late November, 1965: "We should be aware that deployments of the kind I have recommended will not guarantee success. U.S. killed-in-action can be expected to reach 1,000 a month, and the odds are even that we will be faced in early 1967 with a 'no-decision' at an

[29] One possible, and very important, exception to this generalization might be the planning put forward by Westmoreland in July, 1965, that—with "Phase I" about to begin—envisioned "Phase III" of his strategy ending with the defeat of the enemy about the middle or end of 1967. Although I remain uncertain, and curious, about President Johnson's personal expectations at that major turning point, it seems possible that he, and Secretary McNamara, accepted Westmoreland's estimate: i.e., that they believed, for once, that the program on which they embarked in mid-July would *win* eventually, not only "buy time." On the other hand, that program was explicitly open-ended (though this was not emphasized to the public), and even the initial phase was very large. That initial stage was very far from being a "small step" or a well-defined, limited measure promising success in the sense of the quagmire thesis; for the next six months it involved an additional 100,000 men, yet it promised, as usual, to do no more than "halt the losing trend by the end of 1965" [*PP*, III, 482].

even higher level" [*PP*, IV, 623]. According to Bill Moyers, P₁ dent Johnson "began to expect the worst" by early 1966 [*Who W Are* (Boston, 1969), page 269].

After reading the earlier published version of this paper, and after subsequent "immersion in the Pentagon Papers," Arthur Schlesinger, Jr., has acknowledged these propositions, and repudiated his previous contradictory statements, as generously as a critic could ask.

> I was wrong in having written [the generalizations cited earlier, *supra* pp. 49, 50, 52 *fn*.] . . . I was mistaken in the suggestion that the escalatory steps actually taken by Presidents were accompanied by promises that these particular strokes would bring victory or would be the last steps necessary.

Schlesinger goes on to comment pungently:

> No President ever escalated enough to satisfy the military, who always complained about civilian restrictions on military action and kept insisting that they be allowed to bomb, shoot, and drown more and more Vietnamese.[30]

But it was not only the military who told each President that what he had chosen would, at best, restore a violent stalemate. That was, regularly, also the gist of the National Intelligence Estimates[31] (which also said much the same for the more violent or costly measures that the military proposed as well, in expectation of enemy counter-escalation), and it was also the view of those, mainly in State, who believed that a different political strategy was essential.

Leslie Gelb, the official in charge of the McNamara Study, sums up this long period in an important paper:[32]

[30] Arthur M. Schlesinger, Jr., "Eyeless in Indochina," *New York Review of Books*, October 21, 1971, page 24; and page 26, ". . . the 1961 decision certainly did not conform to my description of the policy of 'one more step.' . . . No one promised anything about the program that Kennedy did adopt . . ."

[31] These "NIES" are the formal forecasts of the "intelligence community," chaired and coordinated by members of the Office of National Estimates of CIA, under the Director of Central Intelligence. The persistent, realistic skepticism about long-term non-Communist prospects and about the proposals for improving them—particularly about measures to coerce North Vietnamese leadership—that runs through the twenty-year sequence of these estimates is one of the most striking phenomena of the documentation in the Pentagon Papers. The contributions of the Intelligence and Research branch (INR) of State seem to have been particularly creditable.

[32] Leslie H. Gelb, "Vietnam: The System Worked," *Foreign Policy*, Summer, 1971, pages 140-67. I have been greatly stimulated by discussions with Gelb—

The story of United States policy toward Vietnam is either far better or far worse than supposed. Our Presidents and most of those who influenced their decisions did not stumble step-by-step into Vietnam, unaware of the quagmire.

Indeed, to come this close to the fine grain of official choices on Vietnam is to be confronted with puzzles and doubts, to be mired, indeed, in uncertainties. What seemed clear as one listened to speeches, or observed official actions, or compared the two, is less so when files are opened, and concealed actions, official estimates, and internal arguments emerge. Under the magnifying lens, previously evident overall patterns—like the quagmire hypothesis—dissolve like the canals on Mars.

With respect to the question, "Why did successive Presidents do what they did in Vietnam?" the data from the McNamara Study simply rule out one familiar answer, that of the "quagmire" model: "Because they were told it would probably be sufficient to settle the problem for good." To say that is to place *responsibility* for the chosen course, and to focus one's efforts to understand the process, sharply upon the Presidents themselves, rather than upon their advisers. But the question remains; and the Pentagon Papers do not easily yield up other answers to it.

Almost regardless of his attitudes toward the war, a reader exposed to the internal evidence on decision-making is likely to be baffled and troubled by it. How was it that four Presidents —Truman, Eisenhower, Kennedy, Johnson—in the face of intelligence estimates and program analyses and recommendations like these, so persistently chose programs that were presented at the time of decision as almost surely inadequate in the long run, while potentially costly and risky, instead of measures purported to be either more effective or else requiring *lesser* involvement? And why did they, then, at the time of decision almost invariably mislead Congress and the public thereafter concerning the advice and forecasts they had received?

Before setting out to explore some answers to that question, some caveats seem appropriate. To say that much of what fol-

now at the Brookings Institution, formerly an acting Deputy Assistant Secretary of Defense (ISA)—whose study of the earlier periods preceded my own and who in particular first pointed out that the propositions emerging from my study of 1961 and my experience in 1964-1965 applied as well to decisions going back to the 1940's and 1950's.

lows in these essays seems to me still tentative and transitional is not mere hedging: it reflects an important limitation of the data so far available. Although the Pentagon Papers provide a far more adequate and comprehensive collection of pertinent documents than critics have supposed, regarding high-level recommendations, Presidential decisions, estimates, plans, and studies—they remain opaque as to the motives of the major policy-makers and their decisions.

This is not only because the President and White House staff —who leave only a closely guarded and insubstantial trail of documents—necessarily figure in a shadowy, inferential way in these accounts based primarily on documents. Nor is it mainly because of lacunae in the documentation from outside the Defense Department's office of International Security Affairs, which produced the study.[33] It is because the documents available, even the frankest, do not reveal motives; nor do they provide an adequate basis for inferring the motives, attitudes, or perspectives even of the bureaucrats whose names appear most often or who signed them or who may even have written them.

A related but lesser problem in interpreting documents such as those in the Pentagon Papers is that, as Morton Halperin has put it, "Bureaucrats rarely write what they sign, and rarely sign what they write." More importantly, as representatives of an agency and a boss, they rarely believe precisely what they say, or say *all* that they believe, especially in writing, even when they both write it and sign it.

From the point of view of research and analysis, this means that a satisfactory understanding of the decision process cannot be based upon documents alone, forgoing interviews as the authors of the McNamara Study were constrained to do. Their analyses are, at this stage, practically indispensable as a guide to the documents, and with all their gaps and misinterpretations many of them are far more reliable and useful reconstructions than any other accounts yet available. But when Leslie Gelb describes them as "not history, but *inputs* to history," he is being candid about what they were meant to be and are.

[33] For what was and was not available to the task force working on the McNamara Study, see Leslie Gelb, "The Pentagon Papers and The Vantage Point," *Foreign Policy*, Spring, 1972, pages 25-41.

My own direct knowledge of the policy-making process (and indirectly, of the Presidential and Cabinet-level aspect of it, as interpreted to me with great insight, detail, and relish by my former boss, the late John T. McNaughton) taught me how much there was to know about it that was never written down and that could not be guessed from documents. Indeed, a major function of a special assistant, I soon learned, is to deal with what cannot be written down (see pages 87-88); and there are a great many special assistants in Washington. Thus it was no surprise to me to find a number of interpretations that I doubted or flatly disputed in the volumes of the study dealing with the 1964-65 period that I spent in the Pentagon. (I made only very limited contributions to those volumes; and neither in this book nor elsewhere have I yet attempted an account of that period, nor an analysis of the escalation process in 1964-65, as I saw it.)

Thus, those former officials who claim, since the publication of the Pentagon Papers, that their true views and objectives or those of their colleagues have been misunderstood by readers who take their old memos literally are often both sincere and correct. Accounts based only on documents and analyses like those in the Pentagon Papers or, for that matter, only on interviews or on a memoirist's selective memory, must be read like historical dramas: the names of the characters, and much that they do, are factual, but the interests, personalities, and beliefs that purportedly move them are imaginative constructions of the author and reader.

Yet the fact remains that documents, when available, are the place to start. They define usefully *what is to be explained* by those same officials: why they wrote, predicted, recommended, reported just what they did at that particular time, to that recipient. Most documents raise more questions than they answer, yet those questions are essential. Interviews without documents to prime the questioner, to check and jog the memory and candor of former officials, are as unreliable as their memoirs, which, as the Pentagon Papers incidentally reveal, are very unreliable.[84]

[84] See, most recently, Maxwell D. Taylor's *Swords and Ploughshares* (New York, 1972). For example, compare his account of his troop recommendation (pages 232-48) with his cables quoted above.

Thus, the Pentagon Papers are a beginning, a framework, the basis for new interviews, cross-checks of memoirs and journalistic data, and other further exploration that can eventually approach an adequate understanding.

My own hypotheses and tentative conclusions in the rest of this essay and the papers that follow draw heavily upon personal experience, conversations, and documents and studies other than the Pentagon Papers, including those I encountered during a year spent studying crisis decision-making, with high-level inter-departmental access to files and classified histories, prior to entering the Defense Department in mid-1964. My inferences on domestic political considerations, for example, came initially almost entirely from personal experience, particularly as a special assistant (during a Presidential election year), since this is a whole dimension of policy consideration that is often discussed at higher levels but almost never written down for fear of leaks both within the government and to the public. Nevertheless, explanations of "Why they did it," as distinct from "What they did and said," remain mostly conjectures, in my own work as elsewhere.

What the Pentagon Papers do demonstrate unequivocally is that Presidential decisions were not a simple result of accepting predictions and advice. Which is to say that to go beyond this negative finding, to try to explain a President's choices, we must go beyond the Pentagon Papers for evidence; for all the obstacles described above to inferring individual motives from official documents are strongest for the President. Documentary evidence cannot even tell us reliably what considerations were salient to Presidential attention at a given moment. The President—having no formal need to persuade a superior, to coordinate a proposal, or to justify a decision internally—puts much less down on paper than others. Because of his *overlapping* roles, he conceals or dissembles his own views even more than other participants, except selectively to his closest associates. They in turn guard them closely, for reasons of loyalty, their own access, and politics, even when they later come to write "history."

In fact, certain general considerations caution the analyst/historian not to take the set of bureaucratic inputs to Presidential decision as a close reliable guide to the President's own view of a matter, his private expectations and aims.

First, the President may to some degree—rightly or wrongly —disbelieve not only the optimism of certain calculations offered him but the pessimism of others, whether in the form of military recommendations or of intelligence estimates. He may believe that a pessimistic tone reflects a bias, or an attempt to move him toward an alternative, or a bureaucratic hedge. As for claims that measures he has decided to reject or postpone are "essential," he may feel (often with justice) that this language is largely a bureaucratic ploy, an attempt to tie his hands or to make the record as a future hedge against failure, or even to use against him politically in the future.

Most Presidents probably acquire, fairly quickly, some skepticism about assertions that they "must" act *immediately,* or adopt a proposal in full or on a vast scale, if they are to avoid disaster or have any likelihood of success. They are likely to be drawn to converting a program into a sequential decision, to be made in stages, "buying time, awaiting information, keeping options open." They can also *claim* to be doing so, as a way of rejecting a proposal without foreclosing its proponents' hopes.[35]

Moreover, as Richard Moorsteen has pointed out to me, many Presidents, as successful politicians, are likely to exhibit these same traits for temperamental reasons as well. A strong focus on the short run, a hopeful attitude toward the future, a tendency to put off painful decisions in the hope, and with some confidence, that something will turn up to make the decision either unnecessary, or easier: all these are part of the typical makeup of a politician. A President, as Moorsteen puts it, will have at-

[35] This is what Hilsman claims Kennedy did with the proposal to send combat forces in 1961. "In an interesting example of one type of gambit in the politics of Washington policy-making, the President avoided a direct 'no' to the proposal for introducing troops" (*To Move a Nation,* page 424). Such a tactic could account for the success of efforts to keep secret the Taylor/JCS recommendations to send troops. The hope of still persuading the President would discourage leaks among proponents of the measure. And Sorensen suggests another reason: "Formally, Kennedy never made a final negative decision on troops. In typical Kennedy fashion, he made it difficult for any of the pro-intervention advocates to charge him privately with weakness" (*Kennedy,* page 654). On the other hand, a President may claim to be making a sequence of *ad hoc,* contingent, and limited decisions when he has already in fact made a much larger commitment; see below, pages 113-15.

tained that office only by winning a long succession of long shots; by the time he gets there he is likely to have a strong belief in his lucky star, a confidence that he can get away with what looks like chance-taking where others might not, confidence that "something will always turn up" for him.[36] A Bay of Pigs experience comes to him as a special shock; yet even that will probably not erase this tendency permanently.

These considerations of Presidential temperament and operating traits go part of the way to explain discrepancies between the President's views and choices and the estimates and proposals pressed on him by his advisers. But they can hardly, in my opinion, bear the main weight of explanation. That would imply White House wishfulness, or a general and exclusive focus upon the short run, so extreme as to seem almost psychotic. (Nor do they address the reasons for deception of the public.) Rather, it is likely that such factors produced marginal differences in the President's thinking from that of his advisers, but unlikely that they counted for more than that. There is simply no evidence that, in any instance, a President was *radically* more optimistic about the course he was to choose than the expressed appreciations of odds and possibilities presented to him: this conclusion leaves us still facing the earlier puzzles.

Thus, even after making all allowances, the "stumbling-into-quicksand" image cannot be maintained when one looks at the internal record. Instead one sees, repeatedly, a leader striding with his eyes open into what he *sees* as quicksand, increasing his efforts and carrying his followers deeper in. Why? Presumably, because he sees no alternative and hopes to find a way through, or because the alternatives seem even more threatening, worse in the short run. But what in the alternative future is so "intolerable" that even prolonging and enlarging a war seems a lesser evil? What kind of failure seems so ominous that it must be postponed at such costs, while concealing its prospect from the public?

Looking only at the set of critical decision points listed earlier,

[36] See Schlesinger on Kennedy's "enormous confidence in his own luck" (*A Thousand Days,* page 242); Schlesinger puts great emphasis on this in his recent comments in the *New York Review of Books,* October 12, 1971, page 32.

one sees, not an unwary traveler bogging down imperceptibly, but a different image: Eliza, fleeing across the broken ice of the river, leaping from block to block as each begins to slip. . . . And the question becomes: What whips threaten, what are the hounds that bay on the departed shore?

In one period, at least, 1949-50, the identity of the pursuers was in little doubt. A close look at that decision point—when the lack of previous direct American involvement eliminates several of the hypotheses competing for attention later—suggests an answer to the enigma.

1950: The Edge of the Bog

At the time an American President first left solid ground behind to step directly into the Indochina War, the main pursuers to his rear had well-known faces and names, and their accents were American. The voices included those of such Senators as William Knowland, Styles Bridges, Kenneth Wherry, and Pat McCarran, three "Asia-first" Republicans and a right-wing Democrat, who denounced the China White Paper issued by the State Department on August 5, 1949, as "a 1,054-page whitewash of a wishful, do-nothing policy which has succeeded only in placing Asia in danger of Soviet conquest."[37] And even the voice of Arthur Vandenberg, Republican spokesman for "bipartisanship" on foreign affairs: "I think we virtually 'sold China down the river' at Yalta and Potsdam and in our subsequent official demands for coalition with the armed Chinese Communists."[38] And also, the voice of a man who was to defeat Richard Nixon a decade later—in part on the charge that the Republicans had lost Cuba to Communism—who was granted one minute to address the House on January 25, 1949, and used it as follows:

Mr. Speaker, over this weekend we have learned the extent of the disaster that has befallen China and the United States. The responsibility for the failure of our foreign policy in the Far East rests squarely with the White House and the Department of State.

[37] Norman A. Graebner, The New Isolationism (New York, 1956), page 45.
[38] Arthur H. Vandenberg, Jr. (ed.), The Private Papers of Senator Vandenberg (Boston, 1952), page 536

The continued insistence that aid would not be forthcoming unless a coalition government with the Communists was formed was a crippling blow to the National Government.

So concerned were our diplomats and their advisers, the Lattimores and the Fairbanks, with the imperfection of the democratic system in China after twenty years of war and the tales of corruption in high places that they lost sight of our tremendous stake in a non-Communist China.

Our policy, in the words of the Premier of the National Government, Sun Fo, of vacillation, uncertainty, and confusion has reaped the whirlwind.

This House must now assume the responsibility of preventing the onrushing tide of Communism from engulfing all of Asia.[39]

Thus the Democratic Representative from Massachusetts, John F. Kennedy.

Above all, by the spring of 1950 there was the voice of Senator Joe McCarthy, whose sensational charges of Communist infiltration of the State Department began eighteen days after Hiss was convicted in a second trial—or two weeks after Secretary of State Acheson announced, "I will not turn my back on Alger Hiss"—with his speech in Wheeling, West Virginia, on February 9, 1950.

"How can we account for our present situation," McCarthy was to ask later,

unless we believe that men high in this government are concerting to deliver us to disaster? This must be the product of a great conspiracy on a scale so immense as to dwarf any previous venture in the history of man.[40]

Or more specifically, in a Senate speech on March 30, 1950:

It was not Chinese democracy under Mao that conquered China, as Acheson, Lattimore, Jessup, and Hanson contend. Soviet Russia conquered China and an important ally of the conquerors was this small left-wing element in our Department of State.[41]

In less than nine months, criticism of "our loss of China" had moved from condemnation of our "wishful, do-nothing" policy

[39] Congressional Record—House (January 25, 1949), pages 532-33.
[40] Graebner, The New Isolationism, page 28.
[41] Alan D. Harper, The Politics of Loyalty (Westport, Conn., 1969), page 133.

to discern a more sinister meaning than passivity: treason. As Graebner paraphrases the attack:

United States policy failed, in short, because it had pursued the goals, not of this nation, but of the Soviet Union.[42]

Meanwhile, in December, 1949, Chinese Communist troops had reached the borders of Indochina. At that point, granted Chinese sanctuary, supplies, and expert advisors, it became virtually impossible for the Communist-led nationalist forces of the Viet Minh to lose to the French. But for the same reason, given the domestic environment in the U.S. described above, it had become "intolerable" to the Truman Administration that they should win.

Acheson's White Paper on China in 1949 had concluded:

The unfortunate but inescapable fact is that the ominous result of the civil war in China was beyond the control of the government of the United States. Nothing that this country did or could have done within the reasonable limits of its capabilities could have changed that result; nothing that was left undone by his country has contributed to it. It was the product of internal Chinese forces, forces which this country tried to influence but could not. A decision was arrived at within China, if only a decision by default.[43]

This is a statement that might have suggested itself, in every year from 1949 to the present, as providing the format for explaining a U.S. Government decision to abstain or extricate itself from involvement in Indochina. But it is doubtful if that thought ever came to bureaucratic consciousness; the reception of the China White Paper did not encourage it. The argument simply did not "sell," even though its logic rested on the unarguable facts that opposing forces in China were immense and dynamic, no American troops were engaged, and there was no real U.S. support for their involvement. As Acheson has put it recently, the conclusion above "was unpalatable to believers in American omnipotence, to whom every goal unattained is explicable only by incompetence or treason."[44] What the State Department learned then, and evidently has never forgotten, was the number of such believers,

---

[42] Graebner, *The New Isolationism*, page 45.
[43] *United States Relations with China, with Special Reference to the Period 1944-1949* (Washington, D.C. [Government Printing Office], 1949), page xvi.
[44] Dean Acheson, *Present at the Creation* (New York, 1969), page 303.

and their power to wreck policies, administrations, . . . and careers.

In this atmosphere there was no desire in the State Department to have to start drafting a parallel Indochina White Paper. In Indochina the battle against Communist-led guerrillas, whose ultimate direction—here Acheson agreed with his attackers—was seen to be from "the Kremlin," was being carried by French troops unquestionably able and willing to utilize U.S. matériel. No U.S. troops were needed—at least, to avert defeat, to bring about a stalemate. On the other hand, temporary stalemate was about the best that U.S. estimates offered as the outcome of U.S. aid at that time: at least, in the absence of changes that were extremely unlikely in French willingness to grant real independence to Indochina. Yet the need was urgent; official estimates at the end of 1949 gave French forces in Tonkin only six to nine more months, lacking U.S. aid.

In February, 1949, at the apparent initiative of the new Secretary of State, Acheson, the National Security Council had recommended withholding supplies already earmarked for Nationalist China. Senator Vandenberg argued successfully against the move, even though he admitted that Communist victory seemed inevitable; "I decline to be responsible for the *last push* which makes it possible."[45] The aid continued; even this did little to protect the Administration from its critics, yet it was becoming evident that to have done any less would have been still more risky, more ominously "questionable."

A year later, any proponent of withholding military aid from our NATO ally France, thereby accepting full responsibility for its prompt defeat in Indochina by the forces of the Kremlin, would have been in an isolated position. And this despite the fact that intelligence estimates at the time held out scant hope that France would accept the political strategy based on a truly independent, non-Communist regime in Indochina which alone, it was believed, might offer a significant chance of victory. (In retrospect, even this conditional hope was probably a delusion after 1949.)

No matter how slim the probability of "winning," there was

[45] *The Private Papers of Senator Vandenberg*, page 532; his italics.

little debate within the government as to whether the open-ended
direct aid policy we commenced in May, 1950, with a first install-
ment of $10 million, was worthwhile. It could—and did—buy a
stalemate; and the alternative was to add the Democrats' "loss"
of Indochina to their "loss" of China. That was enough to know.
To postpone the loss of Tonkin beyond the tenure of the Truman
Administration evidently seemed worth more than the several
billion dollars—and the French and Vietnamese lives—that it cost.

What leads one to this seemingly harsh and cynical interpretation is not only the great difficulty otherwise of explaining a
decision to involve ourselves directly in this struggle against what
was perceived within the U.S. Government as a nationalist movement—Communist-led, to be sure, but with the support of the
great majority of Vietnamese people[46]—especially given the extreme pessimism of official estimates concerning French prospects
in the long run, even with our aid. No more in this first instance
than in later ones did the quagmire model apply: "one small step
promising success."

Moreover, other hypotheses on possible motives for accepting
a long shot, plausible in later periods, cannot apply here. In 1950,
it could not be said that we had to carry out prior commitments
or promises; or that our prestige rested on earlier involvement; or
that, our own forces having been engaged, we could not afford
a "military defeat."

The relevant events abroad determining our response had taken
place outside Indochina. These were the fall of China, following
earlier disappointments in Eastern Europe, the Czech coup, and
in general, the Cold War. The public's interpretation of these
events was strongly influenced—to the detriment of the Democrats—by the anti-Communist rhetoric that President Truman
himself had invoked in 1947-48 in order to win Congressional
support for foreign aid.[47] In effect, for purposes of foreign policy

[46] See Book 8 of the GPO edition; for example, the documents relating to the
period immediately after the outbreak of hostilities, pages 91-115, and particularly, the State Department Policy Statement on Indochina, September 27, 1948,
pages 143-49.

[47] Richard Freeland, The Truman Doctrine and the Origins of McCarthyism
(New York, 1972); Athan Theoharis, Seeds of Repression (Chicago, 1971); and
look again at the 1949 quotation presented earlier, page 81, from John F.
Kennedy.

the Democrats in Truman's first term called up a genie of anti-Communism, to which they proved to be domestically vulnerable after Truman's surprising victory in 1948, which kept him in the White House for the inexorable victory of Communism in China, the first Russian atomic test, the second Hiss conviction, and the Fuchs case.

All of these events came within a few months starting in the fall of 1949. The response to them by the Republican leadership likewise reflected the stunning frustration of their 1948 electoral defeat. (Senator Taft's decision to back McCarthy was an important part of this response; in turn, this senior Republican sponsorship was crucial to McCarthy's impact.[48]) After these developments, even had there been no prior U.S. involvement in Indochina, a Communist victory in Asia that the U.S. might have prevented was sure to be read as a "defeat" for the U.S., a culpable failure by the Administration, a basis, even, for charges of conscious treachery.

That involvement posed the likelihood of greater costs in the future, and even risks of a major war with China or Russia if the Chinese Communists should enter, all uncompensated by any significant promise of eventual success: none of which outweighed the credible promise that intervention would "buy time," i.e., postpone defeat and avert the political and personal consequences of being "soft on Communism."

With the outbreak of the Korean War, followed rapidly by public disenchantment (and charges that Acheson had even invited the attack), by the message of Republican victories in the fall, and above all by the entry of the Chinese Communists into the war, all the earlier motives were sharpened for "buying time" in Indochina. But even then, not "at any price." Despite the renewed judgment that the strategic stakes in Southeast Asia were of the highest order, there was even less interest than before in committing U.S. ground troops to Indochina.

The "Never Again Club" in the Pentagon, which opposed any further land wars in Asia, was in the process of consolidating. And controversy over General MacArthur's dismissal in April,

---

[48] See Robert Griffith, *The Politics of Fear* (Lexington, 1970), *passim*.

1951, both mobilized critics of Administration policy and publicized a premise already present earlier in the attacks by the
"Asia-first" Republicans. This was a belief that "victory" was not
only, as MacArthur emphasized, indispensable, but that it could
be had on the cheap, by a show of Administration resolve, based
on an unrestrained use of airpower and the troops of Asian allies.[49]
To have to employ U.S. ground forces against Asians showed
weak strategy, incompetence, irresolution, or neglect of potential
allies; to lose an area to Communism marked either culpable
negligence or treason.

Anyone who has witnessed—as I did—the decision-making on
Indochina from the inside during a period such as the autumn of
1964 (perhaps the nadir of U.S. hopes regarding South Vietnam
in the last decade) will almost surely feel on reading accounts of
the 1948-1954 period that he is observing the genesis of many
bureaucratic-political premises of the later debate. Such books[50]
describe the events that scratched the minds of a generation of
bureaucrats and politicians.

In that bleak fall of 1964, a personal memo to Secretary Mc-
Namara drafted on September 3rd by Assistant Secretary John
McNaughton (soon after I had become his Special Assistant)
began, "The situation in South Vietnam is deteriorating. Even
before the government sank into confusion last week . . ." [PP,
III, 556], and went on to pose the substantial chance that the
situation would shortly come "completely apart" no matter what
we did. Admiral Sharp, CINCPAC, warned the Joint Chiefs later
in the month, "we may find ourselves suddenly faced with an
unfriendly government or no government at all" [PP, III, 569].
(In a period of relative calm in late November, an intelligence
working group noted with relief the current absence of "the flurry
of riots and demonstrations of serious proportions, or of labor
strikes, armed revolts, urban lawlessness, and coup plotting that
seemed [August through October] to be bringing South Vietnam

[49] See Harper, *The Politics of Loyalty,* Chapters 5 and 9; and Graebner, *The
New Isolationism,* Chapters 3 and 5.
[50] In addition to those cited earlier, see in particular Tang Tsou, *America's
Failure in China, 1941-50* (Chicago, 1963); H. Bradford Westerfield, *Foreign Policy
and Party Politics* (New Haven, Conn., 1955); and Earl Latham, *The Communist
Controversy in Washington* (Cambridge, Mass., 1966).

close to the brink of internal chaos and disintegration . . ." [*PP*, III, 651].[51])

In these circumstances, McNaughton's September 3rd memo defined the U.S. objective as being "to reverse the present downward trend. Failing that, the alternative objective is to emerge from the situation with as good an image as possible in U.S., allied, and enemy eyes." We should be alert to chances, preferably "to back the DRV down"[52] or "to evolve a tolerable settlement," but "if worst comes and South Vietnam disintegrates or their behavior becomes abominable to 'disown' South Vietnam, hopefully leaving the image of 'a patient who died despite the extraordinary efforts of a good doctor.' "

One of the first tasks assigned me in my new job was to envision the alternative ways that—despite our efforts—the situation might "come apart"; to calculate their relative pros and cons in terms of U.S. interest; and to propose ways of tempering the damage.

---

[51] The section of the Pentagon Papers on "US-GVN Relations" dealing with this dizzying period (II, 333-50) conveys a *Catch-22* spirit, which reached a high point in an abortive coup of September 13th; "The USG opposed the coup, and also opposed overt violence to suppress it; in particular, USG opposed VNAF [Vietnamese Air Force, under Ky] bombing of Saigon, which was threatened at one point . . . When Khanh and Ky asked for U.S. Marines, the USG refused . . ." State's comments to the Embassy were poignant: "(A) It is imperative that there not be internecine war within VN Armed Forces; (B) The picture of petty bickering among VN leaders has created an appalling impression abroad. . . . (G) Emphasize that VN leaders must not take the U.S. for granted" (page 338). (In a comparable period twenty months later—when I was at the Saigon end of the cables—everyone was less restrained. State Department: "This may require rough talk but U.S. cannot accept this insane bickering . . ." "[U.S. Marine] General Walt heard of a possible VNAF attack on dissident ARVN units in their compounds, and threatened to use U.S. jets to shoot down the VNAF aircraft if they did" [*PP*, II, 374-75].)

[52] The body of the memo proposed preparing a "squeeze" on North Vietnam: "by doing legitimate things" ["from the US, GVN, and hopefully allied points of view . . . under the circumstances"] "to provoke a DRV response and to be in a good position to seize on that response, or upon an unprovoked DRV action, to commence a crescendo of GVN-US military actions against the DRV." "The 'scenario' should begin approximately October 1st," which "allows time for some kind of a 'voice' to emerge which can speak for South Vietnam . . . and it postpones probably until November or December any decision as to serious escalation." (The selection of a "voice" for the U.S. by our own usual process was scheduled for November 3rd) "During the next two months, because of the lack of 'rebuttal time' before election to justify particular actions which may be distorted to the U.S. public, we must act with special care—signaling to the DRV that initiatives are being taken, to the GVN that we are behaving energetically despite the restraints of our political season, and to the U.S. public that we are behaving with good purpose and restraint" [*PP*, III, 557-59].

In effect, I was to imagine alternative ways we might come to "lose Indochina" and to frame corresponding "White Papers." As a Cold Warrior I found this assignment not at all congenial, though conceptually not too difficult.[53] I had not read the China White Paper—or I might have used it as a model—but I had no great hopes that any of the rationales of our failure I was asked to devise could be made to sound very convincing.[54]

I was mainly concerned about the impact of that failure on our influence and security; but McNaughton made sure I realized, before undertaking these tasks, what it could also mean to the Administration, party, and individuals implicated in it. I was directed to discuss these tasks with no one but him, not even my colleagues among the Deputy Assistant Secretaries. I was not to use a secretary but to type my reports myself. McNaughton would discuss them with me and sometimes retype, cut, and paste parts of them into his personal memos to the Secretary.

"You should be clear," he warned me several times that fall, "that you could be signing the death warrant to your career by having anything to do with calculations and decisions like these. A lot of people were ruined for less." He did not have to tell me when that had been.

Yet if I had known the detailed history of that earlier period—as described in the books cited on McCarthyism, the Truman policies, and the "loss of China"—I would have found immediately explicable, in career and party terms, certain bureaucratic patterns whose strength in the mid-sixties was then puzzling to me.[55]

---

[53] One of my lists—not the longest—of "Ways GVN might collapse" is presented in *PP*, III, 696; another in *PP*, III, 599. On the "White Paper" aspects, see "Techniques to minimize impact of bad outcomes," *PP*, III, 700.

[54] One of my contributions is paraphrased in a McNaughton draft of October 13th [*PP*, III, 583]: "Care should be taken to attribute any setbacks to factors: a. Which cannot be generalized beyond South Vietnam (i.e., weak government, religious dissension, uncontrollable borders, mess left by French, unfavorable terrain, distance from U.S., etc.) . . ." When a similar point about making clear that "failure in South Vietnam, if it comes, was due to special local factors" was proposed by William Bundy in early November, 1964, a Joint Chiefs representative commented that this was "a slight paraphrase of Aesop's fox and grapes story. No matter how we talk it up amongst ourselves it could only be completely transparent to intelligent outside observers" [*PP*, III, 624].

[55] For some other bureaucratic legacies of the "loss of China," I recommend periodic rereading of the path-breaking essay that, I suspect, first turned my own thoughts in this direction: James C. Thomson, Jr.'s "How Could Vietnam

These patterns, which persist today, include powerful *inhibitions against:*

(1) Proposing "coalition" with Communists (as Marshall was charged with doing in China), or regarding local accommodation as less than tantamount to Communist victory;

(2) Pressuring an Asian ally toward "reforms," to the point of risking the charge of weakening his confidence or political base or military capability;

(3) Regarding Communist adversaries as anything but terrorists and aggressors (though blessed with "organizational skills" and "ideologically indoctrinated");

(4) Withholding approval indefinitely from military proposals for "victory through airpower";

(5) Strongly questioning the likelihood, speed, or impact on U.S. interests of an Asian "accommodation" to Communists after a Communist victory in South Vietnam (the "domino theory");

(6) Describing a "victory" over Communism in any area of conflict as impossible, or proposing a "no-win" policy;

(7) Describing, for example, the eventual victory of Communists in South Vietnam, or Laos as "inevitable" or highly probable, or in value terms as anything but "intolerable."[56]

(8) Appearing to "do nothing" in face of any possible "loss to Communism" (whether or not an action with any promise of effectiveness is at hand), or failing to favor any "cheap" action—with significant domestic support—that "might" succeed.

An important illustration of the last point was the persistence beyond the election of 1964 of the "good doctor" theme. This had first emerged in McNaughton's memos in September, 1964, in connection with the need to put the best face possible on a defeat

Happen?" (prematurely subtitled "An Autopsy"), *The Atlantic*, April, 1968. The credit due Thomson not only for originality but for his sense of responsibility—in risking his professional ties to speak out candidly to the public—is even more apparent now when one counts how few his imitators have been.

It remains to be seen—with no sign yet, as of April, 1972—whether any of these patterns will begin to erode as a result of President Nixon's trip to China.

[56] This evaluation—unchallengeable, bureaucratically, by prudent rules of the game since 1950—leads directly to the peculiarly sparse form that proposals take throughout the Pentagon Papers, a form that I have elsewhere called the Desperate Proposal Pattern. To avoid an "intolerable" (infinitely negative) outcome, any measure with *some* chance of success is justified, no matter how low its probability of success, or how high its cost and risks. Hence there is no need to report or even calculate the latter considerations; it is enough to say that, unlike current policy, the one proposed is *not certain* to fail.

that we might not be able to avoid (in particular, because of the
political need for U.S. military restraint prior to the election).
On the day the polls closed, bombing the North became a live
option. Representing McNaughton, I was assigned to William
Bundy's task force, which convened in State on election day,
November 3, 1964, essentially to consider alternative escalation
proposals. At this point, the "good doctor" metaphor took on an
almost macabre meaning, as a rationale for bombing even if it
were expected to fail (as, in my understanding, both McNaughton
and William Bundy did expect).

In comparing Option C, "Progressive-squeeze" (a "crescendo
of bombing") with Option A, "Continue present policies," Mc-
Naughton asserted: "Even if Option C failed, it would, by demonstrating U.S. willingness to go to the mat, tend to bolster allied
confidence in the U.S. as an ally."[57] A day later he added: "If
Option C is tried and fails, we are in no worse position than we
would be under Option A; but whatever form a failure took,
Option C would leave behind a better odor than Option A: It
would demonstrate that U.S. was a 'good doctor' willing to keep
promises, be tough, take risks, get bloodied, and hurt the enemy
badly."[58] Read today—six million tons of bombs later—these judgments seem astounding, to use as neutral a word as possible. It is
evident (much more sharply than it was to me at the time, though
I opposed the bombing then) that the sort of reputation to be
guarded by such means is not that of a "doctor" but of a Mafia
chieftain.[59]

To suppose that these sentences and recommendations represent truly and fully the values and personal views of McNaughton
and Bundy would be mistaken; as mentioned in the preface, even
in their personal memos they were often framing arguments and
images for their bosses to use, and some of these reflected their
superiors' views more than their own. One hidden strand to this

[57] *PP*, III, 601; John T. McNaughton memo, November 6, 1964.
[58] *PP*, III, 604; for similar expressions, see pages 557, 559, 582, 594, 659, 666,
and 685.
[59] Looking back in early 1966, McNamara commented in a memo to the President drafted by McNaughton: "The price paid for improving our image as a
guarantor has been damage to our image as a country which eschews armed
attacks on other nations" [*PP*, IV, 54]

particular argument, of which I was aware at the time, emerges significantly when one traces back its origins to the 1950's. The advantage of *demonstrating* "resolve," opposition to Communist advances, even by costly and risky actions that were likely to fail, runs through these analyses.

Demonstrate to whom? Purportedly, to foreigners: both opponents and allies. Yet the confident assurance—mocked by events—that these advantages would outweigh costs and risks might have seemed peculiar, even at the time; unless one were sensitive to the fact that "doing something" to hurt Communist opponents, no matter how costly and unpromising, would be strong protection against *domestic* charges of culpable underestimation of a Communist threat, or of defeatism, or being "soft" on Communism, or even—fantastic as this would have seemed before 1950—of literal treason.

The most explicit and influential expression of the "good doctor's" need for malpractice insurance can be found in McGeorge Bundy's memo to President Johnson of February 7, 1965. Bundy's recommendation of "A Policy of Sustained Reprisal," just after the Pleiku attack, came on the eve of the President's initiation of sustained bombing and may well have been decisive. The final paragraph of his section on "Expected Effect" begins:

We cannot assert that a policy of sustained reprisal will succeed in changing the course of the contest in Vietnam. It may fail, and we cannot estimate the odds of success with any accuracy—they may be somewhere between 25 and 75 percent. What we can say is that even if it fails, the policy will be worth it. At a minimum it will damp down the charge that we did not do all that we could have done, and this charge will be important in many countries, including our own. [*PP,* III, 690]

To read in such a book as Tang Tsou's *America's Failure in China* (arresting title), the list of measures that were proposed for the U.S. in China but not tried—including large-scale use of advisors, logistic support, intelligence and communications assistance, the overthrow or replacement of Chiang, transport, combat air support, large-scale training, U.S. combat units—is to read the list of measures that *were* successively tried in Vietnam. ("Leverage" for reform and for broadening the government was urged in both cases, tried in neither.)

These measures had been rejected in China because, in the judgment of General Marshall and others—almost surely correct—they were unlikely to prove adequate. In Vietnam, the Pentagon Papers reveal that many of the corresponding judgments, at the decision-points of escalation, were scarcely more sanguine; but this time the measures were used anyway. Why the difference? Because Vietnam was more important? Hardly. Because of the difference in scale? But the measures urged for China were not very large, and the actual programs in Vietnam, in the end, were not small. Because the Marshall-Acheson policy in China was proved mistaken? One doubts that many officials in the 1960's believed that.

Almost surely, among the generation of officials who survived the purges of the Asian bureaus in the fifties, it was not the worries of foreigners that they remembered, as the epitaph to the Marshall-Acheson course of cutting losses in China, but the famous charges that this policy exposed Marshall as "a living lie . . . a front man for traitors" and Acheson as "the Red Dean."[60]

This period was surely still vivid to the officials making those strange judgments in 1964-65 that even if bombing the North "fails to turn the tide—as it may—the value of the effort seems to us to exceed its cost."[61] (William Bundy was Acheson's son-in-law; McGeorge Bundy edited his speeches.) They may or may not have known of Vandenberg's argument to Acheson in 1949 advocating aid to Chiang—"I decline to be responsible for the *last push* . . ."—but its bureaucratic echoes had lasted fifteen years.

What had been lost to their memory was Acheson's counter-argument, as expressed at the beginning of 1950 with reference to American involvement in the defense of Formosa: "The Chiefs

---

[60] On the effects of McCarthyism—or McCarranism—on the "Asian experts" in the government, see in addition to James Thomson's article cited earlier, the speeches delivered at the AAS Conference, March, 1969, by Richard Kagan, A. Edmund Clubb, and Ross Koen, reprinted in the *Bulletin of Concerned Asian Scholars*, Number Four, May 1969. Also see the profile of John Stewart Service, "Foresight, Nightmare, and Hindsight," by E. J. Kahn, Jr., *New Yorker*, XLVII (April 8, 1972), pages 43-95.

[61] McGeorge Bundy, February 7, 1965 (*PP*, III, 687).

again objected to the involvement of American forces but proposed some funds for military materiel and a fact-finding mission.
I objected to this *toying with the mousetrap*. . . ."[62] To a reader
in 1971, that last comment appears almost stunning in its cogency
and prescience. Yet to an impartial political scientist writing in
the mid-1950's, it marked an attitude and a set of tactics that were
simply "politically foolhardy":

Now, it may be true that Chiang could have been saved only by very
large-scale intervention by the United States "beyond the reasonable
limits of its capabilities" (as Acheson asserted in the 1949 White
Paper). But it seems to be carrying logic in the conduct of foreign
affairs to self-defeating extremes to make that belief a justification for
attempting to block *all* substantial aid, in order to cut American losses.
By spending expeditiously a few hundred million more on military aid,
as the GOP requested, and by sending as many military advisors as
could possibly be spared, the State Department in 1947 could probably
still have forced the Republicans to share public responsibility for any
later decision to cut the losses. . . . If then the American public had
shown a willingness to press on, the rewards of victory or even of
stalemate would have been vastly greater than was eventually the case
in Korea.[63]

Thus the domestic political case in favor of "toying with mouse-
traps," even if the outcome should be the "rewards of stalemate"—
those rewards we have experienced over the last twenty years in
Indochina—was the lesson that stuck, when it came to drawing
morals from the debacle of China policy. (Likewise, some former
Johnson officials seem to have concluded that the President's
main "mistake" was, in effect, not paying attention to the need
to make Congressional leaders his accomplices, in the escalations
of 1964-66.)

To regard domestic political considerations as being of critical
importance to a particular foreign policy decision is not to say
that *only* these considerations figure in the decision; or that the
officials weighing such concerns are thinking only of themselves
and their Administration; or that domestic and international policy
factors were mutually independent; or that domestic considera-

[62] Acheson, *Present at the Creation*, page 350; italics added.
[63] Westerfield, *Foreign Policy and Party Politics*, page 258.

tions were of one simple sort, e.g., winning the next Presidential election.

Other relevant aspects of domestic "politics" that can influence or be influenced by a particular foreign policy include: the prospects of passing a current legislative program (e.g., the Great Society program in 1964); the composition of the next Congress, with its implications for subsequent programs and elections; a President's chances for renomination by his own party, as well as for reelection (see 1968)[64]; the prospects of tumultuous controversy during primaries and the election campaign, with its implications for effective governing (again, 1968); the future of one's party (e.g., the feasibility in the 1970's of creating a "new Republican majority"); a President's reputation, his place in history, and his own self-respect (thus, the concern of both Johnson and Nixon not to be "the first U.S. President to lose a war"); the potential damage to the whole society, as well as to a party or individuals, of a resurgence of "McCarthyism," or in the words of some Johnson officials, a "bloodbath of recrimination."[65]

Each of these "political" considerations interacts with strategic concerns or with other matters of domestic policy. No President, after all, believes that victory for himself or his party, or the defeat of a particular opponent, is merely of selfish interest to himself and his supporters: important issues of foreign and domestic policy and concern are regarded as dependent on these legislative and electoral outcomes. And a "humiliation" for an American President is seen—especially by that President, but not only by him—as a setback for the prestige and influence of the United States as well.

[64] Michael Janeway has suggested to me that 1964 might be another, less obvious example: that LBJ had reason to fear that if he "abandoned" South Vietnam—which he was not inclined to do anyway—he would be attacked by the political heirs of JFK, Robert Kennedy and his supporters. This would imply a mirror image of Nixon's reported worry in 1969-70 about Wallace and Reagan (see footnote, page 98).

[65] See Jerome Slater on the Dominican Republic crisis of 1965: "With the Cuban missile crisis still a very live memory, and with the rise of the radical right, culminating in the Republican nomination of Barry Goldwater only a year earlier, still a major factor in American politics, reasonable men could and did in fact fear that a successful Communist revolution in the Dominican Republic might well jeopardize the future of the Democratic Party in the United States, if not of American liberalism in general." *Intervention and Negotiation: The United States and the Dominican Revolution* (New York, 1970), pages 199-200

Moreover, to somewhat varying degrees, each one of these post-war Presidents has been a "true believer" in the premises of Cold War policy that have figured consistently in their rhetoric. And they themselves have contributed crucially to making these premises influential factors in domestic politics, matters of potential vulnerability for an incumbent. Thus, in their eyes, the imperatives of domestic politics point in the same general direction as do their instincts of "what is right for America."

In the spring of 1950, although Indochina was surely not prominent among the concerns of officials of the Truman Administration, all the considerations above pointed to one conclusion, sufficient to determine policy: *This is not a good year for this Administration to lose Vietnam to Communism.*

Nor was 1951. Nor 1952. Korea, the Chinese Communists, MacArthur, an upcoming Presidential election, all ensured that.

Nor—for a new Administration that had come to office on charges of Democratic "losses" and with loud talk of "rollback" and of "unleashing" Chiang—was 1953 a good year to abandon Vietnam; or, after 1954, South Vietnam. . . .

A decade after 1950, a new Democratic President inherited the task, among others, that he had defined sometime earlier: "preventing the onrushing tide of Communism from engulfing all of Asia." And not only Asia. In a campaign speech to the American Legion Convention on October 18, 1960, John F. Kennedy stated:

American strength relative to that of the Soviet Union has been slipping—and Communism has been advancing steadily in every area of the world—until the Iron Curtain now rests on the Island of Cuba—only ninety miles away . . . Cuba has been lost to the Communists. Laos has begun to slip behind the Iron Curtain . . . I have never believed in retreating under fire. . . .

Within one year of this campaign speech—and after an election victory whose narrowness was frequently on his mind—President Kennedy had experienced: the Bay of Pigs; the need to seek a negotiated—and probably unstable—settlement in Laos; the Vienna Summit conferences; the Berlin Wall and Khrushchev's threats on Berlin; and the resumption of Soviet nuclear testing. The failure in Cuba had confirmed for future Presidents, especially

Democrats, a "No Second Cuba" policy for the Caribbean, whose burden was felt by the Dominican Republic in 1965.[66]

After all this, John F. Kennedy found 1961, like 1950 and the years between, a bad time to depart from the decade-old "No Second China" policy in Asia, a bad year to make decisions that might lose South Vietnam or Laos to Communism. As Schlesinger recalls: "Kennedy told Rostow that Eisenhower could stand the political consequences of Dien Bien Phu and the expulsion of the West from Vietnam in 1954 because the blame fell on the French. 'I can't take a 1954 defeat today.' "[67]

Likewise, most of 1962. Yet by the end of that year, the situation might have been seen differently, at least on the international front. The Cuban missile crisis had established Kennedy's resolve, split further the Soviets and Chinese Communists, ended the Berlin confrontation and prepared the way for the test ban. Meanwhile, as Kenneth O'Donnell has revealed, the mood of optimism about Vietnam that had set in during 1962 had ebbed in the White House by the end of the year, and still more by the following spring. According to O'Donnell's account, seconded by Senator Mansfield, Kennedy had been disturbed in late 1962 to find himself agreeing with an unexpected argument by Mansfield that he should stop sending more military reinforcements to South Vietnam and then withdraw all U.S. forces from that country's civil war.

A continued steady increase of American military advisors in South Vietnam, the Senator argued, would lead to sending still more forces to beef up those that were there, and soon the Americans would be dominating the combat in a civil war that was not our war. Taking over the military leadership and fighting in the Vietnam war, Mans-

---

[66] According to Senator Fulbright in 1965: "The specter of a second Communist state in the hemisphere—and its probable repercussions within the United States and possible effects on the careers of those who might be held responsible—seems to have been the most important single factor in distorting the judgment of otherwise sensible and competent men" (Slater, *Intervention and Negotiation*, pages 31-32). Slater cites LBJ during the 1965 crisis (page 199): "When I do what I am about to do, there'll be a lot of people in this hemisphere I can't live with, but if I don't there'll be a lot of people in this country I can't live with"; and again, "You can imagine what would have happened . . . if I had not intervened . . . and there was an investigation and the press got hold of [Bennett's] cable."

[67] *A Thousand Days*, page 317.

field warned, would hurt American prestige in Asia and would not help the South Vietnamese to stand on their own two feet, either.[68]

Impressed, Kennedy still did not change his public position on the need for U.S. support of Diem. But when Mansfield renewed the argument in the spring of 1963, the President called him in for a private talk, and O'Donnell (who witnessed it) reports:

The President told Mansfield that he had been having serious second thoughts about Mansfield's argument and that he now agreed with the Senator's thinking on the need for a complete military withdrawal from Vietnam.
"But I can't do it until 1965—after I'm reelected," Kennedy told Mansfield.
President Kennedy felt, and Mansfield agreed with him, that if he announced a total withdrawal of American military personnel from Vietnam before the 1964 election, there would be a wild conservative outcry against returning him to the Presidency for a second term.
After Mansfield left the office, the President told me that he had made up his mind that after his reelection he would take the risk of unpopularity and make a complete withdrawal of American forces from Vietnam. "In 1965, I'll be damned everywhere as a Communist appeaser. But I don't care. If I tried to pull out completely now, we would have another Joe McCarthy red scare on our hands, but I can do it after I'm reelected. So we had better make damned sure that I *am* reelected."

There is no way, starting from O'Donnell's understanding of Kennedy's views at this time, to attribute the continued buildup of advisors throughout most of 1963, or the encouragement of the Diem coup, or Kennedy's continued avowals in 1963 of the domino theory and of our unswerving commitment—to his (a) inattention or inadvertence, or (b) confidence in subordinates' optimistic promises, or (c) perception of there being no alternative because of the involvement or pledges of predecessors, or of international concerns.

Indeed, in the light of these revelations of the President's pessimism and intentions, there seems no way to read his actions in 1963 increasing or confirming national involvement in and commitment to the war in Vietnam, except as reflections of his judg-

[68] "LBJ and the Kennedys," *Life*, August 7, 1970. Mansfield was subsequently quoted in interviews as confirming in substance this report.

ment that 1963 was a worse time than 1965 for him to lose a war to Communists, so that he would just have to keep it going till then.

To be sure, continuing the war in Vietnam did not mean the same thing in 1963 that it did in 1965, or 1970, especially for Americans. As O'Donnell pointed out to me recently (February 24, 1971): "Forty-three Americans had been killed in Vietnam at the time of President Kennedy's death. We lost that many in the last two weeks over Laos." (The difference between the two periods in terms of Vietnam casualties was also considerably smaller.)

Nevertheless, as quoted by O'Donnell, Kennedy was not even claiming that he might avoid or reduce the "McCarthy red scare" by postponing it—"In 1965, I'll be damned everywhere as a Communist appeaser"—but merely that he could prevent it from interfering with his reelection. He proposed to do so by accepting two more years of U.S. involvement, with its evident risks—unless he were "damned sure" to be reelected, and perhaps even then—of later escalation, U.S. combat involvement, vastly increased American and Vietnamese deaths, and domestic disaster.

All these risks were realized. Kennedy did not live either to win the election or to leave the war. Instead he willed the war to a President determined not to be the first to lose one, leaving an escalated U.S. involvement in Vietnam to an insecure successor who had some reason to fear the political consequences—even at the hands of the dead President's heirs, officials, and supporters—of publicly abandoning it.[69]

[69] The risk that "losing" Vietnam would pose some risk from a faction within the President's own party was one that Johnson in 1964 shared with Eisenhower in 1954. Even Richard Nixon has seen himself as facing comparable problems in 1969-71, as his special assistant Henry A. Kissinger has reported in numerous "backgrounders": "If we had done in our first year what our loudest critics called on us to do, the 13 percent that voted for Wallace would have grown to 35 or 40 percent; the first thing the President set out to do was to neutralize that faction." (See Derek Shearer, "Kissinger Road Show: An Evening with Henry," *The Nation*, March 8, 1971, page 297, reporting on an off-the-record meeting with Kissinger at Endicott House, January 29, 1971. The quotation is accurate, although the political judgment seems highly dubious.) It was for this reason, Kissinger explained, that the pace of "withdrawal" had been slow, although, "We are ending the war . . . the war is trending down, and it will continue to trend down. . . ." (Unknown to his audience because of a news embargo, the bombing of Laos had been stepped up that evening to a near-record level, preparatory to invasion.)

Sorensen's final comments in *Kennedy* (published in 1965) on his chief's Vietnam legacy are not unduly upbeat, but they need interpreting. They begin:

He could show little gain in that situation to pass on to his successor, either in the military outlook or the progress toward reform. His own errors had not helped.[70]

In this, of course, Kennedy does not suffer by comparison with his two predecessors, or his successor. Arthur Schlesinger, Jr., spans his account of the Kennedy term in *The Bitter Heritage* with the sentences: "In January, 1961, the Vietnam mess fell to a new American President . . . [in 1963] a new President inherited the trouble." From the President's perspective of 1961, was this failure, or was it reasonable success? Just the same statements, after all, could be made for the comparable milestones of 1953, 1961, 1969. And in no case was this assessment at the end of the respective Presidential terms worse than had been predicted—though this prediction was not revealed to the public—at the earlier moment when the President had chosen to sustain and deepen the nation's involvement. Had any of them honestly expected more (except for intermittent periods)? If not—as seems likely—does this not pose questions about the pressures driving these four Presidents, about their aims and motives?

To go on with Sorensen:

But if asked why he had increased this nation's commitment, he might have summed up his stand with the words used by William Pitt when asked in the House of Commons in 1805 what was gained by the war against France: "We have gained everything that we would have lost if we had not fought this war." *In the case of Vietnam, that was a lot.*[71]

Specifically, that was—as John F. Kennedy had wished for himself, according to O'Donnell—a Democratic victory in 1964. It does not seem enough.

[70] *Kennedy*, page 661.
[71] *Ibid.;* italics added.

The Stalemate Machine: Phase A

Although the data that have been discussed are adequate to reject decisively the quagmire theory of the generation-long process of U.S. involvement, they do not point conclusively to an alternative. But they do begin to suggest some answers to puzzles identified earlier, and it is time to draw these together.

What follows is a discussion of a particular "decision model" —in the form of Presidential decision rules in Vietnam crises. (Presidential decisions significantly escalating the nature of U.S. involvement have occurred, in fact, only in crisis situations of impending failure.) With the actual past perceptions and premises of Washington decision-makers as inputs, this model generates policy choices and Executive performance which conform in considerable detail to those actually obtaining at major escalation points between 1950 and 1968. That is all I can say for it, at this point. I cannot prove, or even feel sure, that any particular President has actually seen his decision problem and constraints in just this way. Similar models but with different emphases can also be consistent with the data; see, for example, Leslie Gelb's paper cited earlier. The same might be true for radically different approaches; however, none that I have seen or considered explains so well so many characteristics of the available data.

One of these characteristics happens to be the striking impression of the *sameness* of the bureaucratic debate, in substance, tone, and agency position, and of its relation to Presidential choice, at decision points throughout the twenty-year period. This is in itself a surprising, if subjective, datum, given the differences in circumstances—e.g., the steadily rising level of prior U.S. involvement—and in the characters of the several Presidents.

The obvious differences between Administrations do not, after all, seem to have made much difference in Vietnam policy; at least, so far as concerns a determination to stay in Vietnam, to do what was necessary at any given time to avoid losing, and not, at that time, much more. As Morton H. Halperin has pointed out, this does not mean that a permutation of the sequence of actual Presidents would have made no difference at all; for example, if Lyndon Johnson—or still more, Richard Nixon—had come earlier than he actually did, escalation might well have started sooner and gone further. But this sameness suggests that a single, perhaps complex, hypothesis might cover the whole set of decisions with more validity than a set of purely *ad hoc* explanations. Thus, for example, I am inclined to put less weight on the impact of the Laos negotiations on Kennedy's decision in the fall of 1961 than I did when I first examined that period, before I had come to see his pattern of decision as typical.

In any case, it appears that an appropriate abstraction of the elements of the initial 1950 decision to intervene—despite the lack of major prior commitment or involvement—fits very well all the major subsequent decisions to escalate or to prolong the war, at least through 1968 and probably beyond.

We have already seen one Presidential ruling at work both in 1950 and 1961: *This is a bad year for me to lose Vietnam to Communism.* Along with some rules on constraints (see below), this amounts to a *recurrent* formula for calculating Presidential decisions on Vietnam realistically, given inputs on alternatives, any time from 1950 on. The mix of motives behind this judgment can vary with circumstances and Presidents, but since 1950 a variety of domestic political considerations have virtually always been present. These have been *sufficient* underpinning even in those years when (unlike, say, 1961) "strategic" concerns were not also urgent.

In brief: A decade before what Schlesinger calls Kennedy's "low-level crisis" in South Vietnam, the right wing of the Republican Party tattooed on the skins of politicians and bureaucrats alike some vivid impressions of what could happen to a liberal administration that chanced to be in office the day a red flag rose over Saigon.[72]

---

[72] This lesson was implanted so powerfully between 1949 and 1954 that some special circumstances of that period, limiting its future validity, may well have been overlooked. Thus, Truman's startling victory in 1948, prolonging almost by accident what was already a sixteen-year Democratic reign, not only assured that Democrats would still be in office for the fast-approaching victory of Communists in China, but assured that this vulnerability would be exploited to the hilt, and beyond, by the madly frustrated Republicans. For a provocative dis-

Starting in early 1950, the first Administration to learn painfully this "lesson of China" began to undertake—as in a game of Old Maid—to pass that contingency on to its successor. And each Administration since has found itself caught in the same game.

Rule 1 of that game is: *Do not lose the rest of Vietnam to Communist control before the next election.*[73]

But the rules do not end with Rule 1. There is also—ever since late 1950, when Chinese Communists entered Korea—Rule 2, which asserts among other things: *Do not commit U.S. ground troops to a land war in Asia, either.*

Breaking Rule 2 (which has some further clauses) will not expose one to the charge of treason, but otherwise the political risks—loss of electoral support, loss of Congress, loss of legislative program, loss of reputation—are believed to be about the same. And many of the very same pursuers who would be howling and pointing at the scent of a violation of the first rule would be among the pack chasing a President who proposed to ignore the second.

It so happens that an intense appreciation of U.S. stakes in a non-Communist Southeast Asia does *not* go, either within Congress or the public, with a willingness politically to support costly or risky or domestically unpopular measures to protect those stakes. On the contrary, it tends to be coupled precisely with a determination to oppose and punish many such measures, because it is typically part of a philosophy which asserts that such efforts are both unnecessary—to a patriotic and resolute Administration willing to rely on Asian allies and the threat or use of U.S. airpower—and dangerous to the economy.

---

cussion of this thesis, see Latham, *The Communist Controversy in Washington,* pages 5-7, 416-23.

Fear of McCarthy's and McCarthyism's power at the polls may always have been overdrawn, even in 1950-52, and still more so today. See Michael Paul Rogin, *The Intellectuals and McCarthy* (Cambridge, Mass., 1967). From one point of view, of course, what matters in explaining the behavior of Congressmen and officials is what they believe their risks to be, and what risks they are willing to take. (See the quotation of Kissinger on Wallace, p. 98 *fn.*) Also, Nelson W. Polsby, "Towards an Explanation of McCarthyism," *Political Studies,* VIII, October, 1962, pages 252-71; and Seymour M. Lipset and Earl Raab, *The Politics of Unreason* (New York, 1970), Chapter 6.

[73] As usual, "election" here is a proxy term for the whole range of "political" concerns; each has its own time frame, but all are linked closely to the election cycle.

Suppose, then, an Administration fears attack by or needs the support of the particular faction that holds these attitudes. (Its core is usually characterized as right-wing—and sometimes "isolationist" or "Asia-first"—non-Eastern Republicans; but it is suspected of being able to mobilize a much larger following on these issues in a crisis). What if the President is informed that he cannot avoid enraging that faction by losing part of Southeast Asia in the near future to Communist control, except by antagonizing other major groups (and perhaps that faction as well) by committing troops, or mobilizing reserves, or risking war with the Soviet Union or China?

In that case, the President is in a bind. The Indochina Bind.

That dilemma is all the more certain to recur because of some other politically derived premises that constrict policy. One of the sacred beliefs, inherited from the late 1940's, which any U.S. official must appear to share (and probably does share), is that toleration of an overt Communist Party in a less-developed country, or a provisional or coalition government including Communists, must inevitably lead to total Communist domination.[74] (Eastern Europe and China—rather than France, Italy, or Finland—are cited as the only relevant examples here.) Any prospects of these developments, then, are proscribed under Rule 1.

But this means that acceptable U.S. long-term aims for South Vietnam must be quite ambitious: the total exclusion from national power of its Communist party; and the assurance indefinitely of a totally non-Communist regime.

As early as 1948, according to a State Department policy statement, our long-term objective was "to eliminate so far as possible Communist influence in Indochina" [*GPO*, 8, 144]. This was reiterated throughout the fifties, and reconfirmed by President Johnson in an internal policy statement on March 17, 1964:

We seek an independent non-Communist South Vietnam . . . free . . . to accept outside assistance as required to maintain its security. This assistance should be able to take the form not only of economic and

---

[74] See, for example, Acheson's cable of May 20, 1949 [*GPO*, 8, 196-97], and Lovett's, September 22, 1948 [*GPO*, 8, 141-42].

social measures but also police and military help to root out and control insurgent elements. [*PP*, III, 50]

These were the U.S. goals stated in internal documents until at least 1969; lest they appear too ambitious or interventionist, they were rarely spelled out publicly, and the public position remained ambiguous. It is not clear yet—and appears doubtful —whether recent changes in public statements emphasizing "free elections" correspond to genuine operational changes in the outcomes perceived as "tolerable."[75]

U.S. intelligence analyses have generally recognized that in the face of the actual strength of the Communist party of Vietnam, such goals could not be achieved—without major U.S. involvement indefinitely—by the narrow, conservative, foreign-oriented, anti-Communist, authoritarian regime (supported mainly by Catholics, the Army, bureaucrats and the rich) that alone among Vietnamese political elements was willing to pursue such an aim. Hence, for the long-run goal of an acceptable outcome at an acceptable cost to the U.S., civilian analysts have regularly stressed "reform" and "broadening" of the Saigon regime.

But this position runs into another sort of bind. For even proponents of those political changes admit that a "broadened" government, or even U.S. pressures to achieve it or to reduce the influence of the Army, would increase to some degree the risk in the short term of "instability"—coups, chaos, military weakening, governmental paralysis—and thus of a quick Communist takeover. Thus any measures—U.S. "leverage," political strategies, genuinely "revolutionary" social-political approaches, broad-based regimes—to achieve such long-term aims conflict directly with Rule 1, and perhaps with Rule 2 as well. The rules have always won out.

It follows that in those periods when major U.S. policy innovations have actually been determined, eventual success at acceptable cost, if attainable at all, has been perceived to depend

---

[75] Continued Administration deference to President Thieu, after his one-man election, and Thieu's adherence to his "Four Nos"—ruling out neutrality, partition, coalition, or an open Communist party—seems to settle this question as of April, 1972.

either on U.S. military measures that involved high domestic risks—unless they were sure to be quickly successful, which could not be guaranteed and which Presidents would tend to doubt—or upon political strategies in Vietnam that posed the equally high domestic political risks of short-term instability and possible defeat there.

The standard resolution of this dilemma has been simply to turn away from long-run aims and the measures associated with them, concentrating almost exclusively upon the aim of minimizing the short-run risk of anti-Communist collapse or Communist takeovers. To this end the policy relies heavily on means that do not raise domestic apprehension and opposition—e.g., military aid, covert actions, "advisors"—but it also includes those types of actions restricted under Rule 2 judged by the President minimally necessary to this short-run aim. Their acceptability and probable sequence of adoption are roughly in the order listed below.

Rule 2 (extended): Do not, unless essential to satisfy Rule 1 in the immediate or an earlier crisis:
(a) Bomb South Vietnam or Laos;
(b) Bomb North Vietnam;
(c) Commit U.S. combat troops to Vietnam;
(d) Commit U.S. combat troops to Laos or Cambodia;
(e) Institute wartime domestic controls;
(f) Destroy Hanoi or Haiphong or the dike system, or mine Haiphong harbor;
(g) Mobilize reserves;
(h) Assume full, overt administrative authority and military command in South Vietnam;
(i) Invade North Vietnam;
(j) Use nuclear weapons.

What specially constrains the use of these actions, and determines their ranking, is their relative disruption of normal life, their impact on American casualties, and their risk of war with China or Russia. Strong political inhibitions against initiating such "restricted" measures are revealed by the prolonged unwillingness of any Administration to introduce any of them until needed to sustain Rule 1: i.e., to prevent defeat in Vietnam before the next election.

The President himself must be persuaded that they are essential for that purpose; this is usually long after their use has been urged by others. Indeed, most of these measures have not yet been used. Most of them have been considered or recommended at various times, often on the more or less plausible grounds that they were essential, or highly important, to achieving real "success," and sometimes on the less convincing promise that they guaranteed "victory." Yet Presidents have not, in fact, been willing to adopt any one of them unless and until it was judged essential to avoiding imminent defeat: i.e., to restore a stalemate.[76]

A general Presidential tendency to preserve flexibility, or to focus on or value only short-term consequences, or to economize on means, could not explain the strength and specificity of these inhibitions. Nor have Presidents been strictly indifferent to longer-term prospects, or to the possibility of "victory." The chosen policy usually employs far more in the way of "nonrestricted" instruments than is needed merely to avoid defeat. These include: non-U.S. ground forces; commitments and assurances to allies, warnings to opponents; clandestine activities; economic and military aid; advisors; combat, logistic, mobility, and air support (even to allied invasion forces).

Moreover, once a restricted action is first used to avoid defeat, its use may be greatly expanded in pursuit of ultimate "success": thus, Johnson's use of U.S. ground troops in South Vietnam and bombing of "military targets" in North Vietnam, after they had been introduced in 1965 to avoid imminent defeat. Yet even in the optimistic mood of 1967 and despite the urgings of his military commanders that new means could bring a "win," Johnson resisted going further down the list—e.g., to drop all White House controls on the target list in North Vietnam, or to invade Laos or Cambodia, or mobilize reserves—in the absence of an urgent need to avert failure.

[76] This paper focuses on decisions up through 1968, and President Nixon's decisions on invading Cambodia and Laos might appear to depart from this rule. In the absence of data on Nixon's decision-making comparable to the Pentagon Papers, it is hard to say; however, it is plausible that this Administration judged that U.S. public opinion has been so sensitive to setbacks ever since Tet, 1968, that any major enemy offensive, whatever its local effects, would spell defeat to Administration aims, and therefore must be precluded.

After March, 1968, de-escalation was subject to limits similar to those earlier for escalation; in this case, choices had the desired effect of avoiding political defeat or collapse of support on the U.S. domestic front: in other words, once more "buying time" rather than winning or losing; buying stalemate; prolonging the war.

Many of the paradoxical features of U.S. escalating decisions as seen from the inside—the "discrepancies" between chosen policies, on the one hand, and internal predictions, recommendations, and long-term aims on the other—can thus be seen to reflect conflict between domestic political requirements on outcomes and domestic political constraints on means.[77]

For example, this analysis explains what some others take as a "given," or attribute to purely personal quirks—the peculiarly strong salience and importance of short-term considerations, which so regularly have ruled out "political leverage" for "broadened government" or other less military approaches. A strong domestic political ingredient in policy-making inevitably sharpens the short-term focus. As Presidents might paraphrase Keynes, "In the long run we are all out of office." And there are always legislative programs and Presidential appointments to get through Congress this year, and Congressional elections no later than next year, even when a Presidential election is not close at hand.

It so happens that in Vietnam, realistic policy alternatives have not allowed a subtle adjustment of long-term and short-term considerations, which appear in sharp conflict. The President is challenged, in effect, to pursue one or the other. Thus, the eventual aim of a self-sufficient and relatively democratic South Vietnam not entirely dominated by Communists seems to demand an approach—e.g., a regime based on Southern, civilian, nationalist, and non-Catholic religious leadership, drawing peasant and union support—that poses relatively high risks in the short run of governmental collapse or of "accommodation"

---

[77] In the light of frequent misunderstanding, it seems necessary to emphasize again that I am not saying that *only* calculations of domestic political interest enter or determine these decisions; nor would I deny that such calculations, themselves, may reflect class or corporate interests. And even when various domestic pressures, as reflected in Rules 1 and 2, seem sufficient to explain behavior, other considerations pointing in the same direction may be equally operative.

to Communists. To decide that short-term interests are very important is to bias policy almost entirely toward a short-term orientation: away from such approaches as that above, whatever their long-range merits, toward support of militarized and "rightist" regimes whose only advantages lie in their higher degree of U.S. control and of security against an imminent "disaster," though they offer a very high likelihood of renewed crisis later.

(Obviously, this pattern is not peculiar to Vietnam. Kennedy's well-known remark to Schlesinger, concerning the Dominican Republic in 1961, shows strong parallels between Southeast Asia and the Caribbean: "There are three possibilities, in descending order of preference: a decent democratic regime, a continuation of the Trujillo regime, or a Castro regime. We ought to aim at the first, but we really can't renounce the second until we are sure that we can avoid the third."[78] But when in the spring of 1967 I asked the former economic minister Au Truong Thanh —soon to be barred from the 1967 Presidential race as an alleged "neutralist"—what he expected the consequence to be of U.S. support for Thieu and Ky in that election, he replied: "After Batista . . . Castro.")

Thus, among the consequences of applying Rules 1 and 2 to policy choices, as officials have perceived the alternatives in Vietnam, are several of the patterns observed earlier:

(1) Chosen policies appear from the inside as oriented almost exclusively to short-term considerations, evidently ignoring or trading off very large differences in predicted long-term costs, risks, benefits, and probability of success in pursuit of small reductions in the short-term risk (tacitly, of "losing" South Vietnam prior to the next election).

(2) Chosen programs are predicted internally to be inadequate—or at best long shots—either to "win" or even to avert defeat in the long run (in contrast to public statements, and to some recommended policies that pose higher short-term domestic risks).

(3) Actual policies emphasize predominantly military—rather than political—means, aims, considerations, and executive responsibility, on both the Vietnamese and American sides, for reasons of short-term security.

[78] *A Thousand Days*, pages 704-05.

(4) The U.S. supports—intervening when necessary to install or maintain—a narrow-based, right-wing, anti-Communist, "pro-American," authoritarian (since 1963, essentially military) regime in Saigon, with heavy Northern and Catholic influence: despite its inability to win wider support for eventual self-sufficiency.

All of these features combine to give American policy its peculiar appearance, seen from inside, of being purposefully dedicated to preserving a stalemate, at ever-increasing levels of violence.

Moreover, at least three other characteristics of U.S. Government performance, not discussed earlier, correspond to the implications of this decision model: lack of "leverage," lying, and self-deception. Let us examine these in turn.

The notable weakness of U.S. influence on the policies, either political or military, of its principal ally—first the French and then the GVN—despite a nearly total dependence on U.S. support to pursue the war, follows directly from the U.S. political imperatives.

Rules 1 and 2 together led us, from 1950 to 1965, to accept the role continuously of adviser and supporter to another government carrying the responsibility for administration and fighting —even when our limited role seemed to risk imminent defeat of the non-Communist efforts. From time to time in those fifteen years, Administration leaders would remark publicly of the ally we were supporting: "It is, after all, *their* fight." But these officials' private perceptions would have been better expressed: "In view of our strategic (and domestic political) interests, it is *our* fight, all right, but they have got to fight it for us; because if they don't, we might have to, and that would be nearly as bad as losing."

Given the domestic political constraints embodied in Rule 1, U.S. leaders saw the avoidance of Communist takeover of all of Vietnam as of very considerable importance, both internationally and domestically. Yet for the same reasons, as reflected in Rule 2, they had to hope urgently they could induce others to do the fighting, and take the responsibility for the failures and the casualties, leaving us only with the burden of dollars, matériel, and advice.

This has never been expressed more clearly than in the State Department Policy Statement of September, 1948, cited earlier:

... We are naturally hesitant to press the French too strongly or to become deeply involved so long as we are not in a position to suggest a solution or until we are prepared to accept the onus of intervention ... [GPO, 8, 148]

And thirteen years later, President Kennedy's cable of instructions to Ambassador Nolting, relaying his decisions of November, 1961, and his hopes for reform and broadening of the Diem regime, ended with the line (foreclosing those hopes): "However [the] objective of our policy is to do all possible to accomplish purpose without use of U.S. combat forces" [PP, II, 119].

This "bargain"—first with the French, then with the GVN —has always seemed in danger of breaking down, facing the current Administration with the loss of South Vietnam or else with the necessity of taking over the combat ourselves. Hence, our officials rarely felt they could afford to strain the bargain by pressuring our ally into fighting better or differently, or into taking political measures to which it was, in fact, adamantly opposed, even when we suspected that such changes were critical to success. In effect the U.S. had no leverage to use, despite the intelligence reports that the military-political challenge of the Communist-led forces would almost surely grow, and the ability of the ally (French, then the GVN/RVNAF) to meet it would decline, unless these changes did occur.

Meanwhile, as an essential part of the bargain with our ally —serving to keep it in power and fighting—high U.S. officials provided verbal and symbolic encouragement and evidence of U.S. concern and commitment. This came "cheap" in terms of current demands on the U.S. public. But it was making ever more certain the provision of U.S. combat forces if that became essential to holding Vietnam.

To convince the GVN (and its Vietnamese critics and rivals) —in lieu of sending U.S. troops immediately—that we would do "whatever necessary" to support them, the Administration had to say so publicly, and to assert that major U.S. interests were at stake; likewise, to warn Hanoi's leaders and deter them from increasing the pressure.

To get sizable enough sums of money out of Congress to satisfy Rule 1, these officials had to say, again, that major U.S. interests were at stake, implying that even major commitments would be justified; but on the other hand they had to suggest that there was very little likelihood that these programs would lead to U.S. combat involvement. The only way in which these requirements could be harmonized was to profess, at any given time, great optimism for the results of the GVN's performance if the U.S. aid were sent (combined with pessimism, and the prospects of major losses for the U.S., if it were not).

Here, then, is the explanation for the news-management recounted earlier. The deceptive games with Congress and public were played for serious stakes. The President's resolution of the conflicting demands and constraints upon him called for supressing any indications of possible inadequacy of the programs he proposed. The penalty for frankness could be to ally against his programs those who might conclude they were not worth attempting at all, and those who would condemn him for not doing much more. Yet the latter could be expected to oppose him if he did ask and do much more, unless he won quickly, which he did not expect; and the former would desert him, he suspected, if he took their advice and lost Vietnam. Honesty, it appeared, would only earn him opposition whatever he did, and sooner than otherwise.

Yet, internal analyses, estimates, reports, planning, recommendations, all indicated that in a variety of ways these chosen programs were inadequate. Thus all these documents and opinions had to be concealed, by secrecy and deception.

In short, the Presidents conclude, the public must be lied to: about what the President's decision is, what advice he rejects, what he was told to expect, what he foresees and intends for the future.

When he decides to go slow and small, as in November, 1961, the fact that much more was considered and recommended is suppressed lest doubts be raised on the meaningfulness of the program. James Reston's remark at the outset of the Taylor mission, that Taylor was not a man who would "blithely" recommend committing U.S. combat units to a jungle war, was presumably right; likewise Taylor's own comment that "any American" would be reluctant to do so "unless absolutely necessary." Nevertheless, that is what Taylor did recommend. The fact that he did so therefore carried an important message about the seriousness of the situation, and the prospects of the lesser course the President chose. To suppress the fact of this recommendation, as the President chose to do, was to conceal this information. And for officials to lie to reporters about Taylor's views—which were shared by Rostow and the Joint Chiefs, and initially at least by McNamara and Gilpatric—was to convey the opposite, untrue impression.[79]

Thus, when David Halberstam's *The Making of a Quagmire* appeared in the middle of the decade, based largely on his reporting for the *New York Times* in 1962-63 (far more accurate reporting than that, public or private, of the U.S. mission during this period), his account of the decision in 1961 to reject U.S. combat troops and to step up the U.S. commitment instead "to a point just short of combat" confirmed to the public the earlier, misleading fallacy:

> The key man in making this choice was Maxwell Taylor. As such, he was in fact a representative of what is known in Washington as the "Never Again Club," a Korean legacy—a phrase meaning that its members never again wanted to place American combat troops on the mainland of Asia without atomic weapons. Above all else, Taylor wanted to keep American combat troops out of the Vietnamese jungles. He and others like him shared a feeling that this was not America's war . . . In effect, the Taylor mission reported that the war could be won, and could be won under the existing government—provided that a huge retraining program oriented the Vietnamese military away from conventional warfare to new concepts of flexible counterguerrilla warfare.[80]

While the *Times* stories did not reveal the officials who put out this misinformation in 1961, General Taylor himself was still denying in public his actual recommendations as late as the summer of 1971, when he stated on television:

[79] To my knowledge, no other paper ever challenged the *Times,* or the Administration, on these versions of Taylor's advice. Nor did any different version appear until the appearance in 1965 of the Schlesinger and Sorensen histories, neither of which drew attention to the fact that they directly contradicted White House statements and all newspaper stories of the time and subsequent accounts.

[80] *The Making of a Quagmire,* page 67.

I did not recommend combat forces. I stressed we would bring in engineer forces, logistic forces, that could work on logistics and help in the very serious flood problem in 1961. So this was not a combat force . . . I did not recommend anything other than three battalions of infantry. Pardon me, three battalions of engineers.[81]

By the same token, when a President finally decided to go in big, the schedule and total commitment were concealed, with increments—actually programmed in advance—being announced as if based on a sequence of *ad hoc* decisions of "small steps," lest public fears be aroused on the costs of the program, and the ultimate risks and commitment. This was the nature of the "public information" program associated with the early bombing campaign against North Vietnam, the buildup of troop levels to 75,000 in the spring of 1965, and the open-ended buildup of troops to 175,000 and beyond, determined in July, 1965.

In the latter case, I helped write a draft speech and a press release for Secretary McNamara stating, correctly, that the decision had been made to add about 100,000 men by the end of the year to the current ceiling of 75,000, for a year-end total of about 175,000. But the White House decided to make the announcement; watching TV at the Pentagon on July 28, 1965, we heard the President say (describing the same decision):

I have today ordered to Vietnam the Airmobile Division and certain other forces which will raise our fighting strength from 75,000 to 125,-000 men almost immediately. Additional forces will be needed later, and they will be sent as requested. [*PP*, III, 477]

[81] *The Pentagon Papers, New York Times*-Bantam edition, page xvi. What Taylor actually said in 1961 about the proposed "dual mission" of the task force was: "The extent to which the task force would engage in flood relief activities in the Delta will depend on further study of the problem there. As reported in Saigon [cable] 537, I see considerable advantages in playing up this aspect of the task force mission. I am presently inclined to favor a dual mission, initially help to the flood area and subsequently use in any other area of SVN where its resources can be used effectively to give tangible support in the struggle against the Viet Cong. However, the possibility of emphasizing the humanitarian mission will wane if we wait long in moving our forces or in linking our stated purpose with the emergency conditions created by the flood" [*PP*, II, 91-92].

Taylor's interview with Martin Agronsky, taped earlier that spring, happened to be broadcast on June 27, 1971; as I remember, it was later this same week that Taylor's Eyes Only cables to the President, cited earlier, finally appeared in the *New York Times*. As I watched General Taylor's account to the American public of those closely held recommendations, now a decade old, I recall thinking—perhaps unfairly generalizing—"The President's men think they have a license to lie that never expires."

Actually, no further request was called for with respect to this "Phase I package"; its total was soon "refined" upward to 219,000 men, of whom 184,314 men were in-country by the end of the year, on a prearranged schedule. What McNamara had brought back from Saigon a week earlier was Westmoreland's estimate of his "Phase II" requirements for an *additional* 100,000 men in the *next* year. Nevertheless, we turned dutifully to revising the Department's press releases to inform the public that "50,000" men would be sent "almost immediately," etcetera.

Meanwhile, the following exchange occurred at the same White House press conference:

QUESTION: Mr. President, does the fact that you are sending additional forces to Vietnam imply any change in the existing policy of relying mainly on the South Vietnamese to carry out offensive operations and using American forces to guard installations and to act as an emergency backup?

THE PRESIDENT: It does not imply any change in policy whatever. It does not imply change of objective.

This too was an artful answer, since the fact was that the policy had been changed *earlier*—without public announcement—from what the questioner and the rest of the public understood it to be, i.e., from what they had earlier been told it was. The President's decision, on approximately April 1st, to change the mission of U.S. ground troops (initially, the Marines) to include offensive ground operations, had been announced internally by McGeorge Bundy (NSAM-328, April 6, 1965) along with the admonition:

The President desires that . . . premature publicity be avoided by all possible precautions. The actions themselves should be taken as rapidly as practicable, but in ways that should minimize any appearance of sudden changes in policy . . . The President's desire is that these movements and changes [in combat mission] should be understood as being gradual and wholly consistent with existing policy.[82]

In the carrying out of this instruction, then, the President himself on July 28th was leading the way.

One pertinent effect of this information policy, from 1961 on,

[82] *PP*, III, 703; also see discussion of the emerging "credibility gap," *PP*, III, 447-61.

was that it considerably distorted the public view, then and later, of what the President thought he was getting us into, what he thought of the chances and the relevant goals, and just what was in the inner pages of the contracts Congress and the public were being asked, implicitly, to sign.

From such a mistaken understanding of these and other choices, bad predictions and prescriptions must follow. It leads to wrong questions and wrong inferences about Presidential motives, and about what changes in his calculations and in the pressures on him might influence his choices.

Thus those who keep secret the past condemn us to repeat it.

The Stalemate Machine: Phase B

These deceptive practices bring us back to the quagmire myth and to the question of why it seems so plausible to the public.

Part of the answer is that the Presidents themselves choose to foster impressions, when new crises and requirements emerge, that their past Vietnam decision-making has been subject to a quicksand process.

This is the effect of repeatedly announcing very limited measures—usually less than is expected privately to be needed, sometimes less than is definitely planned—as if they were believed adequate to achieve ambitious publicly announced goals. By doing so they win public support for programs that will, in fact, assure avoidance of short-term defeat, though probably not much more than that; at the same time they avoid public pressures that could result from frankness on prospects, pressures either to take much riskier measures to win and get the problem over with, or to get out of Vietnam, accepting a defeat that might cut losses for the country but might mean eventual disaster for the Administration, even if the initial public reaction were relief. To these risks of candor, Presidents prefer the risks of concealment and deception.

They do so despite the unfavorable implications—when their aims appear repeatedly frustrated and "hopes" disappointed—of inadvertence, ignorance, inattention, lack of Presidential control, lack of realistic planning, lack of expertise, overly ambitious aims for the means used, overly optimistic expectations. They choose to encourage these particular criticisms—even when these are both damaging and misguided—because either a different substantive policy or a more accurate public understanding of their actual policy seems to them to pose even greater disadvantages and risks.

All very calculated, this. But, it turns out, this posture of secrecy and deception toward Congress and the public, maintained over time, takes its internal toll. An ironic result is that all of the above imputed flaws and limitations increasingly do characterize the Executive decision-making process. And for a number of reasons, as the chosen policy begins to be implemented, internal operational reporting, program analyses, and high-level expectations do gradually drift in the direction of the public optimism expressed constantly from the outset.

Thus real hopes—ill-founded hopes—follow hard upon the crisis choices, eventually replacing phony and invalid optimism with genuine invalid optimism.

Again, the aftermath of the November, 1961, decision is typical. Schlesinger reports it well: the striking advent of optimism in official expectations during 1962, a reversal which the public misread as a vindication of earlier estimates. U.S. combat troops, it now appeared, had not been "essential" after all. (If the President had, indeed, suspected that earlier, he was the only one who seemed vindicated.) But no recriminations blossomed in this atmosphere; only mutual congratulations that the long shot was paying off.[83]

Roger Hilsman reports a meeting in Honolulu in April, 1963:

General Harkins gave us all the facts and figures—the number of strategic hamlets established, number of Viet Cong killed, operations initiated by government forces, and so on. He could not, of course, he said, give any guarantees, but he thought he could say that *by Christmas it would be all over.* The Secretary of Defense was elated. He reminded me that I had attended one of the very first of these meetings, *when it had all looked so black—and that had been only a year and a half ago.*[84]

[83] See *A Thousand Days,* page 508, and *The Bitter Heritage,* pages 41, 42.
[84] *To Move A Nation,* pages 466-67; italics added.

Why the fast reversal? There were several reasons, none peculiar to this case. First, the new programs had been implemented in Vietnam by new American officials directed to carry them to success. They were as unaware as the public of the different recommendations made only a few months before by Taylor and others, and the pessimistic predictions made for the actual courses they were attempting to implement. The recommendations, in particular, had been "closely held" and later denied even within the system, so they were part of no institutional "memory" below the highest levels; and old intelligence estimates are rarely consulted by those with operational responsibilities. Ignorant of past predictions and current realities in Vietnam, they had no strong reason to assume that the tasks they had been given were infeasible with the means at hand. And they quickly learned that Washington tended to rely on reporting up through the chain of operational command; which is to say, their performance in their jobs would be evaluated by their own reports of "progress." As an American division commander told one of his district advisors, who insisted on reporting the persistent presence of unpacified VC hamlets in his area: "Son, you're writing our own report card in this country. Why are you failing us?"

Even when this did not lead to conscious dishonesty at the higher levels in Saigon, it created a bias toward accepting and reporting favorable information from subordinates and from their Vietnamese counterparts, neither of whom failed to provide it.

Thus, it was more mechanism than coincidence that in 1962 and early 1963, as Schlesinger notes, the strategy of unconditional support of Diem combined with the military advisor system seemed to be working—or so at least the senior American officials in Saigon assured the President.[85] Such assurances said nothing more than that the two officials themselves—Ambassador Nolting and General Harkins—were "working"—succeeding—in the two programs they had been sent by Kennedy respectively to manage:

[85] *The Bitter Heritage*, page 45.

Ngo Dinh Nhu made the strategic hamlet program his personal project and published glowing reports of spectacular success. One might have wondered whether Nhu was just the man to mobilize the idealism of the villages; but Ambassador Nolting and General Harkins listened uncritically to his claims and passed them back to Washington as facts, where they were read with elation.[86]

One might also have wondered—but no one ever seemed to —whether Nhu was just the man uniquely to report upon "his personal project"; or whether Nolting was just the man to report the effects and value of reassuring Diem and Nhu, or Harkins the success of the military advisor system, their own respective personal projects.

But to emphasize the role of bureaucratic optimism in this process of internal self-deception is to underrate the influence of the President himself, and of his top advisors. They, too, like Nolting, Harkins, or Nhu, had their personal projects, larger ones, on which they reported to those who controlled their budgets and their tenure: Congress and the public. And they too, thanks to the security system and Executive privilege, "wrote their own report cards": with a little help from their subordinates.

Precisely as at lower levels, but with enormously broader impact, the needs of the President and the Secretaries of State and Defense to use "information" to reassure Congress and the public had its effect on the internal flow of information up to the President. Reports and analyses that supported the Administration's public position and could be released or leaked to that end were "helpful" and welcome, while "pessimism" was at best painful, less "useful," if not even dangerous to put down on paper. Executive values like these (vastly sharpened in 1966-1968, when skeptics and critics were more numerous and vocal, and had to be refuted) translate into powerful incentives at lower levels to give the Chief what he so obviously wants.

Moreover, human wishfulness, a factor at all levels, probably had its greatest impact at the highest. Repeatedly we have seen that a President felt compelled to adopt and promote policies that his chief advisors or official intelligence estimates told him

[86] *The Bitter Heritage,* page 40.

were inadequate, while he told the public otherwise. He could only hope that these best-informed perceptions would prove wrong, and that what he had been telling the public would turn out, for the good of all, to have been correct. In hoping, one finds indications (especially from highly dependent subordinates) that support one's hopes.

At other levels, the same mechanisms. In periods like 1956 or 1962, when the policy "seemed to be working" despite its neglect of factors that had been considered by some experts critical to success, it was easy for all to doubt and gradually forget the earlier warnings. In general, pessimism regarding an ongoing policy is a fragile, unstable phenomenon within a large bureaucracy.

Ironically, even the VC and the GVN (earlier, the Viet Minh and French) played their roles, too, in providing indicators of allied "progress" and intervals when things "seemed to be working." In 1951, 1956, 1962, and 1965, bureaucratic optimism was catalyzed by the actual effects of the new programs on allies and opponents in the desired direction. "In the field," these effects proved very temporary, whereas our reading of them did not. As Kennedy had predicted, the effects of any one "small drink" on friend and opponent faded quickly. What he may not fully have foreseen was the far more lasting afterglow in our own system.

In each case, the aftermath of escalation was an increased emphasis on military factors, and an accompanying alteration of mood from gloom to elation. Thus, when U.S. combat units flooded into Vietnam from 1965 on, the pessimism of late 1964 gave way increasingly to buoyant hopes by 1967 of a military victory, just as it had in the past, as early as 1951, after U.S. matériel and American liaison teams had made their way to Tonkin to join a failing French effort.[87]

Meanwhile, the Viet Minh, and later the VC, had a characteristic response to a new U.S./GVN strategy or to an escalation of our involvement which further encouraged our shift to un-

---

[87] See Senator John F. Kennedy's speech in 1954, cited in Schlesinger, *The Bitter Heritage*, page 27, on official optimism underlying a Truman-Eisenhower "credibility gap" in Indochina.

bounded optimism. After suffering initial setbacks, they would lie low for an extended period, gather data, analyze experience, develop, test, and adapt new strategies, then plan and prepare carefully before launching them. (Nothing, our Vietnam experience tells us, could be more un-American.)

Since so great a part of U.S. and GVN knowledge of enemy activities comes from operational contacts, there seems to be an irresistible tendency for U.S. commanders to believe that data concerning contacts reveals enemy capabilities, i.e., that lessened VC combat operations indicate lessened capability. Another mechanism, then: U.S. optimism grows during VC "inactivity" —periods when VC activities are of a sort we do not observe— reaching a peak, ironically, when extreme VC quiescence reflects intense preparations for an explosion.

Crisis periods, then, are typically preceded by high points in U.S. official expectations. Thus, peaks of U.S. optimism occurred in late 1953 (just before Dien Bien Phu), 1958 (when guerrilla warfare was about to recommence), early 1963 (when the VC had been studying the vulnerabilities of the strategic hamlet program, and meanwhile infiltrating massively), and late 1967 (during last-minute recruiting and preparations for the Tet offensive, including feints at the borders).

If a fever chart of U.S. expectations could be drawn meaningfully for the last twenty years, it would have a recurrent sawtooth shape: an accelerating rise of optimism just before an abrupt decline (Figure 1 is a conceptual sketch of such a graph).* Our perceptual and emotional experience in Vietnam can be regarded as a sequence of two-phase cycles, in which Phase B —optimism—evolves causally in large part from decisions that follow Phase A, a crisis period of pessimism.

(The B-phases in Figure 1 have been drawn with a reverse S-shape, signifying three subphases: an initial period in which the VC suffers real reverses and the GVN stabilizes on the basis of new programs; then a period in which, in reality, the VC have adapted and the GVN is declining, but U.S. expectations remain at a plateau instead of being reduced; finally, a period

---

* The question mark placed at the end of the latest Phase B when this graph was first drawn (in September, 1970) can now be replaced by the heading: NVA offensive, April, 1972.

when the VC begin quietly preparing for a major offensive, causing U.S. hopes to soar.)

If major escalating decisions—enlarging the nature of our involvement, not merely the scale—had actually been made during the B-phases, that would conform to the quagmire model. This has never been the case.

However, although no new major policies or commitments are introduced during the B-phases, U.S. aims may change significantly in the atmosphere of optimism, especially in the last stage, going beyond the goal of avoiding defeat (dominant aim in Phase A and the early Phase B) to that of achieving a victory. At the same time, real optimism leads officials to be much less cautious in public aims and predictions; to give commanders more leeway; to monitor operations less closely; and to indulge in operations that are costly (in many terms) and of low effectiveness but that may speed the coming win. All of these responses lead to toleration of rapidly rising costs, and hence to a feeling, when a new crisis brings the return of Phase A, that the stakes, the investment, the commitment have become still

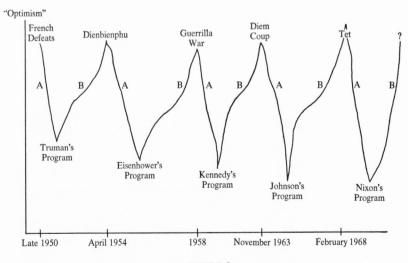

FIGURE I

higher than before, the need to avoid "defeat" being now even greater.

Nevertheless, this post-escalation euphoria, or "quagmire phase" of the cycle, seems to play no essential role in the escalation process. It simply reinforces the Presidential tendency to escalate if and as necessary to avoid an imminent "defeat." As Leslie Gelb has put it: "Each Administration was prepared to pay the costs it could foresee for itself." Political, along with strategic, motives underlying that tendency were already strong enough in 1950 to induce the initial U.S. commitment without any prior or current period of American optimism. And they almost surely were felt strongly enough in subsequent years to have induced much greater escalation than occurred if that had appeared both necessary and effective in the short run.

Consciously oriented as escalating decisions actually were, when chosen, to the defensive aim of averting an immediate Communist takeover, *each of these decisions of the past two decades can be said to have achieved its initial, internal aim.*

In Gelb's phrase: "The system worked," not in terms of publicly avowed long-range aims, but in terms of the successive short-range aims and expectations that were actually—it is inferred here—salient in the White House. In fact, these Presidential policies and tactics, in sequence, had the effect of holding South Vietnam out of Communist hands "cheaply"—i.e., without sizable numbers of U.S. combat troops—for fifteen years, from 1950 to 1965.

Whether efforts and sacrifices, by Americans and Vietnamese, of even these limited but increasing magnitudes could easily have been justified to various parts of the electorate in terms of such limited aims—in starkest terms, the restoration of stalemate and the postponement of a possible Communist takeover in Vietnam beyond the date of the next U.S. election—is another question. No Administration chose to find out.

In this respect, too, the policies "worked." Until 1968 at least, each President avoided the kinds of political damages related to Vietnam that his tactics were meant mainly to avert. In fact, up to the present, no President has had to face a political penalty for losing South Vietnam. Not even LBJ will be blamed in history for that, although he is blamed for other things.

Yet the earlier "cheap victories," year by year from 1950 to 1965, were purchased at a long-term price, one not yet paid in full. Presidential policies and tactics actively sustained and encouraged over that period a high estimate of U.S. strategic stakes in the conflict within the U.S. Executive branch and the military, the Congress, and the public. Meanwhile, they failed—as was highly likely, in the light of repeated internal estimates by the intelligence community, though the Presidents may not fully have accepted these—to strengthen adequately non-Communist Vietnamese efforts; to modify Communist aims; to deter or prevent an increase in Communist capabilities; or, of course, to induce the acceptance by Hanoi's leaders or the revolutionary forces in South Vietnam of the U.S. role, presence, and aims in South Vietnam, or those of the U.S.-supported Saigon regime.

Thus, a hypothetical observer who adopted the view of Presidential motives presented here, and at the same time accepted the view of GVN and DRV/VC behavior regularly presented by the intelligence community, could have calculated during most of that fifteen-year period that there was a high probability that large numbers of U.S. troops would end up fighting in South Vietnam, with U.S. planes bombing throughout Indochina. He would have predicted that they would be sent if necessary to avert defeat, and that they would be necessary.

This is what is meant by saying that there is, I believe, a mechanism at work, a "stalemate machine": not perfectly determinate, but with stable tendencies well-enough established so that one can say usefully, on the basis of an understanding of it, *how to bet,* at various moments and with respect to various activities.

This is *not* to say that any of the Presidents concerned would have bet the same way, with respect to the long run: i.e., that they accepted this model of the "stalemate machine." Almost surely they did not. For example, George Ball is quoted as having told President Kennedy in 1961 that General Taylor's 8,000-man task force "could lead in five years' time to an involvement of 300,000 men." The President answered him, "George, you're crazy as hell!"[88]

Four years later, Ball told Kennedy's successor, on the eve

[88] Martin Agronsky, TV broadcast, June 27, 1971.

(July 1, 1965) of President Johnson's decision to expand from 75,000 men to an open-ended commitment:

The South Vietnamese are losing the war to the Viet Cong. No one can assure you that we can beat the Viet Cong or even force them to the conference table on our terms, no matter how many hundred thousand *white, foreign* (U.S.) troops we deploy. . . . The decision you face now, therefore, is crucial. Once large numbers of U.S. troops are committed to direct combat . . . [and] once we suffer large casualties, we will have started a well-nigh irreversible process. Our involvement will be so great that we cannot—without national humiliation—stop short of achieving our complete objectives. *Of the two possibilities I think humiliation would be more likely than the achievement of our objectives—even after we have paid terrible costs.* [*PP*, IV, 615-16; italics added.]

The President's answer, if any, is not recorded.

So the future, and even the process, was visible—to some officials. Why not to the Presidents? Probably for two reasons. Ball stressed the first of these as he explained to Agronsky Kennedy's answer to his prediction:

"What he was saying to me was—look, I'm not going to do this, I'm not going to let it escalate. I think that he was aware of the fact that when he moved up from the 600 to 700 advisors that we had [to] a very much larger number that he might be starting a process. But I think that he felt that it was a process that he could control."

Johnson in mid-'65, on the other hand, knew he was taking no "small step," knew he was starting a process not easily controlled, and knew that the intelligence analysts offered little promise of victory ever, while no one (except, most of the time, Walt Rostow) promised it quickly. But in terms of his longer-range expectations, Schlesinger's guess about Johnson is probably right:

I still believe he found it viscerally inconceivable that what Walt Rostow kept telling him was "the greatest power in the world" could not dispose of a collection of night-riders in black pajamas.[89]

Thus, neither of these Presidents chose "knowingly"[90] the

[89] "The Quagmire Papers (Cont.)," *New York Review of Books*, December 16, 1971, page 41.

[90] My use of this word in the earlier version of this paper was somewhat misconstrued by Schlesinger (in "Eyeless in Indochina") but it was, I now feel, misleading; and I am indebted to Schlesinger's critique, and to several conversations with him, for stimulating me to rethink and modify this passage.

actual future of a half-million U.S. troops and twelve million tons of shells and bombs. Contrary to the quagmire model, they did know at the moment of their escalating decisions that new crises or challenges to larger efforts would *probably* return. But each of them undoubtedly believed—like Truman and Eisenhower before them—that at some stage long before the actual 1968-72 levels of violence were reached he, or his successor, would have chosen *either* to Win or to Leave: i.e., would have finally accepted one of the two alternatives both of which he was postponing at the moment in favor of Staying: avoiding defeat, regaining a stalemate. What none probably imagined was that he himself, and his successors, would go on making the same conceptual choice again and again—Winning always looking too risky or infeasible, the other side never cracking; but it seeming always the wrong time to Leave. None may have guessed that "buying time," postponing a defeat, would *always* look like a lesser evil to an American President than ending the war as a failure, despite escalation of the stalemate and of the human costs to awful levels.

So we need not infer of any of our five Presidents who have made this war that he acted in full knowledge or acceptance of what it would finally mean to America and Indochina; just that at each juncture in the quarter-century, each chose knowingly to *prolong* the war, and in most cases to expand it. Each always paid the necessary price—in the lives and resources of others—to "stay in the game," always preserving the options to go Up while making it more costly and unlikely for himself and his successors ever to go Out. That pattern covers a generation of Presidents; all the Presidents within the lifetime of a recent college graduate.

Will the tradition of choosing probable stalemate end with the current President? How many more could it encompass? Nothing in the generalizations we have abstracted in this paper from the experience of the last two decades gives a clear hint of a definite breaking point, or a foreseeable change in basic motives and values either for the Communist-led forces or the U.S. Government. That may be a limitation of the analysis, a characteristic —perhaps a defect—of the model suggested.

But perhaps it is a property of reality.

If so, it is a human and political reality, and humans can, in principle, change it. But change would not be easy. Rule 1 has deep roots in politicians' fears and motives, and in public responses, that have been powerfully influential for twenty years, through some hard times and challenges. There is little indication yet that it will not speak commandingly to Presidents after this one. (Of its authority for the present one, there can be no real doubt.[91])

Improved Presidential foresight—even the awareness that might be attained from this analysis—would not probably supersede Rule 1. If anything, it might serve to relax the constraining influence of Rule 2.

In the spring of 1965 President Johnson is reported to have received calls almost daily from one of his closest advisers, telling him (what no one had to tell him): "Lyndon, don't be the first American President to lose a war."

It is true that such advisers omitted warnings of other deadly errors. They neglected to caution him: "Don't, over more than one or two years, lie to the public; or mislead and bypass Congress; or draft and spend and kill and suffer casualties at the rate your military will propose; or abort negotiations; or, even once, allow your generals to describe the enemy as defeated on the eve of their major offensive."[92]

But if they had, and if he had seen the cogency of their warning: Would he then have decided to lose the war? Or would he,

[91] The discussion has gone only through 1968; no attempt is made here to apply the conjectures and generalizations of this paper to the statements and actions of the current Administration. That is left as an exercise to the reader.

Nothing in the past attitudes and history of the current President, or any of his public statements or official actions so far in office, suggests in any way that these generalizations should be less applicable to him than to any of his predecessors; thus this extrapolation should be a fair test. One might, for example, address the question: Which year between now and 1977 might Richard Milhous Nixon consider an acceptable one, for him, to lose South Vietnam to Communist control?

For my own views, see "Murder in Laos," pages 253-74.

[92] No advisor is perfect. There are things Presidents have to learn for themselves. One supposes no one told President Nixon, before the event: "Don't condone the shooting of white students by National Guardsmen just after crossing a national border with troops without consulting Congress, the public, or the country invaded."

mindful of the time constraints, have tried to *win* it within them? The same question applies to earlier Presidents; and later.

Theodore Draper has observed of the Bay of Pigs that it was that rare political/military event, "a perfect failure." If U.S. policy in Vietnam is at all to be seen as a tragedy—rather than a mechanical process, or a criminal one—it might be because its failures have all been imperfect: a series of achievements seen by our Presidents as adequate—though limited and temporary—successes as well as partial failures, each drawing them ever deeper into . . . a Sea of Pigs.

The Faces in the Quagmire

Looking at where their policies and tactics have brought us so far, it is easy to understand why the past four Presidents would want, before and after, to conceal and deprecate their own foreknowledge and intentions.[93] And it is no harder to guess why—perhaps unconsciously—participant-observers of one or another of these Administrations have promoted the same lenient interpretation of foresight and purpose, values and priorities, influence and responsibility, respecting their past colleagues within and outside government. Indeed, they make no secret of the conclusion they wish to convey by the quagmire metaphor and model concerning the responsibility of individuals and groups.

Thus, Townsend Hoopes, acutely and perceptively critical of the policies under Johnson and earlier Presidents, extends what Richard Falk has called "the circle of responsibility" widely indeed, in explicit purpose to relieve the burden of those seemingly at its center. Traumatized by a suggestion made by two reporters from the *Village Voice* that he himself, as Assistant Secretary of the Air Force under Johnson, might have been guilty of war crimes (their subsequent article was titled: "The War Criminals Hedge Their Bets"[94]), Hoopes has published several rejoinders and dis-

---

[93] No event, and no Presidential decision, of course, occurred because it "had" to, in any sense of certainty or absolute determinism. What does? On the other hand, in every major case, from the perspective of existing, inside knowledge and opinion years earlier, what actually occurred in the way of Presidential decision and of resulting developments in Vietnam would have seemed the way to bet.

[94] Judith Coburn and Geoffrey Cowan, *Village Voice*, December 4, 1969.

cussions of the problem of responsibility. In the first of these, he describes his chief concern in the disturbing conversation to be "the broad question of how the *entire nation* had stumbled down the long slippery slope of self-delusion into the engulfing morass." Hoopes then concludes:

The tragic story of Vietnam is not, in truth, a tale of malevolent men bent upon conquest for personal gain or imperial glory. It is the story of an entire generation of leaders (and an entire generation of followers). . . . [Johnson's] principal advisers were, almost uniformly, those considered when they took office to be among the ablest, the best, the most humane and liberal men that could be found for public trust. No one doubted their honest, high-minded pursuit of the best interests of their country, and indeed of the whole non-Communist world, as they perceived those interests.[95]

Arthur Schlesinger, Jr., less generous in his appreciation of some of Kennedy's and Johnson's civilian lieutenants, is no less reluctant to single out them or their Chief as "guilty" in any special way for their role in our vast national undertaking. In the "quagmire" (literally, "morass") passage previously cited in this paper, he asserts:

It is not only idle but unfair to seek out guilty men. . . . we find ourselves entrapped today in . . . a war which no President, including President Johnson, desired or intended. The Vietnam story is *a tragedy without villains.* No thoughtful American can withhold sympathy as President Johnson ponders the gloomy choices which lie ahead.[96]

[95] Townsend Hoopes, "The Nuremberg Suggestion," *Washington Monthly*, December, 1969; italics added. Reprinted, with reply, in "The Hoopes Defense," by Judith Coburn and Geoffrey Cowan, *Village Voice*, January 29, 1970. See also the cogent comment by lawyer Peter Weiss (with reply by Hoopes), *Washington Monthly*, June, 1970, pages 4-8.
In none of his comments (nor in his later *Foreign Affairs* article, "Legacy of the Cold War in Indochina," July, 1970) does Hoopes dissent from this general evaluation of the aims and values of the Johnson advisers, although it would seem fair to reexamine these on the basis of their official performance as it becomes increasingly known, and on their sense of social responsibility for events, shown after leaving office. For some of my own reflections on these matters, see the final essay in this volume, "The Responsibility of Officials in a Criminal War," pages 275-309.
[96] *The Bitter Heritage*, pages 47, 48; italics added. Schlesinger's more recent comments, quoted earlier—"At every stage of our descent into the quagmire, the military have played the dominant role. . . . At each point along the ghastly way, the generals promised . . ."—do, of course, add villains to the tragedy, although not civilian ones. If he no longer thinks it idle to seek out guilty men, he has nevertheless managed to be unfair.

One can read some of these passages as reflections of the sentiment Hoopes expresses: "What the country needs is not retribution, but therapy. . . ." (It is just possible that both are needed, at this point, in the interests of our country and of others.) He completes the sentence, plausibly—"therapy in the form of deeper understanding of our problems and each other"; but in all of these passages and the larger arguments in which they are embedded, one senses that the drive to exculpate, to ward off retribution, is seriously setting back the cause of understanding.

Both the substance of the tentative conclusions in this paper, and my experience of the heuristic process that gradually pointed toward them, warn that a deeper analytical understanding of these well-guarded data and controverted events is not likely to be reached by a searcher committed and determined to see the conflict and our part in it as "a tragedy without villains": war crimes without criminals, lies without liars, a process of immaculate deception.

Many former officials are particularly concerned to defend American institutions and legitimate authority (and surely some of their leaders and colleagues, if not themselves) from the most extreme charges and sanctions: "Lyndon Johnson, though disturbingly volatile," Hoopes remarks, "was not in his worst moments an evil man in the Hitlerian sense." This leads them as analysts to adopt and promulgate a view of the process, roles, and motives involved that is grossly mistaken—as should be known to them from their own experience and access to information as officials.

Thus, an effort—in alleged pursuit of "objective judgment"—to defend against self-perceptions or accusations by others of "immorality" leads in this case to historical and analytical error. And it has political consequences: It underwrites deceits that have served importantly a succession of Presidents to maintain support for their substantive policies of intervention in Vietnam.

Of course, to promulgate a view is not necessarily to have it accepted. But this one has a powerful appeal. We can suspect that the quagmire image speaks for deeper, more emotional concerns when it is presented regularly in the broad strokes of political cartoons in mass-circulation newspapers. That was particularly evident on the nation's editorial pages during the Cambodian invasion.

That week, while photographs on the front page showed unwonted images of *blitzkrieg*—tanks in formation driving across fields trailing plumes of dust, and locust swarms of American armed helicopters moving across new borders—and while reporters offered verbal pictures of the Cambodian village of Snoul being destroyed and looted, the drawings on the editorial pages were of Uncle Sam's and GI Joe's engulfed, bemused, floundering from a swamp marked "Vietnam" to one marked "Cambodia." Images, curiously, of impotence, passivity: ironically contrasting both with the news and the photographs of what Americans in Southeast Asia were actually doing and with the President's announced intent to expunge any notions of America as a "pitiful, helpless giant."

One cartoon, reproduced in *Time*, showed the "U.S. citizen" in tatters on a raft, confronting three enormous, wide-mouthed whales, labeled: "Vietnam," "Cambodia," and "Laos."

Whales?

The imagery, pressed far enough, reveals its key. The relative scale of the parties, and the direction of the menace, have simply been reversed. The actual role of America and Americans in and toward Indochina has been distorted, to a staggering degree, in the very process of suggesting that it be reconsidered. And looking back to the quicksand cartoons, one sees their self-pity, their preoccupation with Uncle Sam's predicament, and one finally asks: Where are the Asians? Where are the Cambodians, the Laotians, the Vietnamese in these drawings?

Presumably—there is no other sign—they are the particles of the bog, bits of the porridgey quagmire that has seized GI Joe and will not free him. . . .

It is not, after all, only Presidents and Cabinet members who have a powerful need and reason to deny their responsibility for this war. And who succeed at it. It is true that the fact of Executive deception gives the quagmire model a reality with respect to the *public,* and even the Congress, that it lacks for the Presidents; the responsibility of those lied to—even given a persistent "need-not-to-know"—is not as great as that of the liars. Nevertheless, just as Presidents and their partisans find comfort and political safety in the quicksand image of the *President-as-victim,* so Americans at large are reassured in sudden moments of doubt by the same image drawn large, *America-as-victim.* It is no more real than the first, and neither national understanding nor extrication truly lie that way.

To understand the war process as it emerges in the documents behind public statements, the concerns never written down that moved decisions, the history scratched on the minds of bureaucrats: to translate that understanding into images that can guide actions related closely to reality, one must begin by seeing that it is Americans, our leaders and ourselves, that build the bog, a trap much more for other victims: *our* policies, our politics the quagmire in which Indochina drowns.

The Stalemate Machine: A Schematic Summary

The following imputed Presidential decision guidelines (A, below) will, under crisis conditions of the Vietnam conflict as perceived by Washington decision-makers, lead to policy choices and Executive performance conforming in some detail to those actually obtaining at major escalation points (not necessarily to behavior in between them) between 1950-68. (Presidential choices significantly escalating U.S. involvement have occurred, in fact, only in crisis situations of impending failure.)

Together with decisions between major escalations, institutional consequences (including consequences for expectations), and external factors—mainly, GVN and DRV/VC behavior operating over time—these rules will generate an evolution of policy, involvement, and conflict very close to that observed over that period (B, C, and D below).

A. *Presidential Decision Rules in Crisis*

Rule 1. *Do not* lose South Vietnam[97] to Communist control—or appear likely to do so—before the next election.

Rule 2. *Do not*, unless essential to satisfy Rule 1 in the immediate crisis or an earlier one:

 a. bomb South Vietnam or Laos;
 b. bomb North Vietnam;
 c. commit U.S. combat troops to Vietnam;
 d. commit U.S. combat troops to Laos or Cambodia;
 e. institute wartime domestic controls;
 f. destroy Hanoi or Haiphong or the dike system, or mine Haiphong harbor;
 g. mobilize reserves;
 h. assume full, overt administrative authority and military command in South Vietnam;
 i. invade North Vietnam;
 j. use nuclear weapons.

[97] From 1949 till June, 1954, for this read "Vietnam" (especially Tonkin).

Rule 3. *Do* choose actions that will:

a. minimize the risk of loss—or public expectation of eventual loss—within the next six months, so far as possible without violating Rule 2.
b. if this risk is significant without certain actions so far "prohibited" by Rule 2, break constraints[98] to use the types of actions minimally necessary (as judged by President) to reduce the risk to a very low level.
c. so far as is consistent with Rule 1, and using fully any action no longer prohibited, maximize the probability of an eventual "win," in the sense of eliminating the Communist party in South Vietnam and assuring indefinitely a non-Communist regime.
d. so far as is consistent with Rule 1, do not take actions that might *appear* to preclude or indefinitely forgo an eventual "win": i.e., a "no-win strategy."

B. *Consequences for U.S. Policy*

Viewed from inside, resultant policies reflecting the above rules show certain "discrepancies" when compared to *internal predictions, recommendations, and stated aims* (as well as to *public statements*), giving policy the internal appearance of being purposefully dedicated to preserving a stalemate.

1. Because of the short-term focus of Rule 1:

a. chosen policies appear—and are—almost exclusively oriented to *short-term* considerations, neglecting or trading off very large differences in predicted long-run costs, risks, benefits, and probability of success in pursuit of small reductions in short-term risk (i.e., risk of "losing" South Vietnam in the next six months, or prior to the next election).
b. chosen programs are predicted internally to be *inadequate*—or at best, "long shots"—in the *long run* either to "win" or even to avert defeat, (in contrast to public statements about them, and to some recommended but rejected policies).
c. actual policies chosen emphasize predominantly military—rather than political—means, aims, considerations, and executive responsibility on both Vietnamese and American sides.

2. To compensate for avoidance of "constrained instruments" (Rule 2), the chosen policy relies heavily upon:

a. allied ground forces;
b. commitments and assurances to allies, warnings and threats to opponents;
c. clandestine activities;

[98] Roughly in order shown under Rule 2, though, for example, any adjacent pair may be reversed, depending on judgment and circumstances.

d. other nonprohibited instruments (including economic and military aid;
    advisors; combat, logistic, mobility, and air support).

3. For reasons reflecting both Rules 1 and 2:

a. U.S. supports (intervening as necessary to instate or maintain) a narrow-
    based, right-wing, anti-Communist, "pro-American," authoritarian
    (since 1963, essentially military) regime in Saigon, despite its predicted
    (and actual) inability to win wider popular support for long-term self-
    sufficiency—*forgoing pressure* for either "broadening" or "reform," and
    accepting a condition of *weak* U.S. influence toward these "aims" or
    upon most other GVN policies or execution. (Between 1946-54, there
    was an exactly corresponding weakness of U.S. influence upon the
    colonial or military policies of its French ally, with the U.S. likewise
    forgoing any use of "leverage" despite correspondingly important sup-
    port.)
b. In communications to Congress and the public, the Administration:
    (1) expresses optimism (exceeding internal estimates at the time of
        decision) on both the short- and the long-term prospects of actual
        programs.
    (2) conceals (if necessary, misleading or lying about) indications of pos-
        sible inadequacy of current programs, including:
        (a) pessimistic estimates or appraisals;
        (b) internal recommendations for more extreme actions;
        (c) planning activity for much greater effort or more extreme actions.
    (3) describes the strategic *stakes* for the U.S. in maintaining a non-
        Communist South Vietnam in the most impressive and grave terms,
        relying upon extended "domino" premises (whether or not cur-
        rently affirmed by intelligence analyses).
    (4) conceals (lying or misleading as necessary) the full extent of pro-
        grams actually decided upon (as well as of follow-on programs
        expected to be approved), instead giving the impression that fully
        scheduled buildups are resulting from sequential, marginal, con-
        tingent *ad hoc* decisions.

C. Institutional Consequences of Escalation

There are bureaucratic tendencies—except during military or budget
crises—to assure superiors, and to believe, that current programs are
adequate and are succeeding; to provide data supporting what the
public is being told and to come to believe it is true. These tendencies
have the following consequences:

1. *Internal operational reporting,* program analyses, and high-level
expectations (though not necessarily intelligence estimates) gradually move, as the chosen policy begins to be implemented, in the

direction of the public optimism expressed earlier; early VC and GVN responses to the escalation reinforce this trend, to bring about a "Phase B" stage of genuine internal "euphoria" subsequent to—and caused by—the crisis-escalation of "Phase A."

2. During this "euphoric aftermath" of the escalation, more ambitious goals are adopted within the Administration (more weight is given to the long-term "win"); these do *not* lead to qualitative escalation by the President—despite urging to do so—but to expanded effort, toleration of rapidly rising *costs,* and increasingly optimistic public *predictions.*

D. *Consequences for Further Escalation*

1. The escalations themselves, and the institutional consequences above, increase the political stakes for a given Administration and its successor, and reinforce tendencies to obey the Decision Rules above when a Communist resurgence or GVN collapse returns conditions of crisis.

2. The recurrent estimates of the intelligence community—that the VC and DRV are *unlikely* to abandon or reduce their long-term aims in South Vietnam in response to U.S. escalation, and *likely* instead to match increased US/GVN efforts to the extent necessary to frustrate them and threaten their defeat—are in fact, *correct:* therefore, the dynamic result of the Presidential decision rules above is what John T. McNaughton in January, 1966, called "an escalating military stalemate" (*PP,* IV, 47).

BACKGROUND:
VIETNAM, 1965-67

I reread pieces like those that follow, written during my two years' service in Vietnam, with very mixed feelings. They recall to me a spirit of hopefulness reflecting illusions and ignorance that did me no credit even in 1965. They recall, too, friends, some as close as I will ever have, now killed or in prisons on either side, or, almost worse, compromised by their inability to denounce or to detach themselves from a lost war whose corruption they know better than most.

Somewhere one of Lewis Carroll's characters reflects: "I wonder what it feels like to believe that." I have little need to wonder when I listen to believers in this war, or in the Cold War; except for the beliefs of some in the efficacy and legitimacy of bombing and torture, there is scarcely an Administration belief so ill-founded or tendentious that I have not managed to believe it at some past time. So it is not lack of empathy that makes me impatient with those who have managed to preserve such beliefs intact through the last seven years of history. My own change of mind did not, perhaps, take unduly long, considering how much I had to unlearn; but it came too slowly and late to be the basis of self-congratulation, considering the human and social stakes involved.

Still, perhaps it is well for the reader to be aware that where the critical content of my writing carries an evident emotional charge, it is one that is the opposite of invidious. To illustrate that point sharply, I include in this section one piece written later—my review in late 1970 of *The Road from War: Vietnam 1965-1970,* a collection of essays by Robert Shaplen. To understand my own perspective on the history and problems of Vietnam five years earlier, one could simply examine Shaplen's earlier book, *The Lost Revolution* (1965). I took up the task of reviewing his subsequent pieces on Vietnam with the special interest of measuring my own trajectory of opinion against that of a sober, experienced observer whose values, beliefs, and aims had, to the best of my understanding, coincided almost identically with my own at the time I arrived in Vietnam to serve under Shaplen's friend, Major General Edward Lansdale.

Thus it was peculiarly challenging to discover that a "journal" whose earlier sections, from the point of view of tone and content, might have been written by myself at that time, preserves the same assumptions and concerns—as in amber—through the accounts written in each succeeding year. Was Shaplen Rip Van Winkle still asleep, dreaming? Or have I dreamed the intervening years, with what seemed their deadening freight of disillusion of the hopes we shared in '65? Neither thought is pleasant. When I comment in the review that the repeated frustrations—faithfully reported and then, it seems, ignored by Shaplen—of those recrudescent hopes "calls into question the very relevance of Shaplen's chosen beat . . . primarily Saigon maneuvering and 'pacification' operations in the countryside," I am questioning the significance of *my own* chosen "beat" in Vietnam, which was precisely the same.

If the tone of the review seems sardonic, it is anything but detached; it is a *cri du coeur,* addressed to more than one of my former associates, trying to call them away from preoccupations that no longer seemed respectable by the time of this book and this review. (My review appeared in the *Washington Post* on November 4, 1970, the day after an election campaign in which the war and the events of that spring in Cambodia were scarcely mentioned as issues, even while American bombers continued to destroy the social fabric of a country that had been at peace at the start of the year.) It is as expressive a comment as I could present briefly of my current opinion of the cogency of my own earlier hopes and attitudes in Vietnam, which are represented in the selections that follow.

These pieces, especially "Visit to an Insecure Province" and "Problems of 'Revolutionary Development,' " suggest how Vietnam itself was perceived by dedicated officials in the field who accepted the viewpoint—as I did when I wrote them—that Vietnam presented "problems," challenges, to Americans. Yet the men I worked most closely with, friends I respected and learned from, were, like myself, far from being only cool problem-solvers in that country. Like Shaplen, like Lansdale, we believed—six million tons ago!—that we had grown to love Vietnam and its people, and that our presence, along with other Americans, could help them. A long letter to friends at home a few weeks after my arrival suggests how much we wanted to believe that:

—I have fallen in love with the children of Vietnam. I have never seen any, anywhere in the world, so gay, so friendly and funny. They all remind me of my own. "It's funny," says an American, "you worry about people being anti-American; but when you walk through the villages, the way these kids come on with you . . . it's hard to believe that their parents could hate us, when they're so friendly." Again and again, a crowd of kids sees us approaching, on foot or in a car, and explodes into a chant, almost in unison: "Okay! Okay! Hallo! Hallo! Number one!" They rush out with hysterical grins—and I remember Robert and Mary running out to climb over me at the end of the day, and my heart turns over. In the hamlets, they want to hold your wrist, pluck the hair on your arms; if you try to catch them to lift them up, they dart just out of reach, till a brave one tries it, then they all want to be swung. "Chao em" (Hello . . . to a child) brings thrilled looks, giggling consultation; "chao ba" to an old lady splinters her old-apple face in a big grin, lips and teeth stained with betel nut. In a village, a province capital, or a hamlet, the children don't leave; they follow you around like a cloud of birds; as you walk, talking to someone, little hands slip into yours from behind; another hand may slap you impudently on the butt. They seem so *pleased* by your existence, by your own friendliness—it's head-spinning. I love them, and I don't want to leave them.

—"Look at this," says the USOM (AID) province representative in Chau Doc, arms encrusted with little girls belonging to his cook and housekeeper. "And they tell you not to get involved."

—Within a week, I know many Americans who are involved. Fanatics, mavericks, losers, non-team-players, fluent speakers of Vietnamese, old Vietnam hands who have hung on or gotten back . . .

"Involved." Yes, we were all involved, my friends and I there, and we paid various prices for it. The province representative in Chau Doc was blown to pieces—though he survived—by a mine under his truck within weeks of my letter. Of the others described in that passage, one had died in a plane crash, shot down by the VC, by the time I wrote; another, John Paul Vann, continued to survive innumerable ambushes, while a third, working for Vann, was captured on the road and is still a prisoner of the VC, if he is alive; a fourth was killed in Laos.

But the price of our presence and involvement was far greater for the children of Indochina. We all knew what war was, of course, and what it did to children, but there was scarcely one among us then who was not blind in some important measure to the real nature, history, and sociology of that conflict and of our crucial twenty-year role in it—and to our place in a much longer history.

"Okay! Hallo!" These greetings began to sound different after a comment I heard once, driving along a road between Danang and Hoi An in I Corps. It was the spring of 1966, during the second Buddhist Struggle uprising. The road had been blocked or cut that morning every half-mile or so—not by the VC but by other factions rebelling against the U.S.-backed Saigon regime. Along the road was a succession of abandoned forts and outposts, of varying construction. There were mud outposts of the Popular Forces, and concrete French outposts, mostly from the 1946-54 war but some from earlier; Japanese pillboxes, from the 1940-45 period, had a different design. And at one point we passed a massive knoll overgrown with grass, which had been, I was told, a Chinese fort. ("You must understand," a Vietnamese friend told me once, "that we think of ourselves as having defeated the Chinese, though it took us a thousand years.") It was not a secure road; we drove fast, between obstacles, with weapons handy; but the children we passed, as always, called out, "Number one! Okay!" And the Vietnamese lieutenant with us re-marked, "When I was their age, I called 'hello' to soldiers too." "How did you say it?" I asked him, expecting him to say "*Bonjour.*" "*Ohayo gozaimasu,*" he answered in Japanese.

There were those of us in Vietnam who hoped—along with Lans-dale and Shaplen—that the nationalist, revolutionary (or at least reformist!) cause had not been "lost" irrevocably to Communist leadership, and we thought of our efforts as aimed at recapturing it; Vann drafted a paper just before I arrived expressing the views shared by most of us, including our friend Tran Ngoc Chau—now Thieu's prisoner in a Saigon jail—entitled "Harnessing the Revolution in South Vietnam."

In truth, Vietnam, and its revolution, had never been ours to lose, or to harness; it was *the* war that had always been ours: to end. If we had known better, my friends in Vietnam and I, in ways I had come to suspect by the time I wrote "The Day Lôc Tiên Was Pacified," it might not have made any difference to the war: but our own personal "involvement" would have taken a different turn, I think, as mine did when I read the early sections of the Pentagon Papers four years later.

My own incomprehension stares at me rather poignantly from a letter to my children only a few days after the one quoted above, written on September 27, 1965. It referred to their visit with me in Washington six weeks earlier, which had unexpectedly taken place just after General Lansdale had accepted me on his team, a week after I had volunteered. I was to leave within two weeks, so the visit had coincided with my getting ready to go.

In between my shots, visas, and briefings, I took them to see historical monuments, mostly at night. One inscription that we read together at the Lincoln Memorial had seemed uncanny in its aptness to the goals of our team, as I understood them, and my son Robert, then eight, had found leaflets at the monument that reproduced the passage. I brought a handful with me to Vietnam and recalled this in the letter:

> I think a great deal of all the things we did together. (I can still see Mary racing around the Washington Monument our first night) . . . Do you remember reading Lincoln's Second Inaugural Address, Robert? You remember that I had you bring some copies of it, because I felt sure that someone in Vietnam would recognize that it applied perfectly to their situation. Today I had the chance to use it: Prime Minister Ky wanted us to help him write a speech, and I got out our quotation and had my boss, General Lansdale, take it over to Ky to show him. The last paragraph is:
>
> "With malice toward none; with charity for all; with firmness in the right, as God gives us to see the right, let us strive on to finish the work we are in; to bind up the nation's wounds; to care for him who shall have borne the battle, and for his widow, and his orphan—to do all which may achieve and cherish a just and lasting peace among ourselves, and with all nations."
>
> I don't know if Ky will use it in his speech, but I'm glad that he had a chance to see it; I think the people of South Vietnam would be glad to know that we are able to understand their problems because we had a civil war

ourselves, and also to realize that now we are united, free, and rich in spite of our own civil war. And Lincoln's thought, "With malice toward none; with charity for all," is important for them to hear. So I owe the chance to pass this on to your visit, and to our trip to the Lincoln Memorial (I told this to all the men I am working with).

What is there to say now about that blend of sympathy and ignorance, brought to Vietnam by so many Americans along with our firepower—a mixture about to explode among the Vietnamese in 1965? Civil war? Like most Americans, I had gotten two parts of our own history, a century apart, confused; it was our "revolutionary" war, our war for independence from foreign control that was the counterpart to the thirty-year struggle of the Vietnamese.[1]

Widows, orphans . . . there are far more of them in Vietnamese society today than when I and some friends in September of that year encouraged Premier Ky to translate Lincoln's words of concern into official Vietnamese.

It was that fall, and the summer before it—when heavy American air and artillery bombardment first began, accompanying the operations of American troops—that the great flow of war refugees within South Vietnam commenced. The total number of refugees—disproportionately children, along with women and the very old—is now calculated at between five and six million people, out of a total population of eighteen million. (The monthly flow of refugees during several months of 1971 was higher than at any time since the Tet offensive in 1968.) The Kennedy Subcommittee on Refugees estimates more than one million civilian casualties in South Vietnam since 1965, including at least 325,000 deaths.

Moreover, Senator Kennedy has reported:

—addressing only victims among "our side," not the NLF—inevitably, tens of thousands of the civilian casualties who survive are physically disabled. Again, official statistics do not reflect the true picture, but as of late 1969,

---

[1] To suppose, as I long did, that analogy falsified by the purported fact that no more than one third or one fifth of the Vietnamese population wholeheartedly supported the revolutionary struggle, or even the war for independence from foreigners, is simply to misconstrue the history of revolutionary and independence movements in general, and our own in particular, of which precisely the same was true. (See, for example, David V. J. Bell and Allan E. Goodman, "Vietnam and The American Revolution," Yale Review, Volume LXI, Issue 1, Fall, 1971, pages 26-34; and John Adams' well-known estimate that one third of the population in America had supported the rebels, one third the British—closer to one half in some areas, like New York—and one third were neutral.)

some 79,000 civilian amputees and paraplegics were registered with the Vietnamese government, as well as some 25,600 civilians who have become blind
or deaf from war causes. In addition, the official register lists some 258,000
orphans and some 131,000 war widows.

Again, it is the children who have paid the highest price in lost arms and
legs, sight and hearing. And this situation in South Vietnam has been now
duplicated in Laos—where American bombing has been vastly increased
since late 1968—and in Cambodia, where operations during and after the
American-South Vietnamese invasion in the spring of 1970 have led to over
one million refugees [two million as of 1972] out of a population of less than
seven million. The burden of American fighting power on the population on
Indochina shows no sign of diminishing . . .

It is another inscription I saw, that night with my children in
Washington, that comes back to me more and more now, as the
widow-making and orphaning goes on. From the walls of the Jeffer-
son Memorial:

Indeed, I tremble for my country when I reflect that God is just; and that his
justice will not sleep forever . . .

VISIT TO AN INSECURE PROVINCE

What follows is Part I of an early trip report to my colleagues on the Lansdale team, most of whom had served in Vietnam before but had not been recently in the field. General Lansdale, who hoped to concentrate on encouraging political development, had been assigned by Ambassador Lodge the thankless job of coordinating U.S. civil activities directed toward "pacification." Assisting him in this role, I began to make extensive field trips; as a newcomer, I wanted to educate myself on conditions in the countryside and the nature of the counterguerrilla war.

Within the band of "fanatics, mavericks . . . and old Vietnam hands" described in my letter quoted earlier, none had a higher reputation than John Paul Vann, who was to become my closest friend in Vietnam. (Vann is now [April, 1972] Senior Advisor in II Corps, the first civilian ever to command all the Americans, including military, in a Corps area in Vietnam.) I had heard of him even before I arrived from David Halberstam, who had written at length about Vann's honesty, nerve, and outspokenness during his 1962-63 tour—when he was an active Army officer, a lieutenant colonel—as Senior Advisor to the ARVN 7th Division (see *The Making of a Quagmire,* Chapters X and XI). That had involved responsibility covering eight Delta provinces. Now back as a civilian in AID, retired from the Army, Vann was being treated with great reserve by his new agency, whose officials had read Halberstam's account of his famous candor from a different point of view than mine. At this point he had spent ten months as an AID province representative in Hau Nghia, a small, dusty, wholly insecure province which functioned mainly as a highway for Viet Cong moving out of the adjacent Plain of Reeds.

When I met Vann in Saigon, he offered to show me his province; in the course of three days' driving with him, I began to learn a good deal. In the next six weeks, we drove to every province capital in III Corps, some of which had not been visited by road for almost a year. In the following report I deliberately included the kind of concrete details I wished I had been given in my reading the year before, in Washington; later this account circulated widely among my former colleagues and superiors in the Pentagon.

Glossary: The following terms and acronyms recur frequently in the four papers that follow in this "Background" section. "Revolutionary Development" (*RD*) is an American name for what the French call "pacification": coined by White House aides because it sounded less French and more competitive with the NLF. (The Saigon regime, which has a better sense than we do of who they are, declined to follow this usage, shunning the word "revolutionary"; they use the title "Rural Construction," equally misleading but less provocative.) An RD cadre team is a 59-man group—originally trained, armed, and paid by the CIA—which carries out various organizational activities in a hamlet to fulfill the six criteria (see "The Day Lôc Tiên Was Pacified") of a "pacified" or "secured" hamlet. PF are Popular Force soldiers: local, lightly trained and equipped militia, operating in squads and platoons at village level. RF are Regional Forces, better trained and equipped, commanded at province level and operating in a district, generally in companies. ARVN are the regular units of the Army of the Republic of Vietnam, organized in divisions. RVNAF comprises all the armed forces of the Republic of Vietnam, including PF, RF, ARVN, air force, navy etcetera. MACV is the U.S. Military Assistance Command, Vietnam; *AID* is the U.S. Agency for International Development. *NVA* is the North Vietnamese army and *DRV* is the government of North Vietnam.

Part III of this report—omitted here—described "Vann theses" on the problems of Vietnam and what to do about them. That section began:

When I asked Vann, Monday night, what lesson he particularly wanted me to take away from our ride through the countryside, he said immediately: "The thinness of control by either the VC or the GVN." Vann believes that control can be wrested from the VC, in many areas by rather simple changes in activity. But these "simple" changes would be revolutionary departures for ARVN and the GVN. And Vann does not think they will happen without major U.S. initiatives and interventions.

Vann and his assistant, Douglas Ramsey, believed that the major "problem" in the countryside was that "the present leaders, bureaucrats, and province and district officials do not come from, think like, know much about, or respond to the wishes of the rural majority of the population." (An obvious solution on the first three counts would be to replace them with NLF officials; but as we saw it then—arguably—that would not surely meet the last criterion.) Many of those who stayed long in the country came to see that as the problem, all right, but remained skeptical of Vann's solution: that the U.S. Government should "accept *responsibility* for actual governmental performance in South Vietnam and act upon it."

I pointed out an obvious objection in my memo:

The "facade" [of Vietnamese authority, which Vann proposed to maintain] would eventually wear pretty thin, and we would lay ourselves open to charges, not only from the VC, that we had taken on a "colonialist" role. (There would be a good deal of basis for this charge; though it should be noted that, given the qualifications described above, the closest past analogy to the U.S. role would be that of a "good" colonialist power: one that was fully committed to granting full independence in the near future and that was making major, effective efforts to prepare the country for viable independence by educating the population and finding and training a spectrum of young, capable leaders and administrators. In other words, the closest colonial analogy would be British policy in Malaya under Templer, not French policy in either Indochina or Algeria.)

I shared this objection to Vann's approach, though I pointed out that it managed at least to address some important problems that were often ignored; within a year I had pinned my own hopes on another form of U.S. intervention that I had mentioned in this memo: "starting an evolutionary process in motion—perhaps by the beginnings of representative government—that will eventually transform the nature of the government, its personnel, and its élan." One more delusion; and looking back, I am more impressed by the similarities to Vann's concept of my own and others' approaches than by what we saw as differences. The actual U.S. colonial approach in Vietnam, of course, has always been essentially French, not British (with a great deal more troops and firepower than either). That, and no more than that, was what my friends and I were criticizing. "*Good* colonialists" was what we were all trying to be, and what Vann is. It was, and is, the wrong aspiration to have.

Late Sunday afternoon, October 17, 1965, I drove from Saigon to Bao Trai, province capital of Hau Nghia, with John Paul Vann, the AID provincial representative. The next day we drove to each of the four districts of Hau Nghia, visiting a number of hamlets, each of the district towns and sub-sector advisor posts, and several refugee relocation centers; we traveled on every road in the province that was not physically blocked.

Vann and his assistant, Doug Ramsey, maintain a map in their office showing the latest status of the roads as "passable—not hazardous," as passable but "slightly," "moderately," "extremely hazardous," and as (physically) "impossible." Over the long stretches of "moderately hazardous" road, Vann drove fairly fast, 80 to 90 kilometers per hour. On brief stretches of "extremely hazardous" road, he drove very fast, 90 to 110 kilometers—with one hand on an AR-15 pointed out the window, extra ammo around his shoulder, and grenades in his belt.

(On the most incident-prone of these portions—18 killed a month on a two-kilometer stretch—our [110 kph] progress was halted for 45 minutes by some cars mired down where the road had been destroyed two days earlier and badly repaired. We pulled a car loose with a tow rope, got stuck ourselves and were pulled out; meanwhile, five individuals had come up separately to tell us, in various ways, to "leave quickly" because there were VC on both sides of the road. We left as quickly as we could.)

Vann drove without bravado, paying very serious attention to what he was doing and to reducing the risks, and giving me running lessons on what to watch for and what to do. ("Vann doesn't take any risks he doesn't have to," an experienced AID colleague had told me, "short of abandoning the roads to the VC.")

Vann's side comments on road security: "The roads are generally clear from mines by ten or eleven in the morning; the VC have either blown them already or RF road-clearing details have found them." (However, a mine was blown at 1500 that day—killing five RF troops in a foot column and wounding seven—on a stretch of road we had driven over at 1100.) The mines are almost all wire-controlled, and the electric circuits sometimes have delays in them; so it is hard for the controller (who may be 400 to 500 yards away) to hit a fast-moving vehicle. It is common for a mine to go off behind a vehicle moving fast; the VC prefer to wait for a convoy, so that they have the best chance of getting one. (One informant led them to a row of twenty 105 mm. shells controlled by a single wire.) "Some day they may catch on that the way to get a single fast vehicle—like Ramsey or me—is to blow the mine just *ahead* of us."

They use enormous quantities of explosives for many of these mines—as much as 100 to 200 kilos of plastic explosive have been uncovered, though 15 to 20 kilos are more normal—so craters are typically six to seven feet deep, with one crater eleven feet deep (sandbags in the car would be of little help). In a road ambush, the local guerrillas do not usually lay an obstacle across the road, though a water buffalo may serve as a mobile barrier. The best tactic is to drive right through it; "they're very poor shots, like ARVN—the weapons are too big for them, and so is the kick— and the guerrillas are not like good regular soldiers; they'll scatter and duck if you fire back in their general direction." (Vann has now driven through three ambushes, one involving fifteen men close in on both sides of the road, and Ramsey has been through two.)

"You're safest in a single, unmarked vehicle, driving fast at irregular times, during the day." (On the way out from Saigon, Vann deliberately avoided joining the province chief's small convoy, but on the way back on Tuesday he gave in with considerable reluctance to the chief's insistence that we ride in his car. "We're *so* much more likely to get our ass blown off in this convoy than in my Scout," he told me.)

Water and Fish

"This is a PF outpost," says Vann; the PF's wave at us, behind their barbed wire and moat, lying on top of their concrete tower. "This one has an accommodation with the VC." How could one say that? "This post has had no contact with the VC in months; no casualties, hasn't been attacked. Now, you see this wreck next to it?" We stopped and looked at a skeleton of a building, only part of the frame and a few sheets of roofing, in the same open field as the PF outpost. It was surrounded by brand-new barbed wire; every section had been cut and trampled into the ground. "That's a PF training center we've been trying to build. The VC have torn it down *five times*. Last time was three nights ago. They ripped the boards and the roofing off, tore up the wire. It's exactly one hundred and seventeen paces to that post. But the PF's didn't hear anything, didn't see anything—didn't do anything." Some workers were lying nearby, taking siesta. "Those are the construction workers. Some of them probably helped tear it down."

Could the "accommodation" simply be tacit: we won't bother you, so you don't bother us? "Hell no, it's not tacit. We get the information; while those VC workers are out there, tearing up the building and making a hell of a racket, they're yelling right into this post: 'We're your brothers. Why are you working for the Americans and the traitors in Saigon?' And most of the time where these little deals are made, the PF leader or hamlet chief has talked face to face with the VC commissar."

When we drove by the post two days later, on the return to Saigon, the last sheets of roofing had been removed from the training center, and the wire was further tangled.

Again and again we rode over a patch where the road had been recently trenched and then filled in, or where a dirt wall had been built across it, or a large mine hole filled; in nearly every case, there would be a PF outpost 50 to 100 meters away. This was no coincidence. The VC were deliberately cutting and mining the road—with much hand labor, pick-and-shovel work that could probably be heard for half a mile—within eyesight and earshot of GVN soldiers, PF posts, and even district towns with RF detachments. The lesson, for the villagers, was pretty plain.

It was also pretty plain that one could find VC local guerrillas when one wanted to, without going very far. The roads were being cut or mined, or ambushes laid, in exactly the same spots day after day, sometimes four or five times in a row. "If I wanted to meet some guerrillas, I'd wait in the ditch any night next to the Sui Sau bridge," the MACV S-2 advisor told me (pointing to the bridge, locally known as "Sui Cide," where we had been stopped for 45 minutes the day before).[2] That there is abundant

---

[2] That incident was the one time I ever saw Vann edgy. It was near that bridge three months later that his assistant, Doug Ramsey, was ambushed while driving, and captured.

information on where to find guerrillas is shown by the record of the Chieu Hoi [VC defectors] platoon; out of seventeen operations in August, armed only with hand grenades, it had made contact each time, killing eleven VC. It went where the VC could be expected to be (on the basis of information and of past patterns of VC behavior).

In the same month, the 49th Regiment of the 25th Division reported conducting more than 1,400 small-unit actions, 605 of them at night. They reported contact with the VC sixteen times; no VC were killed. (Nor were any VC killed in the several large-scale operations; the 49th Regiment killed *no* VC in August.)

This pattern of almost no contact and few casualties inflicted or suffered on offensive operations is not peculiar to the 49th Regiment, or to John Vann's province. On my return, I began checking the countrywide figures: on October 17, 2,677 small-unit actions were reported, countrywide, with 13 contacts; on October 18th, 2,922 actions, 22 contacts; on October 22nd, 2,852 actions, 8 contacts (of these 43 contacts, 13 were at night, when the VC rules the countryside). A live VC is hard to find: for ARVN.

"The theory they give us for the outposts," the American advisor told me, "is that they serve as *bases*, from which they can do night patrolling." In reality, as he and everyone else I asked confirmed, the PF's simply do not move from these posts at night. Most of the posts in Hau Nghia are along major routes, guarding roads rather than villages; even those associated with a village are at one end, on the outskirts. The "security" they provide the villagers at night is not even problematic. And the arrogance of the VC, tearing up roads, killing hamlet officials, and abducting messengers from buses virtually at the front gate of the outposts, underlines the point.

As for the RF's and the 25th Division: (a) most of the small-unit actions reported, especially alleged night actions, are simply fictitious; (b) when they do venture out, it is to go places where the VC can be expected *not* to be (intelligence is good enough for that, too); (c) large-scale operations can be expected to be compromised in advance (the American advisors told me) by VC penetrations of headquarters and supporting units and by nonexistent communications security; (d) according to the U.S. advisor to the 49th Regiment, "nearly every regimental plan is changed in many ways by 25th Division headquarters; and virtually every change is such as to reduce the chance of contact or to allow the VC an avenue of escape: changing the axis of approach, removing the block force, leaving an open flank. . . ."

The sector advisory team and the regimental advisor (I didn't talk to the divisional advisory staff) told me they urge "daily" that each one of these patterns be changed: with what they describe as *zero* success.

In the morning we arrived at Dong Hoa hamlet, part of Hiep Hoa village in Duc Hue district, just after a graduation ceremony for a PF platoon that had received motivational indoctrination training. The province chief and sector advisor and their staffs had arrived for the occasion by helicopter.

This little area illustrated many of the complexities of "security" in Hau Nghia. Dong Hoa is carried on the charts as "blue" ("secured") although it is surrounded by "red." This is because it is the location of a big sugar mill (generally called the "Hiep Hoa sugar mill") which has never been attacked since it was constructed in 1923. "Notice the plate glass windows," Vann said, pointing to the housing next to the mill. The mill's sanctuary reflects the payment of what is reported to be 1,700,000 piasters a year to the VC. It is jointly owned by French and the GVN (inherited, I believe, from Madame Nhu); hearsay is that the French interest is unlikely to be expropriated, because it makes payment of the VC tax less embarrassing. The mill is unlikely to be attacked. But despite the serenity of Dong Hoa, the U.S. advisory staff to the Duc Hue sub-sector had just been removed from the hamlet "for security reasons": because of VC control of the surrounding area.

Meanwhile, Dong Hoa Bac, the hamlet just the other side of the Vaico Oriental River, was likewise carried as "GVN"–the only hamlet west of the river so listed–though it was in "deep red" country. How did its PF post survive? "By an accommodation," says Vann; the hamlet is, in fact, VC-controlled, and the fiction that it is a GVN hamlet is maintained only to permit the province to show one such hamlet west of the river. It was the

PF platoon and Dong Hoa Bac that had just received motivational indoctrination training; why the district chief had picked this particular platoon was not clear. Just two nights before, the VC had broken their truce with the hamlet by lobbing some mortar shells into the PF post—evidently to remind everyone, just before graduation, that motivation indoctrination training wasn't going to change any of the realities of the situation.

However, because of the ceremony, the province chief and the staffs accompanied the PF platoon as they returned across the river, and visited the post briefly. We went along. "This is quite an occasion," Vann told me. "This is only the second time that the province chief has ever been to this hamlet, that is, been west of the river. The previous chief never went. You'll be the first civilian—beside Ramsey and me—to be across the river in a couple of years."

While the chief was in a dugout in the post, Vann motioned me to follow him down a path between the river and a row of huts. "Watch this guard," he said. "He'll be very unhappy when we move off the tour; he probably won't let us go left here." The guard said nothing. "That's funny," Vann said, "they made a big stink when I tried to walk down here last time." (What struck me about these observations—which came early in the day—was that the province chief and his guard were only a few yards behind us, and the apparently "dangerous zone" was separated from the outpost defenses by several paces.) But after a few minutes we ran into the province chief and his guards, who had come around the back way. "Ah, that's it," Vann said. "This is on the tour today."

Close by, we gave a lift to the cadre of the motivational training course, who had flown to a neighborhood village by helicopter. They had changed into civilian clothing and left all weapons and documents identifying them as cadre behind, because they were going to ride on a public bus and didn't want to be abducted from it by VC "road agents" (as were three ARVN soldiers on leave, that afternoon).

Near Dong Hoa we entered Tan Hoa hamlet, now the seat of the village of Hiep Hoa (Hiep Hoa hamlet had become too insecure to be the village hamlet). It is shown as "black"—"undergoing securing"—on the map and has cadre in the daytime; but all of these, including the village chief, move to Dong Hoa every night, to the security of the sugar mill. We drove slowly along a canal to a dead end, then turned back. "These people are pretty surprised to see us," Vann said. "They haven't seen anyone connected with the GVN poke down this street for a hell of a long time." They looked surprised; though when I waved, they smiled and waved back. At one point we passed a gathering of a dozen black-clad boys in their early twenties: draft-age, but not in "our" army. "There's little doubt you're looking at a VC squad," Vann said, so I took a picture. They straightened up and smiled. ("The fact is, they look too clean-cut to be GVN," Vann muttered.)

Back at the marketplace, two blocks on, I got out and took some pictures, till Vann honked the horn. "Let's move out," he said, "they're starting to move away from the car." There was now a noticeable empty space around the Scout. "We're safe for a little while, because they don't expect to see us and it takes them a few minutes to react. But eventually, one of the people back there is going to start thinking about collecting the twenty-thousand-piaster reward and the gold medal the VC gives out for a dead American." As we were leaving, the district chief arrived in a jeep, preceded by a jeepload of APA's (CIA-trained "Armed Propaganda" team). "This may be the most corrupt district chief in Vietnam," Vann said. "We're investigating him. He always uses the APA's as his bodyguard." "But I thought you said no GVN official ever came this way?" I asked. "That was *behind* the wire; see that wire we passed, on the other side of the market, as we started to go along that canal? The district chief isn't going to pass that wire—no GVN official will, or has." The other side of the tracks, in short.

This was the pattern of the day: no doubt familiar to most members of the team, but an education for me. I've described it in detail to convey the impression I got of being closely surrounded in both hamlets and countryside by little signs—visible to all—saying, "To find VC, turn left—about ten feet," "This bridge closed for mining, tonight and every night," "GVN not welcome here," or "GVN traffic on this road only between 0700 and 1800, VC traffic only between 1800 and 0700" (like Washington streets

that are one-way in opposite directions during morning and evening rush hours).

(One road we did not go down. At an intersection, Vann
pointed right and said, "If you want to meet VC with one hundred percent certainty, day or night, just go into that treeline,
four hundred yards off. Some Polish journalists wanted to meet
VC; the VC met them at the treeline, burned their jeep, and kept
them for three days. They got a good story.")

Another impressive hamlet was An Hoa, a Catholic community
with a churchyard and gardens as pretty as a New England
village. The hamlet is very safe ("I'd sleep here any night, without a gun," Vann said)—without barbed wire. "The priest here
says if any VC enters anywhere in the hamlet, he knows of it
within ten minutes—and he reacts." The VC stay clear of it. The
VNAF, however, tore it to pieces early in the year, by mistake,
causing many casualties. Vann and the sector advisor had just
gotten some compensation funds to them: the only compensation
paid during the year, amounting to the first quarter's allowance
for the province.

At various times during the day Vann stopped to talk business
with sub-sector advisory teams, in particular suggesting a range
of projects for them to spend their piaster fund on. He also had
business with Captain Hiep, the district chief of Duc Hoa, whom
he praised as an outstanding officer. Barry Sutherland, the
Australian supervising the construction advisory crew working
throughout SVN, also praised Hiep: "He's a unique Vietnamese;
he gets things done. And he's honest and he cares about the
people." When the district hospital was taken over by the army,
Hiep had gotten another one built by the people. (Vann's comment on many of the self-help projects: "The province chief calls
them 'help self.' The theory is that they're what the people want,
and they'll contribute the labor. The villagers ask for schools,
clinics, soccer fields; but somehow the request comes up through
the village and district chiefs, and the people usually turn out
to want new hamlet offices. The people aren't interested in working on that, so we end up buying labor and using a contractor
anyway.")

Nearly all of the people we passed seemed very friendly, especially to Vann. "I'm usually on hand when anything gets passed out," Vann said. "They associate me with goodies." What surprised me was that the villagers seemed just as friendly in the hamlets we passed through that were controlled by the VC; although VC guerrillas slept in those huts every night and VC political cadre held meetings and discussions frequently. "They *are* friendly. They're friendly people," Vann said, when I asked whether I should take their smiles and return waves as purely hypocritical (hard to do). "They don't hate individual Americans, even in VC territory. And incidentally, they see a lot more Americans now—who are friendlier than the French were—than they *ever* saw Frenchmen, out here in the provinces. On the other hand, even in the places the VC don't control, friendliness doesn't mean these people are going to involve themselves to help you out. These people smiling at us right now would smile just as warmly—and be perfectly honest about it—if they knew that in another ten yards we were going to be blown up by a mine the VC laid last night; and they wouldn't say anything."

(As Vann wrote in one of his monthly reports: "The people have come to believe in VC promises of retribution more than in GVN promises of protection and help," so they aren't inclined to volunteer information. It's true that several bystanders at the Sui Sau bridge did warn us to leave because there were VC in the treelines on both sides of the road, a few hundred yards off; but they were stuck with us in the mud and in the traffic jam, so they couldn't get out of the line of fire.)

"The children are different," Vann said. "No matter what they hear at night, they go by what they see, and if you're nice to them they trust you. I've had kids warn me along the road, a number of times, not to go into a hamlet because the VC were there; I turn right around. I give out a whole lot of gum along these roads."

That night, in a meeting with a Filipino medical team that had just arrived for a two-week stay in Hau Nghia to give standard medical aid, Vann learned that the team actually had surgical background. By the next morning—which began with a half-hour bombardment by B-52's, plainly visible over our heads, which shook the walls of the houses hard though the bombs were falling in the neighboring province, twenty-three kilometers away—Vann was busy drawing on his brand-new contingency fund to make a temporary surgical operating room out of a large provincial meeting hall. By mid-morning, chalk-lines were laid out on the floor to mark partitions and workmen were pounding holes in the cement floor; it was ready by that evening. "Without this fund, it would have taken months to get a project like this all staffed through the ministry," Vann said. "The team would have been long gone." Since the team had brought none of their surgical instruments with them to South Vietnam, Vann was going into Saigon that night to find some and bring them back. (In the attack on Duc Lap after this was written, October 27, 1965, this team was the only surgical team in the area; it treated many casualties immediately.)

We ate our meals both days with the province chief, Lieutenant Colonel Hanh. Vann eats all his meals with Hanh (Vann supplies much of the food and all the wine and liquor). He gets on well with Hanh, they talk business together very freely, and they respect each other. But Hanh is a depressed man. (In part because of troubles with Division and Saigon; though Vann told me, "His real trouble with Division is me. Because of me, he keeps making proposals they don't like.") The only time I saw him smile, rather painfully, was when he told a joke, Tuesday night, surrounded by his wife and seven children at dinner in Saigon. "There are two hundred and twenty thousand people in Hau Nghia, and two hundred thousand of them are ruled by the VC," he said. "I am not a province chief; I am a hamlet chief."

PROBLEMS OF
"REVOLUTIONARY DEVELOPMENT"

In July and August, 1966, I was a member of a Roles and Missions study group, chaired by Colonel George Jacobson, to report to the Mission Council—Ambassador Lodge, General Westmoreland, and agency heads—on "the proper role of each military and paramilitary and police and civilian force in the country."[3] I was asked to frame a definition of "Revolutionary Development" (a trick name devised to avoid the French term, "pacification") and to provide a description of the process. My section began with what was often used thereafter as an official definition of RD:

Revolutionary Development consists of those military and civil efforts designed to liberate the population of South Vietnam from Communist coercion; to restore public security; to initiate economic and political development; to extend effective GVN authority throughout SVN; and to win the willing support of the people to these ends.

The ensuing description of the conceptual framework of the RD program (omitted here) is complimented by the author of the section of the McNamara Study that deals with "Re-emphasis on Pacification: 1965-1967" as "the most logical and coherent approach to returning an area to GVN control and then gaining its support that had yet been produced by a group in either the Mission or Washington" (PP, II, 584). The approach described was also largely a fantasy, in terms of actual RD practices and potential, as I knew from my own observations, having stayed in most of the forty-three provinces of South Vietnam by this time. Therefore, I decided to provide a further discussion, under the heading "Some Major Problem Areas," which began:

The RD program will fail to extend GVN authority significantly or permanently in contested areas unless there is radical improvement in the operation, effectiveness, and conduct of each of the major GVN/RVNAF elements

---

[3] See PP, II, 583-86, for discussion of the group's eighty-one recommendations and the Council's response.

bearing on RD . . . even the modified (less ambitious) concept described cannot be said to be realizable with the GVN/RVNAF system as it is.

The last part of this section—which follows—deals with the "major improvements" needed in the "reciprocal attitudes, expectations, and conduct of GVN representatives—civil and military—and of the people of South Vietnam." (This and other parts of my contribution to the "Jacobson Report" were paraphrased in a memorandum to the President by Secretary McNamara of October 14, 1966. McNamara had read it—along with the preceding "Insecure Province" report and a number of my other memoranda—when I accompanied him and Under Secretary of State Katzenbach to and from Vietnam in October. (See *PP*, IV, 350-51.)[4]

Underlying my analysis of the problems is the viewpoint expressed by another member of the study group, Frank Scotton: to get the public cooperation needed for "Revolutionary Development," he argued, "revolution isn't essential, but radical *reform is* essential; and reform, unlike revolution, must start at the top." Whether "radical reform" was even remotely likely without a revolutionary change that replaced the elites we maintained in power, and whether that change was compatible with the actual interests that propelled U.S. policy, were questions we did not face realistically; we were criticizing programs whose counterrevolutionary framework we did not question or even perceive. Unwilling to see the war as a war of independence and a revolution—because we did not want to admit which side of those two struggles we were on—we did not face up to reasons more fundamental than "poor leadership" for the ARVN soldiers' unwillingness to fight or the unwillingness of the Saigon landholder-politicians or generals to reform, any more than our military acknowledged the true basis for the dedication of the Viet Cong guerrilla.

Two days before his inauguration, John F. Kennedy had talked about Laos with President Eisenhower, who "wondered aloud why, in interventions of this kind, we always seem to find that the morale of the Communist forces was better than that of the democratic

---

[4] At one point, John McNaughton—who was also a passenger on the Secretary's windowless tanker, along with General Wheeler, Robert Komer, and Henry Kissinger—took me aside to relay two requests from McNamara: he would like an extra copy of my report, "Visit to an Insecure Province"; also, would I mind not showing that report to the military passengers, in the interest of not further straining civil-military relations?

forces."[5] Or, as that "old China hand" Theodore H. White put it seven months later, in a private report to the White House: "What perplexes hell out of me is that the Commies, on their side, seem to be able to find people willing to die for their cause. . . ."[6]

Three years later in a briefing to the highest officials in Washington General Taylor describes "two primary causes" for "the present unsatisfactory situation," which he treats as separate, independent, and equally mysterious: "[1] the continued ineffectiveness of the central government, [and 2] the increasing strength and effectiveness of the Viet Cong and their ability to replace losses." Taylor continues:

> As the past history of this country shows, there seems to be a national attribute which makes for factionalism and limits the development of a truly national spirit. Whether this tendency is innate or a development growing out of the conditions of political suppression under which successive generations have lived is hard to determine. But it is an inescapable fact that there is no national tendency toward team play or mutual loyalty to be found among many of the leaders and political groups within South Vietnam. . . .
>
> The ability of the Viet Cong continuously to rebuild their units and to make good their losses is one of the mysteries of this guerrilla war. We are aware of the recruiting methods by which local boys are induced or compelled to join the Viet Cong ranks and have some general appreciation of the amount of infiltration of personnel from the outside. Yet taking both of these sources into account, we still find no plausible explanation of the continued strength of the Viet Cong if our data on Viet Cong losses are even approximately correct. Not only do the Viet Cong units have the recuperative powers of the phoenix, but they have an amazing ability to maintain morale. Only in rare cases have we found evidences of bad morale among Viet Cong prisoners or recorded in captured Viet Cong documents. [PP, III, 668]

Just a month after Taylor spoke, a Rand researcher, Joseph Zasloff, briefed Defense officials on the results of the first six months of Rand's project on "Viet Cong Motivation and Morale," based on long, open-ended interviews with Viet Cong prisoners and defectors. His findings confirmed and went far to explain the high "morale" that so perplexed Eisenhower, White, and Taylor. I remember his briefing my boss, John

---

[5] Clark Clifford's notes on the meeting of January 19, 1961 (PP, II, 637). (This sentence, and the rest of the paragraph—in which President Eisenhower offers his "explanation [that] the Communist philosophy appeared to produce a [better] sense of dedication"—has been deleted from the GPO edition by the Defense Department censors: see the blank page following Volume 10, page 1364.)

[6] Schlesinger, A Thousand Days, page 503.

McNaughton, on a late afternoon in December, 1964; when he finished, McNaughton commented: "If what you say is true, we're fighting on the wrong side." I don't recall the subject being raised again. It was a busy time for us; the sustained bombing of the North began a couple of months later, after much preparation.

Two subsequent years in Vietnam taught me much, but not—I realized later—about the Viet Cong. By the time I left I knew many Vietnamese, including former Viet Minh from the "First War," and a great deal about U.S. and GVN/ARVN operations, but—like all officials, really—I knew relatively little, other than abstractions and allegations, about the National Liberation Front. I had been shot at by Viet Cong, but had never (knowingly) met one.

Meanwhile, Rand field researchers (including Anthony Russo) had gone on to collect over one thousand interviews, some of them as long as sixty single-spaced pages, with Viet Cong and North Vietnamese prisoners. So when I returned to Rand in 1968, I was finally exposed to the detailed thoughts and feelings of "the enemy" to a degree scarcely possible for an American working in Vietnam. Though some of the Rand reports, unlike Zasloff's, were discreditable as analyses,[7] the basic data were unprecedentedly revealing—and affecting. Just as the Pentagon Papers changed the few officials who read them, these autobiographical accounts strongly impressed most of those who worked closely with them. Some of these analysts were cynical "psy-warriors" who had been reading prisoner interrogations for over twenty years, throughout World War II and the Cold War: but never ones like these. Reading their conclusions between 1968-1970 added to my education about the war—legitimating the cause of our opponents and further discrediting our own—in ways that were disconcerting and painful to one already disillusioned, in other respects, by services in Vietnam and by the Pentagon Papers.

But about ten years earlier, without benefit of any classified Rand reports, I. F. Stone had commented brilliantly on the bafflement of Taylor and the obtuseness of most of us who went abroad to serve on the Empire's new frontier:

---

[7] A major exception is Russo's own important analysis, "Social and Economic Correlates of Government Control in South Vietnam," in *Anger, Violence, and Politics*, ed. Gurr and Fierabend (Englewood Cliffs, N. J., 1972). Also see Anthony Russo, "Inside the Rand Corporation and Out: My Story," *Ramparts*, X, April, 1972, pages 45-55.

In reading the military literature on guerrilla warfare now so fashionable at the Pentagon, one feels that these writers are like men watching a dance from outside through heavy plate glass windows. They see the motions but they can't hear the music. They put the mechanical gestures down on paper with pedantic fidelity. But what rarely comes through to them are the injured racial feelings, the misery, the rankling slights, the hatred, the devotion, the inspiration and the desperation. So they do not really understand what leads men to abandon wife, children, home, career, and friends; to take to the bush and live gun in hand like a hunted animal; to challenge overwhelming military odds rather than acquiesce any longer in humiliation, injustice, or poverty.[8]

Discussions of Revolutionary Development commonly emphasize that the central object of the process is to win not only the sympathy but the active commitment and support of the people to the GVN side. This is seen as primarily the mission of the RD cadre. But exactly what is desired of the people: how much and how urgently? And what can reasonably be expected of them: or of the cadre? Exponents of RD differ on the degree of public involvement that is regarded as necessary and attainable.

One influential view is that it is both feasible and essential to achieve a very high level of commitment to the GVN and total involvement in the defense against the VC, on a widespread basis, among villagers in areas currently contested or VC-controlled. This commitment would be embodied ultimately in a "people's self-defense" or hamlet militia effort in which virtually everyone in the hamlet would participate vigorously—old women and children providing early warning, men and women building defenses, and the younger men bearing arms—so as to ward off all but large-scale VC efforts to penetrate the hamlet for propaganda, tax collection, recruiting, or assassination.

In its most ambitious form, this approach foresees a landscape of hedgehog defenses shutting out the VC, who wander rootless and harassed by a hostile partisan militia, unable to get a drink

---

[8] I. F. Stone, *In A Time of Torment* (New York, 1967), pages 173-74. This passage was brought to my attention by Eqbal Ahmad's outstanding critique, "Winning Hearts and Minds: The Theory and Fallacies of Counterinsurgency," *The Nation*, August 2, 1971, pages 70-85.

of water or the time of day—even at gunpoint. "The people" will provide their own security, better than the PF (or implicitly, RF or ARVN) provide it today; they will themselves root out the concealed VC agents in their midst, as the police have so far neglected to do; and all this is to be brought about predominantly by the catalytic influence of the RD cadre. Thus default by the GVN military and police on their responsibilities to protect the people and defeat conspiracy will be made good by an aroused citizenry shouldering the responsibilities themselves, a "country-side at arms."

We do not think this is going to happen.

It is too late in the war. These people have seen too many government promises broken, sooner or later, over the years: promises to remain, to protect them, to bring social justice and lasting benefits. Their resistance to active, visible involvement, now, reflects skepticism and fear that is rooted deep in bitter experience. They have seen Communist guerrilla presence outlast several pacification programs, many province chiefs, and countless cadre. They are beyond the point where enthusiasm, major efforts, and truly deep commitment to a GVN are realistic mid-term demands. To ask of them at this point to take up the heavy burden of their own defense, to choose sides publicly and irrevocably, is to ask too much.

This is not to deny that hamlets and enclaves already exist where religious bonds and leadership or inspiring local officials have produced just the active self-defense that this concept demands. Cadre and officials should indeed be alert to support this spirit where it emerges spontaneously, or where it is a genuine response to GVN efforts. But it is not now something to be programmed and scheduled, or expected or aimed for on a mass basis.

In most of the area that requires RD, a genuine, intense, high-level public involvement, reflected in truly effective "partisan" defense, is simply not to be achieved in a matter of months or a year or two, if ever: not by the cadre as they are, or as they may become, or even in context of all the reforms suggested in this paper. To press for it in every case, to take it as the basic measure of cadre and RD success, is to invite distortion of effort, counterproductive nagging and coercion by cadre, self-deception, and false reporting. It is to ensure another failure, of a sort that grows more costly for the GVN each time.

Fortunately, no such *tour de force* need really be demanded of the RD cadre. What is required in the mid-term is low-to moderate-level public involvement on the GVN side: willing *co-operation* with government authorities, and increasing avoidance of collaboration with the VC. Under present circumstances, this is still an ambitious aim; and it is essential to thorough, lasting success in countering the guerrillas and Communist apparatus. On both counts, it would be an achievement worthy of the considerable efforts and reforms it demands from all agencies of government.

If the people in the contested areas are to cooperate with the GVN in this fashion, they must be persuaded that: (a) the risks of helping the GVN and of resisting the VC are acceptably low; (b) the GVN means to win, and (with Free World help) has the ability to win; (c) the GVN deserves their respect and support.

For most people in the rural areas, these beliefs would represent radical changes in attitude. Their present noninvolvement, passive help to both sides when pressed, or apathy toward the GVN and covert aid to VC, flow from specific attitudes like the following, which must be countered:

(1) The VC will win in the end: after the U.S. leaves or stops fighting, when the whole effort against the VC will collapse.

(2) The GVN will not stay in the local area, despite its promises; the VC will return (and its covert apparatus will remain throughout).

(3) Any willing cooperation with the GVN will be noted by the local VC apparatus and eventually punished; participation as an elected or appointed GVN official is likely to mean death.

(4) The RVNAF will not keep out the VC, will not support people's resistance against VC, and will not even reinforce friendly units under attack; RVNAF troops are a heavy burden upon the people, rather than their protectors.

(5) GVN officials are indifferent to the welfare of the people.

(6) The GVN at low levels is the tool of the landlords and the local rich, at all levels is a means to self-enrichment of officials.

(7) The corruption, lack of motivation, and inefficiency of GVN officials is in dramatic contrast to the VC hierarchy, which (in the

minds of the peasants, including those who oppose the VC for their cruelty, their demands, their Communism or atheism) is incorruptible, dedicated, and efficient.

None of these attitudes can be changed by GVN/cadre words alone. Changing them is not merely a problem of communication or of "carrying the GVN message to the people." The supporting reality—the element of truth underlying each of these beliefs—must change.

Words and actions of RD cadre are scarcely the main evidence that shapes people's impressions of the nature of the GVN. When RD cadre tell the villagers about the government, they are not speaking to the credulous or ignorant. They are speaking to the people who see "the government" every day, people who are experiencing the conduct of government representatives—ARVN, RF, PF, police, district and province officials, technical cadre—even while the RD cadre talk. If that conduct confirms what VC cadre say, rather than what RD cadre say, the latter's words are wasted. Too often now that is the case. The very conception of the RD cadre as a tool to promote a favorable image of the GVN is prompted by the failure of the RVNAF and regular GVN officials to have done so by their normal behavior: indeed, from and tendency of many units and officials to blacken the name of the GVN.

The cadre example at its best will have little lasting impact on the attitudes of the villagers so long as it must compete with the more vivid impressions formed by:

• RVNAF units that fail to provide security; to operate at night or interfere with the movement of armed VC; to support hamlet cadre or outposts under attack at night; or even to protect themselves adequately against surprise.
• Rangers and other ARVN soldiers who steal chickens and pigs (under the eyes of their officers); who take meals and goods in the towns without paying; ignore police and civil authority; commit petty crimes without punishment; and terrorize the towns with drunken rampages, rape, and undisciplined shooting.
• PF or RF units whose leaders hire them out to collect rents for rich landlords.
• Village and district officials and police who set a price on every service they provide; who sell supplies provided for "self-help" proj-

ects; who not only provide for a decent living and their "old-age security," but manage to grow unjustly rich through corruption.

• ARVN and sector artillery practices that contribute to insecurity and demonstrate indifference to welfare by erratic, unobserved, indiscriminate firing.

• National Police who charge tolls at [contraband] checkpoints.

• Officials and technical cadre totally lacking in competence, training, motivation, or discipline.

• GVN neglect of the welfare even of its own representatives and its most committed supporters; e.g., the low pay, poor medical care, and lack of dependents' housing and support for RF/PF.

In securing vitally needed collaboration by the public, VC arguments and coercion are most effective in the context of real GVN failings and abuses. GVN campaigns to win support and end the collaboration cannot wholly succeed while the abuses continue. (At best, some good impressions will join the bad, so that feelings toward the GVN progress toward ambivalence.) Before a change can be expected in the people's attitude and conduct toward the government, there must be a change in the government's attitude and conduct toward the people.

Of first importance is improving the behavior of those government representatives whose misconduct the people see most widely and frequently and feel most acutely: *the soldiers.* The arrival of a Ranger battalion is generally regarded now by townspeople and peasants alike as the coming of a scourge.[9] (One province chief recently threatened to put trucks on the runway if a certain battalion of Rangers, already en route by air to his province, was not ordered back. In two provinces, villagers reportedly asked the VC to deliver them from the Ranger battalions then afflicting them.) It is easy to believe that such troops have been worth far more to the VC than to the GVN. But this is only an extreme; most other units abuse the public less flamboyantly but more steadily, daily demonstrating in a multitude

---

[9] Partly to underline the importance of ARVN conduct, one of the eighty-one recommendations of the Jacobson Roles and Mission study group was that Ranger units "because of their frequently intolerable conduct toward the populace, be disbanded with individual Rangers reassigned" (*PP*, II, 584). The Pentagon Papers analyst notes: "This was a recommendation which MACV particularly opposed, arguing that it 'would seriously reduce ARVN combat strength.' Westmoreland added that he could not countenance the disbanding of units which had just received a Presidential Unit Citation."

of ways their feelings of isolation from the public, their lack of responsibility to the people or respect for them. No GVN program or "psy-war" measure could have such widespread, immediate, and favorable impact as change in such attitudes and conduct by the soldiers; without that change, other efforts to improve the image of the GVN and induce more willing cooperation have scant chance of success.

The first step must be to bring about understanding in the RVNAF—starting with the highest military commanders and working down to the junior officers and troops—of the importance of proper, disciplined conduct to Revolutionary Development and to winning the war. (ARVN battalions newly committed to support of RD, in particular, need troop reorientation training.) Effective "motivational training" aims first at just such understanding, plus understanding of the nature and aims of the war and the soldiers' role in it, to generate a sense of dignity, self-respect, and purpose—prerequisites to self-disciplined behavior. *All troops and officers* in RVNAF need that indoctrination (as does the civil side of the GVN): backed up increasingly by the example of dedication, purposeful direction, and command discipline in their superiors. Second, the troops deserve more evidence of concern for their welfare by their government and country: above all, by pay protected from inflation and by adequate dependents' housing and other dependents' benefits (so that soldiers and their families will have less basis for the resentful belief that peasants, refugees, and Chieu Hoi ralliers [VC defectors] should be doing "civic action" for *them.*)

These measures are just as relevant to the achievement of higher combat performance. Within this framework of better understanding and incentives, *military discipline should begin to be rigidly enforced at all levels within RVNAF ranks,* to the ends both of adequate observance of military orders and regulations and of proper conduct toward the public. Probably no other program could so surely or with wide approval stamp a government of Vietnam as truly "revolutionary."

A comparable program of reform on the civil side of the GVN is likewise essential to the success of RD. Just as the RD cadre need effective military performance in their area—lest inadequate security or undisciplined troop conduct *negate* their efforts—so they need good civil government over them if they are to carry out their mission.

As representatives of the national government, RD cadre are often correctly described as indispensable links between the district level, where national government has traditionally stopped, and the hamlets and villages. But bridging that gap is of conditional value to the villager. Links to an indifferent, incompetent, or corrupt level of government are not worth very much to him. Cadre can testify to the intentions of the government to serve and protect the people; they can be a channel of grievances, aspirations, and intelligence to higher authority. Yet if the government neglects to demonstrate those intentions in action—if the district and province officials and technical cadre fail to *act* upon the cadre information, to resolve grievances, satisfy reasonable aspirations, exploit intelligence—the cadre will have, in the end, little impact.

Moreover, experience already shows that the cadre teams themselves need the supervision and guidance of alert, dedicated district and province officials if they are to work effectively. The support of the district chief is most critical to their performance. Where the district chief is conscientious, sees the RD cadre as "his" workers, and understands their mission, they are showing encouraging promise. Where the district chief is apathetic toward the cadre and accepts no responsibility for them—perhaps still the majority of districts where RD cadre are deployed—they act distressingly like most other "cadre" of recent years, i.e., they are prone to do almost nothing at all. (Mechanical census-taking threatens to succeed the mechanical fence-building of yester-year.)

Ultimately, it is a delusion to imagine that RD cadre could persist as an honest, highly motivated element in what continued to be a corrupt, apathetic administrative system. Where the district/province officials are corrupt, the cadre will be forced to buy their appointments and promotions (and draft deferment), and to kickback on their salary; immersed from the start in a traditional pattern of petty corruptions, they will scarcely be inspired to be avid reformers in the hamlets. *In the end the GVN will get the cadre it deserves:* just as it now has the RVNAF and police it has deserved.

But what is true for the cadre is true for the district chief: and on up the line. There is a deadly correlation between corruption at high levels in an administrative system and the spread throughout the system of incompetence, as higher-ups encourage and promote corrupt subordinates, protecting them from the consequences of poor performance of duty or direct disobedience of orders. Such a system demoralizes and "selects out" the able and the dedicated who do not play the game, and thwarts any attempts at reform initiated at intermediate levels. There is no escape from the requirement that reform, unlike revolution, must start at the top.

Today the government of Vietnam and its armed forces need urgent radical reforms, starting from the top; including in particular, throughout the GVN structure: (1) *marked reduction of corruption;* (2) *encouragement of leadership and initiative;* and (3) *promotion on merit.*

Such reforms must replace the current tendency to make appointments and promotions primarily on the basis of diplomas, nepotism, political alliance, and kickbacks. The consequences of the present system are incompetence, lack of discipline, apathy, and encouragement of further corruption.

The military and administrative challenge posed by the Communist apparatus cannot be met by a government suffering these defects: they deprive the GVN of the ability to execute its programs. At the same time, the contrast (in the belief of most Vietnamese) to the Communists in these particular respects is an intolerable burden to the GVN in its political struggle with the VC for public and elite support.

The true urgency of these reforms does not emerge when one focuses upon the war against mobile, large-unit, regular Main Force and NVA forces, where Free World Military Assistance Forces have blocked military defeat and can continue to win significant successes without major help from RVNAF or the population. It is in the ultimately vital war against VC guerrillas and apparatus for allegiance and control of the people in the countryside that GVN/RVNAF capability is and will remain crucial; and in which changes such as those discussed above mean the difference between potential success and almost certain failure. Very bluntly: present VC control in the countryside *will not be rolled back significantly or permanently by the GVN/RVNAF system as it now functions.* Nor will the political struggle in the countryside be won at all unless the GVN and RVNAF become capable of winning it.

An apparent alternative to high-level, thoroughgoing reform would be for the U.S. to substitute its own authority and capability for that of the GVN: bypassing the GVN in direct relations with province chiefs, RD cadre, and troop commanders, or relying wholly on U.S.-executed military and civil programs. Unaccompanied by an increase in GVN capability, this approach would fail in the long run. It would fail for many reasons, but one of the most fundamental is simply that the Vietnamese people do not expect the U.S. to remain in Vietnam bearing such responsibility indefinitely. Therefore, it is to the relative capabilities for struggle of the GVN and the VC apparatus that Vietnamese will look for answers to the crucial question: "Who is going to win in the end?"

Until the GVN begins to appear capable of gaining adequate popular participation and of countering a Communist resurgence on its own, after U.S. involvement has lessened, Free World Military Assistance Forces successes will appear to most Vietnamese (including the VC) as no more than holding operations postponing eventual GVN political defeat. That belief will preclude widespread Vietnamese commitment, adequate cooperation or involvement in the struggle against the VC: hence, in turn, block real progress toward GVN (and U.S.) aims.

Thus a U.S. "takeover," whether blatant or tacit and pragmatic, does not provide an adequate answer. At the same time, the radical changes required *within* the GVN and RVNAF seem most unlikely to occur without the strong, focused, and coordinated exertion of U.S. influence at high levels. The goal of such private U.S. "intervention" must be a GVN capable of winning the support of its population and of winning the war. But in this pursuit as well, the main bulk of the steady pressure and energy for reform must come eventually from Vietnamese. And in these efforts, as in the fight against the VC, there is need both for popular participation and for dedicated leadership.

Many of the young Vietnamese needed for success in a long political struggle—capable of able leadership and of tireless, selfless commitment to a cause that inspires them—are in VC cadre ranks today; and there are many more outside the VC, but fewer devoted to the GVN. To attract these young potential "activists" to the GVN effort—both from the uncommitted ranks, and eventually, from within the VC—initial steps toward reform are needed; but also more than reform: a chance to work toward meaningful public goals.

It is a striking fact that both sides, VC and GVN, proclaim publicly almost identical goals for South Vietnam (a tribute to their validity in Vietnamese terms, despite—save for unification —their "American" ring: security, freedom, independence, democracy, village reform, social justice, development and modernization, public welfare, and happiness.

On the VC side, much of this "platform" is cynical and expedient in the minds of the Communist elite, whose covert ideals call for "modernization" on a fifty-year-old blueprint of forced-draft industrialization under totalitarian controls, capitalized by exploitation of the peasants and preceded by a bloodbath to destroy or terrorize potential opposition: a vision so stark and repelling it must be kept esoteric.

There is no such ideological obstacle on the GVN side to giving unprecedented substance to the popular principles—of *government responding to and serving the welfare of the people* —it already professes. There are only obstacles of inertia, shortsightedness, and past despair.[10] These can be overcome.

The war with the VC for the allegiance and the governing of the people of South Vietnam can be won: but only by RVNAF soldiers who have come to feel and act as protectors and friends

[10] And of class and status interest, the history, politics, and sociology of ruling elites, their total dependence on foreign (U.S.) support, the short-term domestic political needs of the foreign rulers and the long-term economic interests of the foreign ruling groups, to name a few more obstacles I had missed—not so easily overcome.

of the people, and GVN officials who come to feel and act as servants of the people. That means today, it is in *their* hearts and minds, and conduct, that revolutionary development must first take place.

Or as General Taylor put it two years earlier in the November, 1964, briefing cited in the prefatory note (*PP*, III, 668):

If, as the evidence shows, we are playing a losing game in South Vietnam, it is high time we change and find a better way. To change the situation, it is quite clear that we need to do three things: first, establish an adequate government in SVN . . .

THE LOST COUNTERREVOLUTION

A review of Robert Shaplen's *The Road From War: Vietnam 1965-1970*, Harper & Row, New York, 1970, which appeared in the *Washington Post* (November 4, 1970).

Vietnam, 1965-70: the road from war? An unsettling title, for a book three-fifths of which covers the years of American buildup and escalation in Vietnam. And the irony has sharpened since the manuscript was sent to the publisher. It then consisted of twenty-two of Robert Shaplen's articles for the *New Yorker* (shortened and edited), the last of these having appeared January 31, 1970, under the regular caption, "Letter from Saigon."

Shaplen's next *New Yorker* piece, three months later, bore a new heading for the series: "Letter from Indochina." Shaplen had clearly not anticipated that the road from war in Vietnam lay, for some U.S. troops, west through Cambodia; or that what we were on was, all along, the road to the Second Indochina War.

If that last phrase would be a better title for this book, it will serve for his next, and most readers might be well advised to wait for that. But it is questionable whether Shaplen should repeat the experiment of his present format, which lays successive pieces of current reportage end to end. Shaplen's distinguished reporting—complex, reflective, and experienced—is produced in the form of long, dull essays. Hence the temptation simply to reprint them as a "journal," preserving their present tense, their burden of false starts and alarms.

But the effect is cruel to content. It calls into question the very relevance of Shaplen's chosen beat, the "political" side of the war as Shaplen defines it: primarily Saigon maneuvering and "pacification" operations in the countryside. Most of what Shaplen covers does, indeed, go unreported elsewhere; but it is hard to find that negligent when one rereads these columns in sequence.

Is there really need, still, for even one reporter to alert us monthly or quarterly to new "challenges" to the cohesion of Saigon elites and the reformist instincts of corrupt military juntas, "tests" that—as subsequent reports reveal unsurprisingly— are *never* met; or "new" pacification gimmicks by CIA and MACV, which invariably turn out to be hollow, brutal frauds; or new "opportunities"—certain to be missed—for the U.S. Government to reduce its well-intentioned "mistakes" and shoulder "revolutionary" and "democratizing" missions that bear no relation to the aims or perceived interests of any American administration? Shaplen's own memory for such "lessons" seems, sometimes, as short as that of the American officials whose "deliberate ingenuousness" he deplores.

Shaplen plausibly disdains the military focus of most news coverage in this war. (His own essay here at combat reporting, "Below the DMZ," is perhaps a parody; meticulous notetaking has left nearly every sentence so studded with numbers—unit designations and pointless statistics—as to be comically unreadable.) Yet he demonstrates here that there is as much froth to report about "politics" as about military operations. Most of what Shaplen chooses to recount, in fact, is exactly as transient and meaningless as wire service dispatches on kill-ratios and (imaginary) changes in the level of ARVN night patrolling. And nothing shows that so clearly as this very book.

How can Shaplen still take seriously all these non-events, this gossip and scheming, these clumsy rediscoveries of French colonial techniques? In his preface, after all, he reiterates the message of his earlier (1965) title, *The Lost Revolution:* that at some point in the preceding twenty years we had "lost" the nationalist revolutionary cause in Vietnam to the Communists. (In reality, we can never be said to have sought such a cause, and a nationalist revolution, obviously, could never be ours to lose any more than Vietnam—or China—was ours to lose). In any case, time and again Shaplen asserts that its "capture" by the Communists was irreversible, "incurable," perhaps in 1945, certainly by 1965.

Why, then, do we keep confronting, sometimes in the same columns, restatements of the uncertainty or "question," or "challenge," classically expressed (page 31): "It remains to be seen whether somehow, late as it is, the true nationalists [i.e., non-Communists, especially those friendly to and supported by the CIA] can recapture the revolution from the Communists after twenty years of bitter and futile strife?"

After eight years of Shaplen's own reporting from Vietnam this would seem as much of a non-question, or as weak a vehicle for maintaining readers' suspense, as the recurrent speculation throughout the first half of the book whether Nguyen Cao Ky would try to run for President.

If the hopes of those, to paraphrase Shaplen's dedication, who believed that American intervention could further "revolution with freedom" in Vietnam were ever faintly realistic (and whether they were or not, I once shared them), it is hard as this book wears on to read the avowed persistence of such hopes as anything but wildly wishful or obscurantist, a cop-out from the moral and policy implications of what Shaplen really knows about Vietnam.

THE DAY LỘC TIÊN
WAS PACIFIED

From late November, 1966, until I left Vietnam in June, 1967, I was Special Assistant to Deputy Ambassador William Porter, who was in charge of all U.S. civil field operations in Vietnam. My job was primarily to make field evaluations for Porter of programs and operations, particularly those that dealt with pacification and other joint military and civil operations.

One morning in December I was talking to Wade Lathram, Director of Operations of OCO (Office of Civil Operations), who was leaving that afternoon for briefings in Washington. I was encouraging him to be frank and realistic in his description to Congress and elsewhere of the prospects (in my opinion, very limited ones) for pacification in the coming year. I told him of a trip I had just made to a "pacified" hamlet.

When I finished the story, Lathram urged me to write it down for him, fast, so he could take it to Washington and show it around to illustrate concretely why progress in pacification was so slow (or, often, nonexistent). In the next couple of hours, using notes I had made at the time, I wrote as fast as I could, and managed to hand the account that follows to Lathram at the airport.

The morning of December 9, 1966, three neighboring hamlets in Cần Giuộc District of Long An Province were to be formally declared "pacified," joining the fifteen other "secure" ones among the 183 hamlets in the district. Revolutionary Development cadre teams had been working in the three hamlets for about ten weeks, and although the U.S. district advisors were dubious that anything very fundamental had been accomplished or that the area could reasonably be called "secure," the district chief, an ARVN major, was satisfied that the six-point pacification criteria had been met and the cadre could move on.

"They're anxious to finish up their 1966 program so they can get started on the 1967 hamlets," the major who was the MACV

(Military Assistance Command, Vietnam) district advisor said. There was to be a formal ceremony at the main hamlet, Lôc Tiên II, to celebrate the official acceptance of the hamlets as "secure," with all the district and village officials and the MACV and USAID district advisors taking part. I went along with an interpreter and the assistant MACV advisor, a captain, to talk to some of the villagers and cadre.

At 0820 it was raining as we got into jeeps in the district headquarters compound. An old woman was keening loudly in a corner of the courtyard, where some newly painted coffins rested on sawhorses in a shed. She was a relative of one of the Regional Force (RF) soldiers killed in an ambush the morning before. Other women had chanted and cried, standing around the coffins in the light of candles, through most of the night. In the candlelight—and now, on a dark morning—the colors of the wooden boxes were very gay: orange with painted flowers. There were six of them.

The ambush had taken place on the main road from Saigon, a few kilometers south of the district headquarters. A Regional Force platoon, on a mission to clear some dirt roadblocks the VC had put up the night before, walked past a Popular Force outpost without checking in at it—they assumed the PF had already cleared the road ahead—and two hundred meters further on at 0900 on a bright morning they were hit by a VC company. "I missed that one by ten minutes," the district advisor said. "I was on my way by jeep—about ten minutes away—to visit the schoolhouse below the PF outpost. That's where the roadblocks were, at the schoolhouse, and that's where the ambush was. I heard the firing and stopped at the outpost."

The old woman was rocking on her heels on the muddy ground, and she gestured rhythmically with one hand as if, in her wailing, she were lecturing to the little girl facing her. But the little girl was looking past her expressionlessly, once in a while turning her eyes to the woman, whose voice rose and fell and sobbed without stopping. The MACV captain said: "I've been trying to get the district chief to move the mortuary out of this courtyard. I think it's depressing to the troops that sleep here. And these funerals have been happening too often."

After a while of sitting in the jeep I asked the major what we were waiting for. "After we came outside, the district chief got word that the force he sent out to clear the area between here and the hamlets wasn't through yet."

"You mean you need a special clearing operation to get to these pacified hamlets?"

"Oh, I doubt if we'll have any trouble today," he said. "With all the troops they'll have in that village during the ceremony— with all the officials there—I'm only taking a pistol." The captain, in the other jeep, shrugged and tapped his M-16. I got out of the jeep and came back with a weapon. About this time the sun came out and a radioman announced that the clearing operation was finished. The district chief and his party emerged from his office, we all shook hands, and the convoy set out.

The three hamlets were a few kilometers northwest of the district town, along red dirt roads. By the time we got there it was very hot. The entrance to the main hamlet was marked by a high wooden arch over the road with the name of the hamlet —Ấp Lộc Tiên II—neatly painted across the top; this was one of the accomplishments of the RD cadre. (It fell in the category of "self-help and development projects"—though the villagers were supposed to do these themselves, as well as any fortifications, to give them a sense of commitment—which was the fourth of the six criteria for a pacified hamlet.) "Their other big contribution was to build the hamlet 'fortifications,'" the major said. "See that berm over there?" He pointed to an earth embankment about three feet high, stretching out from the road and curling around a clump of bamboo in the distance.

"What good is that?"

"Useless. They worked hard on it, I'll say that. The villagers couldn't care less. They know it's ridiculous. It's over a thousand meters long: a real Chinese Wall. It would take a battalion to man it for it to mean anything, and what they've got is twelve PF. But it helps meet one of the six-point criteria." (The first one: area cleared of VC, and local defenses set up.)

"As a matter of fact, it's been more of a help to the VC," the captain added. "The Claymore mine they set off last week, the one that killed five RD cadre, they set up on top of that berm

—it's just the right height—next to the road pointing down toward the hamlet, with the wires trailing outside. The cadre were just leaving the hamlet, coming up to that sign."

"Are you saying that five cadre were killed here last week?" I asked.

"They weren't the only ones. They've had six Claymores here in the last couple of months, four detonations. But the worst thing was last week the VC came into the other two hamlets, just down the road from this one, and kidnapped the two hamlet chiefs that had just been elected and their families." (Election of hamlet officials is the sixth "pacification criterion.")

How could they be holding the ceremony this week, then?

"Oh, the cadre held another election quick, and the assistant hamlet chiefs were elected chief."

"Aren't they afraid?"

"Don't worry, they won't be sleeping here at night; they'll be in the district town."

The convoy had stopped at a cluster of buildings, decorated for the day with banners and slogans. There were a lot of soldiers of different types about; the major pointed out there were even some troops from the 46th Regiment on duty. On one side of the road, classrooms filled with children surrounded a neat courtyard. The ceremony was being held across the road in a garden so filled with flowers and vines that the faces of the officials were hidden when they sat down on the porch. In a corner next to the porch stood the village notables, flanked by a double row of little girls, sitting up straight in white *ao-dais*. They were all pretty, all with long black hair combed smooth down their backs. The district chief and the MACV and USAID advisors took their places under the banners and the vines, and a cadre leader in black pajamas stepped up to a microphone. The captain and I watched from across the street, and the little girls stole side glances at us as the cadre leader began the morning's speeches; the district policeman saw this and smiled. It was a cheerful occasion.

Our interpreter translated a few sentences: "When we came to this hamlet ten weeks ago, there were six VC agents in the hamlet infrastructure . . ." (ridding the hamlet of VC "infra-

structure"—agents, informers, political organization—is the third
of the pacification criteria). Then we turned back down the road
to talk to some of the villagers. First, we visited the new outpost,
My Loc, just in back of the house where the ceremony was being
held.

"Don't judge other outposts around here by this one," the
MACV captain said. "This is one of the best in Vietnam." It
was built as the base for an RF company. We had to work our
way through an elaborate maze of barbed wire to reach the
moat surrounding the thick mud walls. Inside, the bunkers were
covered not only with the usual sandbags but with concrete. Narrow slits in the bunker walls looked out over cleared fields of
fire; I looked through one to see the house where the pacification
ceremony was going on, the girls' black hair against white silk
showing through gaps in the vine leaves. In the center of the
little fort was a heavy cement communications bunker; next to
it, the familiar wooden arrow, studded with cans of kerosene-
soaked sand, pivoted horizontally to point out the enemy to
planes during a night attack. The sergeant who had left his ham-
mock to show us around was proud of the post, which had just
been finished and which Premier Ky had visited ten days earlier.
He said it would take more than one battalion of VC, maybe
two, to overrun it.

"They're safe enough in here," the captain said. "I think they
could hold out in here against five hundred men. Of course,
whether they make the people around here feel much safer
depends on how much the RF's move around *outside* the barbed
wire. Too many posts like this—the VC could walk into the other
end of the hamlet whenever they felt like it." Apparently, the
presence of the RF's had not deterred the VC from kidnapping
the two officials a few hundred meters down the road.

The ruins of the old post that this one replaced lay just across
the road, again in close sight of the ceremony. It had been
manned by PF's. One night the previous spring the VC had
overrun it, and the reaction force the next morning—our interpreter had been part of it—had found the PF's inside, beheaded,
lying in a row, with their dependents, wives and children, lying
by the opposite wall where they had been machine-gunned.

That had happened in this hamlet just nine months before. It would be much harder to destroy the new fort; but I wondered, looking at the grass-covered ruins of the old PF post (the interpreter warned me not to step inside—it had been mined), how long it really took for the local people to unlearn lessons like that.

The houses of the hamlet were widely spaced; the first one we came to was about fifty yards down the road. We passed through a garden, and said good day to a middle-aged woman on the porch, who was surrounded by children. She was joined by her husband, a man of about 45. As we asked questions, an old woman peered out at us from the darkness of what seemed a very large room.

I asked, through the interpreter, what the RD cadre had done for them.

"They came one afternoon, drank tea, and took a census," the interpreter translated.

Had the cadre ever talked politics or asked about grievances? "No."

Was that all the cadre had done?

"They formed everyone into groups, organizations."

Which organization did the husband belong to?

"The men's organization." ("Organizing the people" by interest-groups and by age and sex, for purposes of self-defense, was the fifth criterion.)

What was the purpose of that organization?

"When the cadre came to drink tea, they just told him, 'You are in the men's organization.' He doesn't know what the purpose of it is."

Did the cadre stay at night in the village?

"No. They came in the morning. About five o'clock he would see them wandering back, along the road; he doesn't know where they went."

Had VC visited the village in the past year?

"Often."

Did he think they still would, with the RF post so near?

"Perhaps not. But they had come into the neighboring hamlets last week and taken off the hamlet chiefs."

Did he think the new hamlet chief would sleep in the hamlet at night?

"Not now: now he sleeps in the district town. But that is because he is not yet confirmed by the province chief. When he is confirmed by the province chief he will sleep in the hamlet."

Why so?

"After he is confirmed by the province chief, if he is killed or kidnapped by the VC his family will get death benefits. But not now."

Reflecting on the last point, we moved on to two houses that were another fifty yards down the road. In the first, we asked an older man and a very old woman many of the same questions, and got the same answers. No, the cadre had never slept in this house at night; the cadre went away at night, they didn't know where. The cadre had been polite during the one visit they had made. They were taking census, and they had left the metal door sign—"22/7," in red letters on a yellow background—which was up on the porch. ("Taking census is what the cadre like to do best," I had been told by advisors in different parts of Vietnam. "In fact," the comment usually ran, "that's about all they do do. That and some fortifications.") Interrogation—supposed to identify grievances and aspirations, along with census data—is the second of the six pacification criteria.

Had ARVN soldiers ever taken food, chickens or ducks, without paying for them?

"They used to do that, when there was only a PF squad in the hamlet. But now that the RF outpost was there, they don't think the ARVN soldiers will do that any more."

Finally, the captain suggested we visit some houses several hundred meters off the road. As we started along the embankment between two flooded rice paddies, the convoy passed by down the road, leaving the hamlet. The officials waved at us from the jeeps. The ceremony was over; now Ấp Lộc Tiên II and the other two hamlets would be colored blue on district and province pacification charts: little patches of blue about the size of a grease-pencil stub, because red areas ("VC-controlled") pressed close on either side of the road. "We won't go too close to that line of trees," the captain said, pointing to a bamboo thicket about five hundred yards off. "That's all deep red, beyond that."

As we walked in file—the rice chest-high on either side—distant shots rang out. I had heard the first ones back in the outpost: some far, some fairly close. "Soldiers shooting birds," the captain said. "Or checking their weapons. Or having fun. You can't stop them. Sometimes you hear one answering another: dut, dut . . . dut. We call it a commo check." Now artillery began to fire . . . sporadically, far off. The sound joined bird-calls, wind in the rice, bamboo clicking, low thrumming of a helicopter moving slowly a mile off: Delta sounds on a quiet, hot day.

The captain told me more about the ambush the day before. For three nights, the VC had put up dirt roadblocks on roads in that area, but there were no mines, and no harassing of the clearing parties. That was all it took to lull the RF's; that was why they hadn't checked with the PF outpost about the road ahead, or put out a point on the fourth morning. The VC were waiting in the grass and had caught them off-guard. Now, for a while, they would be more cautious.

Two hundred meters off the road, we came to a thick grove of bamboo, palms, fruit trees, and bushes rising among the rice fields. It looked wild and wholly dense, but through a gap in the vines we could see water, a moatlike fish pond surrounding a bare, clean yard and a shaded hut. "People think there's no cover in the Delta," the captain remarked. "There's plenty of cover. We couldn't be seen from the air right now; there could be a company in here. And look around." Even before the forest began, the paddies were broken by treelines along canals and other thickets as dense as this one. Standing in the shaded path we talked to an old man wearing shorts and shower sandals. He was dignified, his face deeply lined and handsome; his good-looking twelve-year-old son stood by smiling at us, very interested in my camera.

The cadre had visited his house once, to fill out his family book and take the census. They did not stay in the area at night, because it was not safe for them. VC came every now and then; sometimes they spent the night. Government troops also came once in a while. Some of them paid for food, some took it without paying. The ones who paid did not pay much; but that was all right, he didn't mind. It was the war.

No one from the government had ever asked his opinions, he said, but he did not have any opinions about politics; he was an old man, who was only tending his rice fields, and neither side bothered him very much. The VC collected taxes at harvest time (he also paid rent to a landlord), but they didn't talk politics. The RD cadre, like the VC, were polite. In one way the RD cadre were better than the Strategic Hamlet cadre of three years ago, who had made the people build the fortifications. The RD cadre built the wall around the hamlet themselves.

The captain started to ask the old man some detailed questions about the VC village two kilometers to the north, and I walked around the thicket to see if anyone else were at home. The fish-pond moat surrounding the clearing had no bridge that I could see. At one point I looked through the thick, wall-like vine leaves enclosing the moat to see a young woman squatting across from me, scrubbing clothes in the pond. She looked up and smiled. The yard behind her was swept spotless, if dried mud can be called that.

The captain and the interpreter caught up with me and we set off along another embankment. "I wouldn't put too much stock in what that man had to say," the captain said.

"Why not?"

"I asked him what he did when VC squads came near his house. Who did he tell? He said he didn't do anything; he didn't tell anyone. I asked him how he thought the war would ever be over, how would there ever be security so that his son could grow up in peace, if everyone acted like that: if he wouldn't even tell the district officials when the VC came through. He said he was an old man. The government soldiers couldn't protect him—the post was far away—and the VC would make trouble for him if he talked to the government. It wouldn't do any good for anyone, and he didn't want to get into trouble. He said the war had gone on for a long time, and I told him it would go on for a lot longer when people like him refused to take any part in it." The captain was very irritated. I could see the old man's point of view—we were pretty far away from the road now—but I didn't argue with the captain.

I wanted to see one more household, so we headed for another clump of bamboo a hundred yards further from the road. "About as far as we ought to go," according to the captain. Again, the house was hidden from us until we penetrated the screen of bamboo, brush, and palm trees; then we were in a large dirt courtyard, surrounded by flowers in neat rows and lined on two sides by large ceramic flowerpots. I reflected again on how clean it was, in contrast to the rural slums of Cần Giuộc, the district town a few kilometers away, where refuse littered the mud in the yards and ragged holes held stale water and sewage.

A man and his wife, each looking about 55 but perhaps much older, greeted us warmly. After a few questions, they invited the three of us inside, where they had been having tea. The wife brought new cups; her husband returned from a back room with a plate of store cookies. We each took one with our tea, and they did too, then refilled the plate. They seemed pleased to have company. A little later the host—who had a round, witty face, and who darted, like his eyes, when he moved—brought out a package wrapped in pink tissue paper and began to unwrap it. I protested, but he spoke to the interpreter and went on unwrapping what seemed to be halvah, which he added to the plate. The interpreter explained, "He says he wants to have some, too." This seemed to be true, so we relaxed.

The house looked prosperous, with heavy, carved furniture, brass lamps, screens, religious scrolls and pictures: very Victorian. The old man listened carefully to our questions and answered at length, gesturing with his eyes and hands; his wife, sitting over on the smooth wooden bed, frequently added her comments, sometimes intensely.

We started with some of the same questions, but as the captain had predicted, moving off the road three hundred yards gave a twist to some of the answers we heard. Yes, the cadre had come by, once. They had taken a census, and left a door sign. The man suddenly left the table, got a ladder, and climbed up to a loft over the bed; he poked around under some tiles, then came down brandishing a yellow sign with red numbers on it. When we nodded, he replaced it in the loft, returned to his tea, and waited for our next question.

Finally, I asked: "Why isn't it on his door?"

The interpreter listened to his answer and said: "Last week many VC came to the house next to this and took down the door signs and tore up the family books. They didn't come to this house, but he thought he had better hide what the cadre gave him, to keep it safe."

We sat and looked at each other for a while, drinking our tea.

The interpreter was very good. He put his questions in a gentle voice and listened carefully; the people seemed to trust him. He had lived in this area a long time. The MACV advisors respected him very much; they thought he could be a good district chief.

The captain asked the husband what he knew of Phouc Lâm, the VC village two kilometers to the south. "The people in Phouc Lâm are much less happy than the people in Lôc Tiên."

Why was that?

"Because they get much artillery; they cannot live a peaceful life." The same was true, he said, of the VC village two kilometers to the north.

The captain spread out his map and showed me the two villages, one on either side of Lôc Tiên II. "You see how crazy it all is," he said; "they talk about this village being secured, while right up there, two kilometers away, there's a VC base area that ARVN won't go near. When ARVN gets close to it they start hitting mines and heavy harassment; they just don't go into it. But the VC come out. And they live there; and the same down below here." The villages were frequently hit by artillery—"though nobody will go in to find out what's happened." The district chief was reluctant to use air strikes within the heavily populated district.

Were they bothered by artillery near this house? "Not now," the man said cheerfully to the interpreter. "Last year, when there were only PF's in the outpost, the VC came often and there would be much artillery." But now that there was an RF outpost, he did not expect there to be shelling, even if the VC did probe, unless they attacked the post. I recalled the earlier comment, that the presence of the RF's meant that ARVN was less likely to steal poultry from the hamlet, and I began to see an ironic meaning to the welcome "security" that a permanent government presence in the hamlet brought to the villagers.

While he spoke of the artillery, the shelling we had heard earlier grew much louder and closer. Light was reflected off the glass of a picture frame behind the man's head, holding a red sheet of paper with Chinese characters on it; a sudden roll of artillery shimmered the light on the glass like the surface of a pond. "That may be Phouc Lâm they're shelling right now," the captain said, "though it sounds closer."

"I am a Cao Dai," the man said. He gestured toward the religious ornaments around the room. "I pray every day for peace."

When did he think the war would end?

"I am an old man," he told the interpreter. "I have only a few years left. The war will not end while I am alive."

Who did he think would win?

He pointed up to the sky and answered briefly. "He says Heaven will decide," the interpreter said. "He does not know who will win."

Which side, then, would he *like* to see win? There were only two answers he could give us, I thought: he was indifferent, or he wanted the GVN to win. "He does not care which side wins; he would like the war to be over."

Would it make a difference to him if the VC won? I asked. How does he think his life would be different if the VC should win?

"He does not know. The VC who come to collect his taxes do not talk politics; so he really does not know what they would do or what they would be like if they were the government."

How does he think the long war started? Who began it?

"People in cities have magazines and newspapers, and listen to speeches; they know about things like that. But people who live in the hamlets do not have a chance to learn about such things. He does not know how it started."

On the subject of taxes, he said that his paddies yielded 50 *gia* per hectare (one *gia* = 20 kilos, a hectare = 2.5 acres); the landlord took 20 *gia* and the VC took 5.

Did either the GVN or the VC troops do any bad things in this area? "Both government troops and VC troops always behaved correctly. The government troops did not always pay when they needed food, but that was to be expected."

The glass in the picture frame shimmered violently; but this time it was from a burst of automatic weapon fire that came from only two hundred yards off. The captain started up, took his weapon, and went outside with the interpreter. The old man and woman paid no attention as they drank their tea; they didn't blink at the small-arms fire any more than at the shelling. I thought: they have heard this summer thunder, in bright daylight, for a long time. The captain and interpreter came back and sat down again; but the captain said he thought we should be going soon.

We asked a few more questions, then got up to go, thanking them for their tea. The man spoke, smiling, to the interpreter, who turned to me and said: "Now, before you go, he would like to ask you one question."

As he said this, the automatic weapon opened up again, a long burst, this time from no more than a hundred yards away. The captain went outside. "What is his question?" I asked. The man spoke to the interpreter.

"He says: You are Americans. He would like to ask you, in your opinion, when will the war end?"

I glanced out the door; the captain was looking alert but calm. I turned back to the old man, who watched my face intently, with a polite smile, while I chose my words for the interpreter. "Tell him," I said, "that I am glad he has prayed to Heaven for peace. Say that I think that he is a virtuous man; therefore, I believe the war will end while he is alive."

As the interpreter translated this, the captain stepped inside the doorway and said that he thought we should be moving along. I picked up my weapon, but the old man touched my arm and continued his question.

"He says that he is a Cao Dai, and though he has prayed for years for peace, peace has not come. However, he knows some Catholics; and they believe that peace will come in the two thousandth year. In the Catholic calendar, this is the year 1966

So he thinks that perhaps peace will come in the year 2000. What do you think?"

"Tell him I hope it will come much sooner than that," I said, backing out the door as a third burst sounded, about as close as the last. The interpreter finished my answer, then came out, as our hosts waved good-bye. He walked quickly past me to the captain; they spoke briefly, and the interpreter moved out around a corner of the thicket.

"With that automatic weapon, it could be a squad," the captain said softly. "Three or four, anyway. I don't know what they're firing at, probably harassing the hamlet because of the ceremony. We can't very well go back the way we came; it's too open. I think we'd better try to get them before they get us. Okay?" He asked me to cover him; he pulled back the bolt on his subma- chine gun and cocked it; I did the same. As we moved through the bushes around the yard, I glanced back. Our hosts were standing in the doorway, watching; when they saw me looking, they waved again.

On the other side of the thicket, the captain moved in a crouch along a paddy embankment toward a second grove, in the di- rection of the shots. It was now very quiet, except for the ar- tillery. When he reached the grove he squatted next to a palm and gestured to me; I moved over to him, bending below the level of the tall rice, trying to remember what I had learned a long time ago about moving quietly. As I came up, he slid into a stream of water, moved across it, climbed up on the bank, and disappeared into thick brush. After a moment I followed, feeling the cold water move up my boots, my pants, to my crotch as my boots hit mud at the bottom. Trying not to splash, but unable to avoid the sucking sound as my boots pulled out of the mud at each step, I crossed the stream and crawled up. The captain had moved next to a hut, apparently deserted. As he peered around the far corner, there was a short burst, very loud, though it did not have the sharp crack of bullets aimed directly at us. The captain, however, had pulled back quickly from the edge of the hut, and we moved around the other side and tried to make out movement in the undergrowth. He saw nothing.

In the next twenty minutes, we crossed another stream and a

pond, continuing to move around the outer edge of the thicket. The cold water was no longer a shock. The captain was concerned about finding the interpreter. Finally, he said, "If there *is* a squad, with that weapon, we're not well off here, with just two of us. We'd better try to find Wa. Anyway, I don't think they're shooting at us." There had not been any firing since we left the last hut. On the other side of one more canal we found Wa, who had been circling in the other direction. He said he couldn't tell what the firing was. We walked back along an embankment, keeping a watch to our rear. When we reached the road, we walked back to the jeep. Our clothes were drying fast in the sun, except for our socks.

I wanted to talk to the hamlet chief before we left, but a villager standing next to our jeep said that he had gone back to the district town with the convoy.

It was now almost noon. As we drove out of the hamlet, past the berm the cadre had built, we saw several cadre in a hut next to the entrance arch. I had the driver stop, and they came over to us; one turned out to be the leader of the RD cadre group. He had bushy hair and looked about fourteen, but was probably five years older.

I asked if the cadre had slept in the hamlets while they were working there.

"Yes," the interpreter translated, but smiled slightly at me.

Where had they been when the two hamlet chiefs were kidnapped?

The answer was: the cadre groups were "mobile" and they had warned the hamlet chiefs to move with them, but the chiefs were foolish and stayed in their homes.

Did the leader think that the new hamlet chiefs would be safe enough to stay in their hamlets at night?

The cadre leader looked back at the RF outpost as he answered. "He says that if the troops in the outpost are active and operate at nighttime, the hamlets will be safe enough and the chiefs will sleep in the hamlet."

An "if" answer to a direct question (like replies beginning, "The *plan* is," or "It has been ordered, or . . . agreed, that . . .")

was familiar to me after sixteen months in Vietnam. The best counter, sometimes, was another question.

Did the cadre leader believe that the troops in the outpost *would* be active enough, and operate at night?

The interpreter looked doubtful about putting the question. "These men are RD cadre, they are not military . . ."

"Ask him anyway," I said, "I only want his opinion. Does he believe . . . ?" The interpreter asked him.

"No."

Then, in his opinion, would it be safe enough, and would the hamlet chiefs stay at night?

"No."

But at this point, the cadre leader bent over the jeep and began talking quietly and seriously to the interpreter. He talked for a long time; he suddenly seemed much older. At last the interpreter translated, while the cadre leader looked down the road with a somber expression.

"He says there is no security here. This hamlet is too insecure to be pacified. Twelve PF's are not enough to protect the people. If ARVN troops would come, and stay here, and operate at night, there would be a chance; but when ARVN comes at all, the units leave at four, five o'clock, and at night the VC come. The RF outpost will not make much difference to the people, because the RF's will stay inside their post at night. The cadre were not here long enough to accomplish anything; but even if they had been here much longer, they could not have changed the people's attitudes, because the people are afraid. The six-point criteria have been met, but only on paper."

How about eliminating the VC infrastructure? I asked. How had that criterion been met?

"One member of the infrastructure was shot," one of the cadre by the jeep answered. "There were six. The other five moved out of the hamlet while the cadre were there; they will come back now that the cadre are leaving."

"Anyway," the leader added, "there are other people still in the hamlet who would inform the VC when they come through. There are many people in the hamlet who sympathize with the government: but they are afraid to identify themselves to the cadre. They are afraid to say anything good about the government. And that is still true, after ten weeks' work."

After a pause, I asked the interpreter to thank the leader for being so frank with us. We saw that he was sincere, and that he had done what he could.

"Ten weeks is not enough to do anything, in an area like this," the leader repeated. "But it doesn't make any difference; ten months would not have been enough, either. We worked hard, and we did the best we could; but the people do not really want to talk to us because the VC are all around and they are afraid. Maybe somewhere else we can do more. Or here, when things are better."

We offered the group a lift into town, and they all piled into the jeep. As we moved out toward Cần Giuộc, and dry socks, I asked the interpreter to ask the cadre if they knew what the firing had been about. Could they hear it?

One answered, and the interpreter said: "He heard some firing. He thinks perhaps it was some other cadre."

I looked at the captain. He shrugged. "Could be. I doubt it, that far off the road. But who knows?"

"Ask them what the cadre would have been firing about," I said to the interpreter. Another cadre, hanging on behind me, gave an answer.

"He says they may have been shooting to celebrate, because they had finished their work here, and the hamlets were pacified."

U.S. POLICY AND SOUTH VIETNAMESE POLITICS[1]

On April 15, 1970, I left the Rand Corporation to join the Center for International Studies at M.I.T. as a Senior Research Associate. My need to speak out publicly in the spring of 1970 on the role of the U.S. Government, in particular, that of Ambassador Ellsworth Bunker, in connection with Thieu's repression of my friend, Assemblyman Tran Ngoc Chau,[2] had convinced me that I should separate myself entirely from association with the Government before some new crisis arose calling again for comment or action and posing new dilemmas for Rand and for me.

Rand's top management had won my increasing respect for their willingness to bear the strains and risks imposed by my insistence on speaking—they supported my right to speak, I am afraid, too well for their own good—but it did not seem fair to continue putting them and my colleagues at Rand to this test. Everett Hagen, Acting Director

[1] Testimony before the Senate Committee on Foreign Relations, May 13, 1970. Published in *Impact of the War in Southeast Asia on the U.S. Economy,* Transcript of hearings before the Committee on Foreign Relations, U.S. Senate, Part II, pages 257-346 (hereafter cited as *Hearings).* The following text has deleted the testimony of the other two witnesses, Charles Cooper and David Schoenbrun, and most of the responses to it by Senators Fulbright, Gore, Pell, Case, and Javits, who attended. This text has also been lightly edited to improve readability.

[2] See "The Statement of Tran Ngoc Chau," translated, annotated, and with an introduction by Tran Van Dinh and Daniel Grady, *The Antioch Review,* Fall/Winter 1970-71, pages 299-310. Also see my two memoranda on Chau, *Hearings,* pages 342-46.

of the Center at M.I.T., had assured me that I could write anything that I wanted there—I was thinking at that moment of an article on Chau—without clearing it with anyone and without getting anyone else in trouble. On this basis, I accepted his offer.

Another specific reason for leaving Rand immediately, once I had decided to go, was that I had been invited to testify before the Senate Foreign Relations Committee on May 13, 1970. I had no intention of clearing my testimony with the Defense Department beforehand— or of testifying in a way that could have been cleared—so it was desirable to put as long an interval as possible between my resignation from Rand and my appearance there.

My session of the hearings, in Senator Fulbright's opening words, called for "testimony concerning the historical, political, and economic impact of U.S. policy on Vietnam and Southeast Asia" by, respectively, David Schoenbrun, myself, and my former colleague from Rand, Charles Cooper. The hearings were planned to be educational and uncontroversial, reflecting the mood of the Senate and public in the early spring of 1970, but within these limits I had decided to comment frankly on the nature of the U.S.-supported Saigon regime, and on the specific case of Tran Ngoc Chau, whose illegal trial had taken place in March (I entered two long memos on Chau into the record of the hearings as part of my testimony, which are omitted from the following version of the testimony).

But shortly before I was to testify, President Nixon launched the Cambodian invasion. On Friday, May 8th, I flew to St. Louis to speak at a teach-in at Washington University: it was my first public speech against the war, as well as my first teach-in since I had represented the other side, the Department of Defense, in several of the early ones five years before.

I flew back to Washington to find it taken over by more than two hundred thousand students protesting the invasion. That evening my wife and I walked through clouds of tear gas on Pennsylvania Avenue in front of the White House, which was protected by a line of buses end to end; groups of students were beginning to sit in the main intersections, improvising masks against the gas. (Marshals from the New Mobe finally dissuaded them from trying to shut down traffic and normal business; in retrospect, considering the highly unusual mood of Congress and the country that week, the chance was missed for a more promising occasion for mass civil disobedience than might ever come again.)

In this atmosphere I took part in *The Advocates* TV show Sunday night on the Cambodian invasion, associating myself with Senator Goodell, and against Senator Dole and William Sullivan, my former colleague at the State Department, who defended the invasion, and then prepared my statement for the hearings on Wednesday. With the Senators focused on the Church-Cooper bill, and besieged by delegations of professionals and short-haired, clean-cut college students from campuses that had never marched or protested before Kent State, Jackson State, and Cambodia, no one proposed to compete for attention by changing the relatively innocuous character of the hearings. Instead, the staff of the Committee looked forward to important hearings on the whole Vietnam decision-making process—dramatically exemplified by the new invasion—using the Pentagon Papers as a major resource. These hearings would be held as soon as the deliberations on the Church-Cooper amendment were ended. I had by this time given all of the Pentagon Papers—including the volumes on negotiations—to the Chairman and Committee staff; the Committee had been so far rebuffed by Secretary Laird in its request for an official copy.

Since I wanted to preserve my availability as consultant and possible witness for these more comprehensive hearings, I did not rise fully to Senator Fulbright's invitation to add some comments on the 1964 history at the end of my testimony here on U.S. intervention in Vietnamese politics. But, by the time the Church-Cooper bill was passed, U.S. troops had been withdrawn from Cambodia, and the furor of the public and Senate receded so abruptly that the prospect of hearings on the Pentagon Papers again disappeared. The Church-Cooper amendment exhausted the energies mobilized by the invasion and Kent State and by the Administration's deception and callousness; it prevented the reentry of U.S. troops into Cambodia, but not the reentry of U.S. bombers or of U.S.-supported Vietnamese troops into Cambodia or Laos. Thus it failed to prevent the invasion of Laos in the spring of 1971, or ground and air operations that made refugees of 2 million Cambodians out of a population of 6.7 million in the next year and a half. (Only some 150,000 tons of U.S. bombs were expended in Cambodia in the course of turning one third of the population into refugees, in contrast to South Vietnam, where it took 4 million tons and more than twice as long to create 6 million refugees, one third of the population of 18 million.)

Needless to say, the South Vietnamese politics fostered by our involvement over the past twenty-five years have not changed perceptibly in the two years since I predicted in these hearings the return of "Diemism without Diem." Tran Ngoc Chau remains in prison, held there without any pretense of legality, or of regret by our government, although the Vietnamese Supreme Court subsequently found that his arrest, his trial, and his imprisonment were each unconstitutional: a decision which Ambassador Bunker had earlier described as "the crunch," prior to which official U.S. criticism was inappropriate. His cell is near that of Truong Dinh Dzu, runner-up to Thieu in the 1967 election. (Dzu's son, David Truong, has informed me that they share a copy of the Bantam edition of *The Pentagon Papers*.) Don Luce estimates that there are 100,000 political prisoners in South Vietnam; the U.S. has allocated money for the construction of new "tiger cages" on Con Son island since the time Luce and Representative Anderson exposed the old ones.

I suggested before the Committee that Thieu's policy toward Chau had revealed his decision to discard constitutional legitimacy: "the emperor in full public view had taken off his clothes, and the question was, will we notice?" It took another year and a half, until the single-candidate "election" of 1971, before the Administration gave signs of noticing, and then it was with sadness rather than shock or reproach. Of local governors in hot, savage regions of the empire, it seems, not much is expected in the way of clothes.

This attitude was not exactly news to me. Five years earlier, while I was in the Embassy in Saigon, Ambassador Henry Cabot Lodge had commented to Washington:

It is obviously true that the Vietnamese are not today ready for self-government, and that the French actively tried to unfit them for self-government. One of the implications of the phrase "internal squabbling" is this unfitness. But if we are going to adopt the policy of turning every country that is unfit for self-government over to the Communists, there won't be much of a world left.

. . . The idea that we are here simply because the Vietnamese want us to be here . . . that we have no national interest in being here ourselves; and that if some of them don't want us to stay, we ought to get out is to me fallacious. . . . Some day we may have to decide how much it is worth to us to deny Vietnam to Hanoi and Peking—regardless of what the Vietnamese might think. [May 23, 1964; *PP*, IV, 99–100]

Two months after this cable, I sat in for my boss, General Lansdale, at a meeting of the Mission Council at the Embassy, Saigon. The first topic discussed was preparations for the elections in the fall to the constituent assembly which was to draft a constitution (the one later to be violated, with impunity, by Thieu's arrest and trial of Chau). Lansdale was greatly concerned about these preparations, so I took careful notes; my memo to him began:

Ambassador Porter began the meeting with the comment that General Thang had made some very interesting remarks to General Lansdale the other day. "He [Thang] is concerned with making the elections as well-run and honest as possible. I recommend that Lansdale be requested to ask Thang just how we can be most helpful to him. That might mean helping Thang move about the country or helping other people move. If anyone has any suggestions as to how we might help, they should tell Lansdale. It is good luck for us that Thang has the Ministry of Interior at this particular moment and that he is the kind of man he is.

"Lansdale should, of course, keep in close touch with the political section on this. We are going to come in for a good deal of criticism on these elections—the newspapermen are watching very closely and they are quite critical already—and we want to come out as well as we can."

Lodge responded to this opening with a good deal of reserve, launching into a rather long commentary that put him on distinctly different ground from Thang, Porter, and you. He began: "When you talk about honest elections, you can mean two things: (1) lack of intimidation—this we must have; (2) the fear in some quarters—not, I think, in the highest quarters—that we won't be nice enough to the people who would like to tear the whole thing down. When I see some of the cables coming in just now . . . I'm reminded of a song that they had during World War II, 'Don't Let's Be Beastly to the Germans.' " Porter nodded and interjected, "Don't let's be beastly to Tri Quang." (This was clearly a reference to the Limdis cable in that morning from State expressing concern about exclusion of ex-Struggle Force candidates [Buddhists, led by Thich Tri Quang] from the lists, among other things.)

Lodge continued, "You've got a gentleman in the White House right now who has spent most of his life rigging elections. *I've* spent most of my life rigging elections. I spent nine whole months once rigging a Republican Convention to choose Ike as a candidate rather than Bob Taft. If that was bad . . .

"The issue here is whether you can have open primaries. The fact is that in Southeast Asia in wartime you simply cannot have open primaries. The next question is then, who decides who can run? What worries me about the newspapermen is that they set higher standards for these people than we set for ourselves at home. Nixon and I would have taken Chicago in 1960 if there had been an honest count. The Republican machine there was simply lazy; they didn't get out the vote, and they didn't have anyone watching the polls. But I don't blame the Democrats for that, I blame the Republicans. There is just a limit to how naïve or hypocritical we can afford to be out here." Lodge turned to Porter and said, "Is that responsive to your question?"

Porter, looking slightly taken aback, said, "I just thought General Lansdale should stay close to General Thang on the issue of elections."

Lodge replied, "Well, I want General Lansdale to stay close to Thang on the subject of elections; and I want General Lansdale to stay close to Thang on the subject of pacification, which I think is a great deal more important."

Later Lodge reiterated, "Get it across to the press that they shouldn't apply higher standards here in Vietnam than they do in the U.S. They talk about corruption in Vietnam but not about expense accounts in New York. . . ." (This morning in Saigon 1895 Lodge puts it slightly differently: "The first steps for us in Saigon and in Washington are to make it clear to the press and to Congress that Vietnam should *not* be judged by American standards.")

This report was not encouraging to the Lansdale team; but when we gathered soon after at Lansdale's house to meet Richard Nixon, who was passing through Saigon on a visit, our hopes revived. Nixon had known Lansdale in the fifties when Lansdale had worked for the Dulles brothers, before he worked for the Bundy brothers. If Lansdale could persuade Nixon of the importance of free elections, this would carry weight, we hoped, with Nixon's former running-mate.

The opening moments of that visit have often come back to me. After shaking hands with each of us, Nixon asked: "Well, Ed, what are you up to?"

Lansdale replied: "We want to help General Thang make this the most honest election that's ever been held in Vietnam."

"Oh sure, honest, yes, honest, that's right"—Nixon was sitting himself in an armchair next to Lansdale's—"*so long as you win!*" With the last words he winked, drove his elbow hard into Lansdale's arm, and, in a return motion, slapped his own knee. My teammates turned to stone.

Not that any of this really mattered.

THE CHAIRMAN: The Committee will come to order. The Committee is meeting today to hear testimony concerning the historical, political, and economic impact of U.S. policy on Vietnam and Southeast Asia.

Mr. Ellsberg, will you proceed, please.

MR. ELLSBERG: Senator Fulbright, I heard you ask the first witness [Charles Cooper] if we have a vital interest in Southeast Asia. I would like to begin by giving you the thought that came to my mind.

I found that my answer after the events of the last ten days or so is that the United States of America has a vital interest in getting out of Southeast Asia, getting out of Indochina.

I have participated, in the Government and outside the Government, in a lot of discussions over the last ten years as to what constitutes our "vital interests" and what that phrase might mean. I believe that this morning it has come to me with greater clarity than ever in my life what it means for us to have a vital interest —which is an interest that concerns the survival of this nation— in circumstances other than invasion or nuclear war.

Personally, I have thought during the last couple of years of protest in this country that it was still possible to exaggerate the threat to our society that this conflict posed for us. I feared that we might come to a pass in which there would be a major threat to our society but that we were not there yet. I am assured now that we do still survive as an American nation by the protest to the recent Presidential decisions on Cambodia. But I am afraid that we cannot go on like this—as it seems likely we will, unless Congress soon commits us to total withdrawal—and survive as Americans. There would still be a country here and it might have the same name, but it would not be the same country.

I think that what might be at stake if this involvement goes on is a change in our society as radical and ominous as could be brought about by our occupation by a foreign power. I would hate to see that, and I hope very much that deliberations such as the Senate is undertaking right now will prevent that.

THE CHAIRMAN: If I understand your reply to the question I asked Mr. Cooper, it is that our vital interest is in disengaging. There is no vital interest in remaining and controlling Vietnam.

MR. ELLSBERG: Absolutely. I am saying that earlier I felt we had no vital interest one way or the other, although a considerable interest in getting out. I now think it is vital that we get out, and fast.

THE CHAIRMAN: Yes.

MR. ELLSBERG: The subject I was asked to speak about some months ago was the impact of our policy upon politics in South Vietnam.

This might seem undramatic and less relevant than some other topics as of this week.

But I think that is not true. I think, in fact, that the question of politics in South Vietnam and the question of self-determination in Vietnam are crucial to the question of our ability to withdraw from South Vietnam even sooner than the year, or eighteen months, or whatever, that people are discussing right now. Specifically, I believe that moves toward self-determination in South Vietnam would mean allowing a greater voice and greater role of leadership to those Vietnamese who speak for the mass, I believe, of Vietnamese, who want this war over and who believe that American involvement is prolonging the war. That development may be the key to achieving a cease-fire and the prompt, orderly American disengagement that the health of this nation demands. (It can also greatly improve the political prospects of non-Communist elements after our departure.)

I will proceed with a brief statement; it is the first time in my life, I think, that I have obeyed orders to write a brief statement, so I will elaborate on it a little and I will be glad to have questions.

It concerns mainly what I take to be a central untruth at the heart of American explanations of our involvement in this war, and that applies over a generation of Presidents, five Presidents, going back to 1950.

This Administration, like previous ones, has stated repeatedly that the primary purpose of U.S. involvement in Vietnam is to support and promote self-determination by the Vietnamese people, their right and ability to "choose freely their own form of government, without outside interference." That statement has never been true in the past. It is not true today.

Obviously, "self-determination" has never been the *effect* of our involvement. Not one of the regimes we have supported, from the Bao Dai regime controlled by the French, through Ngo Dinh Diem, to the military junta that rules today behind a constitutional facade, could have resulted from a process of public choice that was truly free, or free of our own outside influence.

Not one of them has "represented" even a majority of the non-Communist Vietnamese it ruled, either in terms of composition, of political origins, or of responsiveness to values with respect to social justice or the issues of war and peace. Nor has our Government in its private estimates ever imagined otherwise for any of the regimes it has supported with money, advice, and, increasingly, with our armed forces.

This last is the perspective which I would like to add to the comments of Mr. Schoenbrun, which I thought were very accurate, extremely pertinent, and regrettably unknown to almost all officials in the Government. I think I can add some knowledge of how these matters were seen in the Government at various times, from my own participation in it and from studying these matters with official access.

One of the startling things, I think, to someone coming from the outside and studying the official estimates and documents, is to realize how clearly one particular fact has been seen at virtually every phase of our involvement; namely, that the Saigon government we were supporting at that time was one that did not command the loyalty or support of the majority of its own citizens, even of its non-Communist citizens, and that it almost surely could not survive even against non-Communist challenges without our strong support in a variety of forms.

Few American officials, I think, have asked themselves whether we had a right to support such governments and thus to impose them on the majority of their citizens. They felt we had a necessity to do so, and hence the question of our "right" did not arise. Yet, as I say, I have increasingly felt that necessity to point in the other direction.

But the evident lack of self-determination in South Vietnam has not meant the failure of our policy. "Freedom of choice" has not been the effect of that policy, but neither has it ever been our intent. On the contrary, in certain specific senses, it has always been our determined purpose, on which we have acted effectively, to prevent certain forms or outcomes of self-determination by important segments of Vietnamese society. I do not speak here only of the Communists.

Our actual intent has been expressed both in our actions and inaction, words and silences, and in our internal policy statements. It is expressed most clearly in the internal statement of U.S. objectives in South Vietnam adopted as official Presidential policy in March, 1964. That statement said: The United States "seeks an independent, non-Communist South Vietnam." A further provision is that the South Vietnamese Government, while it need not be formally allied to the United States, must be "free to accept outside assistance."[3]

SENATOR GORE: What was the date of this?

MR. ELLSBERG: March 17, 1964, sir. It could as well have been written in 1954. It was our policy in 1954, it was our policy in 1950, '58, '60, and I believe it is our policy today. (Although the formal wording in the internal documents has been changed by the present Administration to omit the requirement "non-Communist," many aspects of Administration behavior convince me that it is still there in spirit.) I would like to make clear that this was by no means a policy that was first adopted in 1964. On the contrary, that statement merely put into words American objectives that had often been reflected in our policies before but not always explicitly in internal documents.[4]

---

[3] NSAM 288, March 17, 1964 (*PP*, III, 50). (All footnotes have been prepared for this text and did not appear in the original testimony.)

[4] See, for example, Statement of Policy by the National Security Council, "United States Objectives and Courses of Action with Respect to Southeast Asia," June 25, 1952 (*PP*, I, 384-90).

SENATOR GORE: Whenever stated it is in contravention of the Geneva Accords.

MR. ELLSBERG: That is correct, sir, and that is one reason that it has involved, as I mentioned, one of the central untruths of our policy. The policy has, in fact, been far more knowing, and one would have to say cynical, to insiders, in its contravention of the Accords and of our announced goals of self-determination, than an outsider would easily imagine. Again I would have to say this of the Administrations of five Presidents, three Democratic and two Republican. At each time they have been aware we were undertaking actions in contradiction to past policies of the United States, in this case our anti-colonial policy, but more importantly in contradiction to treaty commitments and public declarations of various kinds.

This is one of the moral burdens which our leaders feel they are called upon to accept from time to time: the responsibility for such choices and deceptions.

In the fifties it was often spelled out in internal policy statements quite sharply that it would be gravely against the interests of the United States, if there should be a Communist takeover in South Vietnam after 1954 (or anywhere in Vietnam, before 1954) "by whatever means." That was a very significant clause, as you will recognize.

The policy statements made it quite clear they were not referring only to a breach of the principles against invasion or armed aggression across borders. They felt that a Communist-dominated South Vietnam after 1954—no matter how it occurred —would jeopardize our interests in terms of influence and prestige; it would lead to Communist takeovers in other countries, in other parts of Southeast Asia and ultimately elsewhere, and thus would jeopardize our national interest. And that specifically meant whether it occurred by means of infiltration, subversion, or, as it was delicately put, by political activity, which is to say by "free choice." Another way to put it, if that is too nice a phrase —and people have questioned whether we should use it about our own elections, I have found—at any rate, by some sort of representative process.

Our officials, civilian and military, have typically interpreted this requirement for a non-Communist regime as inconsistent not only with acceptance by us, or by a regime we supported, of immediate Communist domination or even participation in a Saigon regime, but as inconsistent with an attitude of tolerance toward political activity by Communists or others that could possibly lead to an increasing Communist role.

I might say that those words, those particular words emphasizing our aim of a "non-Communist" regime, do not merely lie dusty in safes but have been brought out quite regularly since 1964, particularly by the Joint Chiefs of Staff, as a specific refutation of any proposal of political processes that could possibly lead eventually to a Communist Vietnam, or to any proposals of neutrality, or of negotiations with the other side that could lead to a coalition.

The JCS, the Joint Chiefs of Staff, in particular, missed no opportunity to point out that such proposals were in direct contradiction, as they read it, of the policy statement—which was NSAM, National Security Action Memorandum 288 in March, 1964—that we wanted an independent non-Communist South Vietnam.

Thus, we have supported only regimes whose policy has been to exclude totally the Communist element of Vietnamese society from any organized or even individual participation in political activity, and if possible to destroy it as an organization.

There have always been arguments as to exactly how large the organization of Communists is in Vietnam and how many people maintain loyalty to it. I have never seen any estimates below about 10 percent, and have seen arguments as to whether it is 15, 25, or 30 percent, and possibly higher at such times as 1964. But if we consider it even as 10 percent and consider it as a minority as well organized as the Communists are and with the prestige accruing from the victorious liberation struggle against the French, and then consider that we were backing policies to exclude totally that organization and destroy it, one sees, I think, the questions that must be raised of both the legitimacy and feasibility of such policies. In fact, both in terms of legitimacy and feasibility, this project has been comparable to an attempt to exclude totally and destroy the Communist parties in France or Italy. It has required, eventually, an enormous investment of foreign—that is, American—money, arms, troops, and lives.

But the effect of our intervention has by no means been limited to excluding this one minority element from representation. We have also thrown our weight against the emergence of any governments, although non-Communist and representative of a majority of the population, that would not be, in our opinion, sufficiently reliable in safeguarding our own dominant interest, preventing eventual Communist domination.[5]

Our main support went, instead, to those most reliably "anti-Communist": as distinct from the mass of "non-Communists" that may indeed make up the majority of the population of South Vietnam today. I might mention that the distinction between anti-Communist and non-Communist is one that is very often made by almost any Vietnamese you get into a political discussion. But it is one that is not really familiar to Americans, including officials, who tend to translate the assertion that "the people do not want Communism" immediately into the phrase that they are "anti-Communists," and read into that that they are dedicated to the support of the GVN, at least as a lesser evil, and are willing to risk their lives or make sacrifices for that regime.

That last is not true, and I think the truth is captured better by this distinction between anti-Communist and non-Communist, with the strongly dedicated "anti-" being a very small minority, scarcely larger, if at all larger, than the Communists.

These "anti-Communists" have comprised parts (not all) of

[5] Compare Jerome Slater's conclusion concerning U.S. motives in 1965 for opposing the victory of forces in the Dominican Republic that proposed to restore President Juan Bosch, who had been elected in 1963 and deposed by a military coup later that year. Although neither Bosch nor the groups supporting him were believed to be controlled by Communists, Slater points out, "There is not the slightest doubt that the primary, indeed the overwhelming factor in the U.S. decision to intervene was the belief in both the Embassy and the State Department that the apparently imminent constitutionalist victory would pose an unacceptable risk of a Communist takeover. . . . As both the Embassy and the State Department saw it, even if Bosch should be reinstalled in the Presidency, he would *soon be discarded* by the better organized and more determined extremists, and there would be a Communist takeover within six months" (*Intervention and Negotiation,* page 31; italics added). Similar dynamic models, and similar caution, in the minds of American officials, have worked against the prospects of "Third Force" politicians in Vietnam for twenty-five years.

the French- and U.S.-trained army, the civil service, the Catholics and especially the northern refugee Catholics, and all of the land-lords and businessmen: in general, those who feel they have most to lose from a Communist takeover, or whose families have al-ready suffered from Communists.

SENATOR CASE: Excuse me. Since you made that distinction, does this mean that the people whom you describe as this third group, the non-Communists, want to be under Communist rule or are indifferent to whether they were under a Communist re-gime or just that they are rather apathetic? They are not activists.

MR. ELLSBERG: That is a very crucial question, which, I believe, has been wrongly answered by many analysts within our Govern-ment over the last decade.

SENATOR CASE: I think it is rather important.

MR. ELLSBERG: I think it is terribly important.

SENATOR CASE: Because if it is just a matter of their not caring who governs them and not having any views about ideology, let them go. But if they are anti-Communists and even though they are not activists, that is a different situation, it seems to me.

MR. ELLSBERG: Sir, I have found within the Government great assurance that what we were doing in Vietnam, basically in pur-suit of our own interests, was legitimate because it did, after all, accord with the interests and desires of the majority of those people, even if they did not have the opportunity to express those desires democratically.

We have been convinced that the people "do not want Com-munism" and, as I say, that comes into official policy statements very frequently, and always in terms of justifying our involve-ment.[6]

[6] See McGeorge Bundy—on his first visit to Vietnam—in his memo recommend-ing sustained bombing of the North after the Pleiku attack, February 7, 1965: "The energy and persistence of the Viet Cong are *astonishing*. They can appear anywhere—and at almost any time. They have accepted extraordinary losses and they come back for more. They show skill in their sneak attacks and ferocity when cornered. *Yet the weary country does not want them to win*" (*PP*, III, 311; italics added).

I think when there is evidence that that does not mean or seem to translate immediately into dedicated support to the Saigon Government, we then go to the second model that you suggested, which was, they do not want Communism but then they do not want very much of anything very intensely. To put it less politely, what lies between the lines is that they are dumb peasants. They are illiterate and apathetic. If we look at a book by John Mecklin, who was the U.S.I.S. Director in Saigon at a certain period, we have the extraordinary statement, and I think very revealing one, that for the half of the adult rural population that are illiterate, their "power of reason . . . develops only slightly beyond the level of an American six-year-old."[7] In other words, one takes reassurance that even if they are not strongly with us, they are indifferent, they are childish and apathetic and probably malleable, and if our policies can be rearranged slightly and publicized properly, perhaps we will get their ardent support.

The actual model, to answer your question as directly and as accurately as I can, is I think, that the mass of the Vietnamese people have a considerable antipathy, not indifference, both to the Communists and to the GVN. That has been described by a former Ambassador of South Vietnam to this country, Vu Van Thai, as a "double allergy," growing more and more intense. That can lead to behavior similar to that of apathy, of course, or to a sort of self-seeking opportunism, but on other occasions it can beget other sorts of explosive phenomena.

The fact is, I believe, that even those who back the GVN regard it at best as a lesser evil. And one of the most significant statements I have ever seen on the problems of the Vietnam War is by a Vietnamese nationalist, now in the Senate, named Dang Van Sung, who said in 1963: "Man is so constituted that he will not willingly make great sacrifices or risk his life merely for a lesser evil, although he will gladly die for an illusion."

I think it is because we have offered, with our backing, the mass of the Vietnamese at best a lesser evil that we have not ever found them wholeheartedly backing—

SENATOR CASE: But you would not want to offer them an illusion, either, that they would die for.

[7] *Mission in Torment* (New York, 1965), page 76.

MR. ELLSBERG: Sir?

SENATOR CASE: You would not offer them an illusion that you just spoke for, the man you quoted.

MR. ELLSBERG: The striking difference between the two sides is that those who back the Communist side do not on the whole regard it as a lesser evil, but as a cause worth dying for.

SENATOR CASE: I am not really trying to take a position here at all. I am just trying to find out exactly what we are talking about. It seems to me it is quite conceivable that people who are completely apathetic about the outside world, who want to be left alone to till their few acres and worship as they please and to honor their ancestors in the same place that they believe they have been for a long time, may be entirely much more aware than we are of the destruction of their environment.

MR. ELLSBERG: I certainly agree with that. I am just taking exception to the phrase "they only want to be left alone," because I believe that has lulled our officials considerably.

I take two points of exception to it. One, I think they are not at all indifferent to the nature of the officials who rule their districts and their provinces, and the battalion commanders and the regimental commanders who control firepower within that province. They know very well that the control of armed forces, police, allied units like our own, and GVN units depends very much on those officials. They hold bad troop behavior, extortion, and indiscriminate firepower very much against the officials, and they are not at all indifferent about such matters. I say this because people ask, "Do they care about elections; do they care about officialdom at all?" As my friend Tran Ngoc Chau, now in prison in Vietnam, used to say, "Peasants would appreciate very much the chance to throw out an oppressive, rotten, or inhumane official if they could. Elections are not the only way to do that, but if elections gave them that chance, they would take to elections very quickly."

The other thing that they are not at all indifferent about is the continuation of this war. And they know very well that is beyond the control of village or province officials. . . .

The phrase "the people in between" is a phrase that has often struck me in Vietnam. The model, the description I have given of attitudes with, say, very roughly, 20 percent perhaps on one side and 20 percent on the other, leaving a great mass of people not committed to either of these parties and not indifferent at all to the carrying on of the war, supports an understanding of the plight of "the people in between." Again, if I may quote Vu Van Thai, who said to me recently: "The problem in Vietnam is that of a people ground down between two competing authoritarian regimes."

On the other hand, if you ask, "Is there anything we can do about this?" the answer is yes; we have been doing something about it for a very long time. We have shown the ability to *preserve* that situation, essentially, to prolong it, and we are seen as doing so by the Vietnamese people. We can keep on doing that if we really want to pay the price. It is not a very idealistic program.

SENATOR CASE: Do you not think it is really true, despite the concentration on the situation in Vietnam that we have given verbally over all these years, that our real concerns have been geopolitics on a larger scale?

MR. ELLSBERG: This has led to what I described as untruth actually. We have felt compelled—and perhaps one should be glad in some sense that our leaders did feel compelled, although we paid a price for it in the frankness of public discussion—to say we were not pursuing our own interests entirely at the expense of the Vietnamese people. But that in fact would have been the accurate thing to say. . . .

Senator Case, I would like to mention something else that your question suggested to me. Even in years when I felt that our policies there were unsound and unwise and should be stopped, I did not have the strong feeling that what we were doing was wrong and intolerable until I began to become aware of much of the history and the background that Mr. Schoenbrun has made a great effort to bring to the American people over some time. My reading of that history, after my return from Vietnam, influenced me a great deal. And I might mention I do not think I have ever met an American official of the Deputy Assistant Secretary level or higher connected with the problems of Southeast Asia who could have really passed a simple college seminar quiz, or I should say a high school quiz, on any of the dates or facts on which Mr. Schoenbrun has properly put such emphasis. . . .

Your question suggests to me one that I asked a Vietnamese in this country named Hoang Van Chi, the author of a book called *From Colonialism to Communism,* which is a classic study of the Communist takeover in North Vietnam. He had been an official in the Viet Minh in the war against the French and then gone to work for the Diem government and ultimately over here.

I asked him if North Vietnam, his native region, would be better off today if Ho Chi Minh had not headed the revolution, and he said, "Oh, yes" right away, which did not surprise me because he is known as an anti-Communist. When I asked him to go into more detail, how it would be better, he said, "My country would not have been destroyed or divided." He said, "If Ho Chi Minh had not headed the liberation someone else would, not a Communist. If one other than a Communist had headed the liberation movement against the French, the United States would never have supported the French with money, weapons, planes, and napalm, and many of my countrymen would not have died.

"Moreover, the liberation would have applied to the entire country."

Frankly, when I heard him say that, it made the hair on my neck stand on end, to realize as an American that the greatest reproach that a Vietnamese could make against Ho Chi Minh would be that he had been responsible for triggering a more or less reflex destructive action over twenty years, by the United States. . . .

THE CHAIRMAN: Yes, I would. I would like to make this observation. This question, of course, arose in the early days of the hearings before this committee, particularly with Secretary Rusk. If my memory serves me correctly, it was quite clear then that the decisive question was not the balance of power other than the ideological obsession we then had. Much of it grew out of our domestic situation. That is the influence that Senator McCarthy had developed here. It had great domestic political implications, which, as you have already described, caused Secretary Dulles to decline to even participate personally in the Geneva Accords.

In the many questions at that time, I think we reduced it to the point of asking if Ho Chi Minh had not been a Communist, do you think we would ever have intervened? I think it is quite clear we would not have. It was the ideological aspect that triggered our intervention, and this was true of situations not only in Southeast Asia, especially, but in Europe. I mean, in the fear of Stalin and his effect.

I always thought our departure from our traditional role, in supporting the French colonial power, was because of our fear of French weakness in Europe.

MR. SCHOENBRUN: Yes, sir, and the French have played upon that, as you know.

THE CHAIRMAN: . . . I never followed the idea that it is all history and it is not important. What do we do now? I think what you do now is based fundamentally upon your understanding of how we got there.

MR. ELLSBERG: Mr. Chairman, having studied the documents of a number of administrations and found the internal rationales in terms of strategic interests palpably inadequate, I have more and more come to look at the domestic political contexts in which those decisions were made year after year This is something that rarely gets into the internal documentation, and if it is even talked about in the Executive branch, it is done very privately, one or two people at a time. I am speaking of the relation of these strategic moves to domestic politics.

THE CHAIRMAN: By strategic you mean in the interest of the security of our country?

MR. ELLSBERG: That is right. As a friend of mine, Morton Halperin, said recently, people other than the President, bureaucrats in fact, make their decisions on the basis of bureaucratic and agency considerations, and Presidents typically make their own choices in terms of domestic political considerations, far more than the public realizes; but in describing their motives and reasoning to each other and to the public, both talk a language of national security and strategy, which creates certain confusions.

In this particular case, I would say that since 1949 no American President has been willing to see the fall of Indochina added to the fall of China during his Administration. And that, I think, has warped very much his perception and weighing of priorities with respect to short-run and long-run interests of this country.

I believe that each President really has been willing to invest major resources to take considerable risks in order simply to postpone the fall of Saigon. He has not wanted to be in office, in effect, when the red flag went up over Saigon.

THE CHAIRMAN: That is, for political reasons here at home and not strategic reasons?

MR. ELLSBERG: Essentially political reasons. And this has led us to take strategies that were risky and costly but did promise that they would postpone this event, even if they offered little hope of averting it indefinitely, that is, of "winning" at acceptable cost.

SENATOR CASE: Can I throw out a suggestion? This unwillingness to be in office at a time when Saigon fell might be based upon a consideration that the people of the country don't believe it is a wise thing to let happen—

MR. ELLSBERG: That is right.

SENATOR CASE (*continuing*): And not for unworthy reasons, but from some deep instinctive feeling about what is in the national interest. Presidents, in following this feeling, haven't therefore been unworthy of the move. That is not the least worthy, I suppose, of motives: To an important degree to follow what I think is our basic guide here, and that is the instinctive movement of the people of this country in one direction or another. And that doesn't mean that everybody hasn't got the obligation to do his own thinking. But the people of this country, when they have been sufficiently informed—and they have an amazing way of getting information, including, I think, osmosis as well as watching television or listening to people on the radio and reading newspapers or listening to political speeches or whatnot—the people, I think, probably are our best reliance when it comes to great policy.

MR. ELLSBERG: I agree completely. I think that is one of the premises that goes into the President's mind, and I am talking now, as I keep repeating, of five Presidents. I should say I know of the premises of the most recent, Nixon, only from newspapers; the others from considerable documentation.

But I think the problem, as the President sees it, is a little more complex than that in this area. He sees, in the first instance, as you say, that the people may well punish him politically if he lets Indochina fall, and, to that extent, acting to prevent that is doing the people's will, which is his democratic responsibility. But at the same time he reads his intelligence analyses and his operational estimates, which tell him what will be required to prevent that from happening, and he compares those calculated requirements with what he thinks the public and the Congress will let him do. And there always has been a great gap between these sets of considerations.

Each President has seen, I think, that although he will lose prestige and power—that is, lose votes—if Indochina falls, he probably cannot get Congress or the people to let him do what his advisers tell him is needed to keep it from falling, reliably and indefinitely. That has meant various things. First, it meant backing a colonial regime, which we did with some distaste. We accepted that. Later it meant backing an authoritarian police state, which we did, though we didn't want to publicize it. Third—

when that began to fail in 1963 and 1964 (I came into the Department of Defense in August, 1964)—the President's military and civilian advisers believed strongly that unless we were prepared to bring direct military pressure on North Vietnam, the situation was irretrievable. Finally, ground troops appeared necessary.

Now during that whole period bombing and ground troops looked perhaps ultimately necessary but were ruled out. Thus, up to 1965, each President was led to take steps short of those measures, steps which he believed to be probably inadequate to the situation. He hoped these lesser steps might work and believed they would at least postpone the dilemma of using troops or bombing or of losing.

This put one further pressure on him to mislead the public as to how these lesser measures were working. We were under great pressure to imply, since advisors were all we could afford to put over there, that advisors were doing the job; or Diem was doing the job; or earlier the French were doing the job. And this meant consciously distorting what our reports were conveying to the President.

SENATOR CASE: We have had direct experience with this again and again, for what, fifteen, twenty years.

MR. ELLSBERG: Yes. When the President starts lying he begins to need evidence to back up his lies because in this democracy he is questioned on his statements. It then percolates down through the bureaucracy that you are helping the Boss if you come up with evidence that is supportive of our public position and you are distinctly unhelpful if you commit to paper statements that might leak to the wrong people.

The effect of that is to poison the flow of information to the President himself and to create a situation where a President can be almost, to use a metaphor, psychotically divorced from the realities in which he is acting. . . .

MR. ELLSBERG (*resuming his statement*): Most Vietnamese on both sides of the struggle see the hegemony of this particular minority grouping, which I described earlier—the Diem coalition of army, Catholics, civil servants, landlords, and businessmen— as the result of American policy and decisions. They are basically right. They do not thank us for it. As Tran Ngoc Chau said to me in Vietnam a few years ago, "The United States gets very angry and disappointed when it finds that the leaders it has se- lected for Vietnam do not command the loyalty of the Vietnamese people." I believe Vietnamese feelings go beyond that now. Any group of leaders who had won the support of the majority of the people right now, I believe would have done so by appealing to end the war.

Has anything in this matter changed lately?

President Thieu's successful campaign from November, 1969, to March, 1970, to imprison the oppositionist Assemblyman Tran Ngoc Chau, in disregard of the 1967 constitution, indicates strongly an open return to the familiar form of politics, described above and known to Vietnamese as "Diemism."

THE CHAIRMAN: As what?

MR. ELLSBERG: Diemism. Diemism without Diem. And perhaps I should describe Diemism more fully. It implies a narrow po- litical base for the regime; exclusion of all other groups such as the Buddhists, the students, unions, the Hoa Hao and Cao Dai, from any participation in power and the use of divide-and-rule tactics on them, an authoritarian police state regime; suppression of free speech; suppression of political activity; total unwilling- ness to negotiate with or tolerate the existence or activity of the Communists; and extreme reliance on the Americans. This con- stitutes the context which is "Diemism."

Watching President Thieu pursue Chau despite the obstacles of the constitution, which made Chau supposedly immune from the particular tactics Thieu was using, all Vietnamese that I spoke to and of whom I heard in Vietnam, immediately said, "We are back to Diemism." Shortly after Chau's imprisonment in March, I spelled out at some length what seem to me the implications of such a conclusion in a memorandum I shall submit for the record of these hearings.

More recent repressive actions by Thieu against students, veterans, political rivals, and newspapers all point strongly in the same direction.

If self-determination were truly our aim. Thieu's policies would be directly thwarting it. But, as we have agreed, we have really other interests that we are pursuing.

How does Diemism without Diem serve these other interests? Well, it does not serve our announced interests in a negotiated settlement—that is certain.

Thieu's policies show a clear intent to monopolize governmental power in the hands of a narrow group which coincides with those least willing to see any reduction in U.S. presence or aid or, indeed, an end of the war that would bring about such a reduction.

Again to quote Vu Van Thai, who represented essentially the same group as Ambassador to Washington, a period that he is not proud of at this point: they are precisely those who could not survive politically an end to the war and American presence; so their status and prestige and power depends entirely upon a prolongation of the war. Even winning the war, even victory would end this power. Prolongation is precisely what they want, with American presence.

This same grouping of forces will accept no compromise of a rigid anti-Communist policy that precludes the concessions required for negotiated settlement. United States policy, in turn, that predicates any agreement with North Vietnam or the NLF upon its acceptance by this Saigon regime, cannot lead to successful negotiations, and one can say that to choose continued support of this regime is knowingly to choose against negotiations as a way out of the Vietnam War for the United States.

Does Diemism without Diem serve our policy of Vietnamization? That depends on what Vietnamization means. Not if it means the aim, for Americans, of leaving Vietnam altogether, leaving it with a government worthy of United States and Vietnamese sacrifices and one that can survive to fight or negotiate or coexist with Communists without us. Even with President Diem, a far more authoritative national leader than Thieu, Diemism failed to achieve this or to survive at all, even against non-Communist opposition. I should say I believe that in continuing there with U.S. troops to support the Thieu government, there is increasing likelihood we will be called upon, unless we change that policy, to support the survival of the Thieu government against non-Communist opposition devoted to ending the war. We will be called on to support it by use of our own military forces, just as we lent transport planes to Ky to suppress the Buddhist uprising in 1966.

Thieu would be even less likely than Diem to successfully build an anti-Communist authoritarian regime that would be strong and stable without either popular support or an American presence.

But the signs are that the Nixon Administration privately knows this quite well and that Vietnamization means something else to it. Since the political component of that policy is clearly predicated on support of Thieu, including his repressive measures of the last six months, it almost surely presumes a large American presence as well. I believe that Vietnamization, as shown more clearly by support of Thieu, is not a policy of withdrawal at all but of reduction of forces to 100,000 or 200,000 troops expected to stay there indefinitely. A slogan that paraphrases views I have heard from officials in the last few months would be: "There is nothing wrong with Diemism that a hundred thousand U.S. troops can't cure."

That in turn, I might say, reflects another attitude, a very nostalgic attitude, for the earlier days of Diem, which could be similarly paraphrased: "Diem would have won if only we had assassinated David Halberstam instead." Again, this imagines that events in that country depend entirely on events and decisions in this country, that they are swung by them and that the realities were leading to victory over there, when in fact that was very far from the case.

The recent U.S. adventure in Cambodia, with the U.S. Administration imitating in Presidential style Thieu's "loose construction" of his own constitution, warns clearly that this Administration is no more ready to contemplate the "loss" of Indochina to Communism, during its term of office, than any of its predecessors.

It is in the full tradition of earlier Administrations, hopeful of victory in the long run but obsessed with avoiding defeat in the short run. They have their eye on the ball, and avoiding short-run defeat is an objective that is worthy of a great many American and Vietnamese lives in their opinion, I am sorry to say.

This Administration is no less ready than earlier ones to incur escalating risks and domestic dissent to avoid or postpone such "humiliation." The rhetoric has changed, and I refer here to the fact that we talk more about self-determination than we did in some recent years, but the policy has not. It is one that condemns Vietnam to endless war and Americans to endless participation in it in support of a corrupt and unpopular military dictatorship.

THE CHAIRMAN: Thank you very much, Mr. Ellsberg.

That is a very dismal conclusion, but I have no quarrel with it. I think if the policy persists and if the Congress is unable or unwilling to change it, I would predict that it will go on as you say. . . .

[There follows a discussion of the view that the war in Vietnam principally serves the interests of the Soviet Union.]

MR. ELLSBERG: Important people who are supposed to have been concentrating on American interests, in successive Administrations, have been oddly blind, I think, to the question of when conflicts of interest on the one hand or harmony of interests on the other were showing up.

There are indications, for example, that President Nixon, even before he took office, was counting on the secret plan of acting upon a supposed harmony of interests with Russia. Now what this analysis is pointing to is that that may be a very unreliable basis. There have been other supposed harmonies of interest in our actions that again we failed to notice were actually in conflict. I think we have never been sensitive to the conflict of interest between this country, ever since it became interested in getting out of this war, and the interest of the Saigon government. On the other hand, we have never noticed the harmony of interest in a certain peculiar sense of the Saigon government with the Communists who almost surely see their own long-run interests served by having power among the non-Communists monopolized, prior to their takeover, by Saigon regimes of the precise character of those we have supported or, in effect, we have chosen to impose.

Several Vietnamese said to me during the elections of 1967 in Vietnam, before Thieu replaced Ky as our candidate: "There are only two people here who agree they want to see Ky as the President of South Vietnam, Westmoreland and Ho Chi Minh." And in fact I think there was a harmony of perception of interests between those two gentlemen, and some other Americans, and it was not based, in my opinion, on a very clear knowledge of where our own interests lay. . . .

THE CHAIRMAN: Mr. Ellsberg, were you stationed in Vietnam, and while you were there did you ever become acquainted with Tran Ngoc Chau?

MR. ELLSBERG: He was a very close friend of mine.

THE CHAIRMAN: You know him. Do you know anything about his relationship with the CIA, which has been in the press? This is not related to what I asked you to discuss, but since you are here I thought I might ask you to comment on it.

MR. ELLSBERG: Well, I had anticipated that questions about Chau might come up. I have a file of various background papers on Chau, some of them memos of conversations that I had with him at the time. If you would like I could enter into the record a memo bearing on that particular subject. I wrote it in 1966 when I was assigned to liaison with Chau, who was then head of the Revolutionary Development (called Rural Construction by the Vietnamese) cadre program. It does not present a comprehensive picture of Chau's relations with the CIA, but it does throw important light, I think, on the origins of friction between them.[8]

THE CHAIRMAN: I think it would be interesting because we have had some difficulty in getting information from the Administration on this subject. They always plead some kind of security. We asked Ambassador Bunker to come before the Committee in open session, but he declined. He has agreed to come in executive session. I don't know whether or not he knows Mr. Chau, but being in Saigon and responsible for our representation, he at least came to him secondhand. He should know about it, but I think it would be well to put in the record the memorandum about Mr. Chau. As I understand it, the Supreme Court in Saigon has declared his conviction unconstitutional or illegal.

MR. ELLSBERG: That is right. The Supreme Court, in what would be in normal terms an encouraging move, almost unprecedented for them in terms of challenge to their Executive, has declared that the manner of his arrest was unconstitutional, that he was tried in the wrong court and that his imprisonment was unconstitutional. They did not, however, order him to be released.

THE CHAIRMAN: He is still in prison?

MR. ELLSBERG: He is still in prison.[9] It has been reported in our newspapers that the U.S. Embassy in Saigon had taken the position that our Government should not be critical publicly of Thieu's behavior in this case until the full constitutional workings of their system had run out. It said, after all the Supreme Court may rule on this, and if they rule, presumably the Execu-

---

[8] See *Hearings*, pages 342-46. The original grounds of this conflict involved Chau's concern that the Office of Special Assistant (CIA) was exercising an undue influence on the policies and administration of this program, particularly in the eyes of the Vietnamese.

[9] As this goes to press, April, 1972, Chau remains in prison, over a year and a half after the Vietnamese Supreme Court removed any shred of legality from his arrest, trial, or imprisonment—with no known protest from the U.S. Embassy.

tive·will obey its guidance. As I read the account of our Embassy views, which sounds very plausible to me,[10] it was put to our State Department that our judgment should be reserved until that time. Well, the time is now. I believe that the attitude of our Government toward obedience or nonobedience by President Thieu to the clear legal implications of this Supreme Court ruling is a test not just of Thieu but of us and our attitude. At the time I felt that Thieu's behavior showed that he had clearly decided to discard constitutional legitimacy, simply to rule without it. I felt the emperor in full public view had taken off his clothes and the question was, will we notice? If our purposes there do not call for any such legitimacy, any pretense of legal restraints or self-determination, then I would call on the President to discard that particular vein of rationalizing our intentions and our presence there.

THE CHAIRMAN: I have seen no indication that our Government is going to respond to that finding.

MR. ELLSBERG: Perhaps you will learn the plans when you see Ambassador Bunker.

THE CHAIRMAN: I doubt that very seriously. Mr. Ellsberg, were you working at the Pentagon at the time the bombing of North Vietnam began?

MR. ELLSBERG: Referring to the Tonkin Gulf reprisal?

THE CHAIRMAN: Either at the time of the Tonkin Gulf incident or the succeeding February. Were you there during that period?

MR. ELLSBERG: I was very closely involved in that decision-making, leading up to the bombing campaign from February, 1965, on, as a staff assistant.

THE CHAIRMAN: Would you tell us a bit about the first one. Perhaps that is the way to start.

[10] This account of the Embassy's position was correct.

MR. ELLSBERG: Well, after——

THE CHAIRMAN: What were your responsibilities? Were you Assistant Secretary of Defense to John McNaughton at the time of the Gulf of Tonkin incident?

MR. ELLSBERG: I was the Special Assistant to the Assistant Secretary of Defense.

THE CHAIRMAN: What were your responsibilities at that time?

MR. ELLSBERG: Really to help him as a staff assistant on particularly sensitive issues of various kinds which were not handled in the normal staff work.

THE CHAIRMAN: The reason I think it is appropriate and timely to ask you this now is that the Committee on Monday voted to repeal the Gulf of Tonkin resolution. The Majority Leader has scheduled it for consideration after the arms sales, so it will be coming up right away. It is history, but I don't believe we have ever had your testimony. I think it is very appropriate since you were one of the people involved. Were you personally aware of the decision-making in connection with the retaliation after the second incident?

MR. ELLSBERG: I was, but almost by chance. I might say, this is a long story.

THE CHAIRMAN: Would you make it as brief as you can? I don't know of any other opportunity I will have to put it in the record. It isn't all-important, but I personally am very interested and I am sure that certain scholars and others will be interested. It is a matter of interest, so if you don't mind I would like any memoranda you have relating to it. Could you give us a very brief summary?

MR. ELLSBERG: I don't have memoranda, but I would be glad

to comment on it in particular because I have been sensing very strong similarities in the last few weeks to the mood of the Government and perhaps to the behavior and planning of the Government in that period, 1964-65 period, very ominous similarities. And I feel that, without knowing in fact precisely what has been planned or proposed lately, or really anything beyond what has been in the newspapers. But some of the terms used and the nature of the process as it has been described just seem to me awfully familiar.

I entered the Government with the intent in fact of learning about the decision process by participating in the workings of the Government; I had previously been studying Presidential decision-making and crisis decision-making. When I entered the Government in August, 1964, I found myself with some surprise surrounded by a mood almost of conspiracy, a situation where the people on the inside felt a great tension and discrepancy between what they thought was necessary for the nation and perhaps for their Administration, and what the public would allow them to do. They felt this tension very greatly.

They felt that the policies that they had been pursuing some years in Vietnam were failing and were about to fail drastically, although they had been protecting the public from full knowledge of that through the spring of 1964.

THE CHAIRMAN: This is the spring of 1964 you are talking about?

MR. ELLSBERG: Yes. I am talking about the period just before I was directly involved.

By coincidence, it was one, however, which I had to go back to while I was working for John McNaughton, to a closer look at the documents, just to understand how we got to where we were, at the point where I found myself.

I came in in August of 1965, and actually one of my first memories—

THE CHAIRMAN: August of 1965?

MR. ELLSBERG: August of 1964. One of my first memories in my participation on Vietnam was the night of the Tonkin Gulf reprisal, when we stayed in the Pentagon most of the night waiting for the raids to take place and then for the reports to come in.

THE CHAIRMAN: That was 1964, the 4th of August?

MR. ELLSBERG: The 4th.

THE CHAIRMAN: There were two incidents.

MR. ELLSBERG: I am talking about the one when we retaliated.

THE CHAIRMAN: That was the 4th. That was the second incident when we sent the sixty missions over Vietnam. Would you summarize it for us?

MR. ELLSBERG: Yes. There have been questions raised whether there was an attack or not, and they still persist.

My predecessor as special assistant to Mr. McNaughton had been due to become Deputy Assistant Secretary at some time later, but they decided they needed an investigation for public relations purposes, in effect, of what had actually happened so quickly, that they swore him in as Deputy Assistant Secretary a little prematurely and rushed him over to the Tonkin Gulf area to interview the people who claimed that they had evidence of an attack and so forth.

THE CHAIRMAN: Who was that?

MR. ELLSBERG: Alvin Friedman.

THE CHAIRMAN: Go ahead.

MR. ELLSBERG: The investigations proceeded and I think mainly concluded that there *probably* was an attack, or as sometimes put, there almost surely was an attack of some sort, or a pass at any rate. There were boats out there and they made threatening passes, at least at the ships, and may have fired 50 caliber, possibly even a torpedo.[11]

One thing I do remember very vividly, though, from the day which has been reported already to your Committee. I was reading the cables, which had a very dramatic quality, "five torpedoes have just gone by," then "the count is now 11, 14," I think it got up to over 20 torpedoes which had been fired. One imagined a sea full of torpedoes, and finally this famous cable came back which has been made public, I believe, that said in effect, "Hold everything. Apparently we have been getting sonar echoes of our own wake, and radar echoes, and it is possible that there have been no torpedoes or perhaps not more than one."

The commander on the spot——

THE CHAIRMAN: Was that Commander Herrick?

MR. ELLSBERG: I have forgotten his name, sir. You can well imagine that I remember this incident very vividly, but not all the details, the names.

That did slow them up a bit at Washington for the moment. They looked for a bit more reassurance and thought they had found it.

What emerges very clearly in retrospect is not, I think, that the decision was taken upon information that was in fact totally false, but that it was taken upon information about which enormous doubts were present, or should have been recognized, at

---

[11] So I believed myself, from August, 1964, until 1971, when I read the closing chapter of Anthony Austin's *tour de force* of investigative reporting and induction, *The President's War* (New York, 1971). Clinching a tightly reasoned analysis with new evidence he had turned up, Austin totally reversed the odds in my own mind: I am now persuaded that the alleged second North Vietnamese attack—to which we "retaliated"—almost surely did not occur. (I still believe that Secretary McNamara mistakenly concluded that it had, having arrived at this conclusion by evidence whose inadequacy and contradictions he concealed in his testimony to Congress, along with his own earlier doubts.)

The passage on this episode in the Pentagon Papers (*PP*, II, 183-90) is one of the weakest in the entire study. It happened to have been drafted in the spring of 1968, during the very period that McNamara was testifying about the Tonkin Bay incident for the second time before the Fulbright Committee. The author was an officer on active duty, who demonstrated independence and perceptiveness elsewhere in his account of the 1964 decisions; but he prudently followed the Secretary's misleading testimony in discussing the Tonkin Bay incident.

the time. In fact the degree of certainty whicn the decision-
makers later attained reflected to a large degree evidence that
came in later, after the reprisal had actually been made. So there
can be no question, I think, that the incident revealed more than
a readiness, a strong eagerness, to take that particular move. And
I think that was related really to two things. One was this feeling
that had been growing ever since the start of 1964, or before I
became involved, that nothing would really achieve our objectives in Vietnam unless North Vietnam could be induced to
turn off the war.

That was often put in terms of supplies, but that was a
euphemism. That last word itself is a euphemism. It was a deception because it was known that the supplies were not critical.
What was really wanted was for North Vietnam to exercise its
degree of coercive power, its control, its authority, over the
branch of the Lao Dong Party in South Vietnam to *call off* the
war and that was believed feasible—by our military and civilian
policy advisers, though not by civilian intelligence analysts—if
we brought military pressure to bear directly on Vietnam.[12] This
is a long story and I won't go into it now.

---

[12] This significant point has not, I believe, been brought out elsewhere. It was
much more present in the minds and discussions of officials in Washington in
1964-65 than is evident from the Pentagon Papers. But note the following statements (italics added):

Assistant Secretary of Defense McNaughton, November 6, 1964—"Action
against North Vietnam is to some extent a substitute for strengthening the
government in South Vietnam. That is, a less active VC (*on orders from DRV*)
can be matched by a less efficient GVN. We therefore should consider squeezing
North Vietnam" (*PP*, III, 599; also see page 603).

William Bundy/McNaughton, November 26, 1964: "Increased U.S. pressures on
North Vietnam would be effective only if they persuaded Hanoi that the price
of maintaining the insurrection in the South would be too great and that it
would be preferable to reduce its aid to the Viet Cong and *direct* at least a
temporary reduction of Viet Cong activity" (*PP*, III, 657).

Most significantly of all, General Taylor, November 27, 1964: "To change the
situation, it is quite clear that we need to do three things: first, establish an
adequate government in SVN; second, improve the conduct of the counterinsurgency campaign; and, finally, persuade or force the DRV to stop its aid to
the Viet Cong and *to use its directive powers to make the Viet Cong desist* from
their efforts to overthrow the government of South Vietnam. . . . In any case,
we feel sure that even after establishing some reasonably satisfactory government and effecting some improvement in the counterinsurgency program, we
will not succeed in the end unless we drive the DRV out of its reinforcing role
and *obtain its cooperation in bringing an end to the Viet Cong insurgency*"
(*PP*, III, 668-69).

THE CHAIRMAN: That was not the official story they gave us in presenting the Tonkin Gulf resolution. The excuse was that this is the way to avoid a war. It wasn't to enlarge it. The whole purpose as they presented it was to do this and then North Vietnam would be induced to call off the war. That was the official line in our own record.

MR. ELLSBERG: I am making a small technical distinction. I think that our officials believed that Hanoi controlled the war.

THE CHAIRMAN: That is right.

MR. ELLSBERG: They did not, however, have conclusive evidence that that was the case. They believed it; they believed the evidence they did have. Moreover some of the evidence which they felt was very critical was of an intelligence nature that they could not reveal to the public. Therefore, they had to talk about a kind of physical support rather than control and to describe it as being quite critical, knowing in fact from our own intelligence estimates that it could not honestly be regarded as critical. In other words, they could talk about supplies, which one could photograph, and infiltrators, which one could capture and interview, small as that might be in terms of the war, rather than talk about the intangible problem which they thought was really critical, the messages from Hanoi that actually controlled the war, and the messages that could call the VC off.

I mention this because it did involve the Administration later in considerably exaggerating the importance of the physical process of sending men and matériel down, and I might say that exaggeration was one I was later involved in.

One part that I played in the onset of the Rolling Thunder bombing campaign was to help prepare the White Paper that the State Department officially put out talking about this matter. . . .

THE CHAIRMAN: [Concluding a discussion of a classified study of the Tonkin Gulf incident] This classification of historical incidents is a dubious classification. Anything that might be embarrassing to a political leader is classified. He doesn't have the right to classify. I think there should be some reasonable limits to the right of classification. It should have some relation to the security of our country and the immediate security of our forces or even to the security of an intelligence-gathering agency. We all recognize that. But here is a study made at Government expense, paid for by the taxpayers, and withheld from the Committee. I don't see any justification for such classification.

MR. ELLSBERG: It is important that such few attempts at learning from our experiences should be exploited, be understood by those people who are involved in decision-making.

I would wish, first of all, that President Nixon could have access to the information in that study and in other studies that were done directly for Mr. McNamara of our involvement. I would doubt very much whether anyone on the National Security Council staff has taken advantage of those.

You asked earlier, how could we ignore this evidence of the past? The sad thing that we are seeing now, I think, is that Republicans are not able to learn from Democrats any more than Democrats learned from the French.

THE CHAIRMAN: In reiteration of what was said in the beginning, it seems to me the function of the Committee to a great extent is the giving of information to the public. This study would be valuable in judging how responsible are the decisions now made to go into Cambodia, for example, which are very current. How the decision was made in that instance has a relationship to how they are made today or maybe made tomorrow to go into Laos. Who knows?

I think if we are to have any real function in giving the public information on which they can make up their minds as to the wisdom of our public policies that involve the lives of our people, we ought to know it.

I can't subscribe to this extension of the concept of classification to prevent our knowing about the past. It is difficult enough to make a judgment on it with information. Without it, it is impossible. It doesn't give democracy an opportunity to function at all. If you don't have the information, that is what it comes down to.

You were talking about these torpedoes. This is a sidelight. Subsequently we captured a commander in the patrol navy of North Vietnam. His evidence disclosed that those particular boats called Swatows didn't even carry torpedoes, but were simply little patrol boats carrying 50-caliber machine guns. They were not capable of carrying torpedoes in the first place.

The first attack was by other boats, many of which were destroyed. In this second case the commander who was captured sometime later said there had been no attack at all. He testified clearly and consistently to what we alleged happened on the 2nd of August, but he said there wasn't any attack on August 4th.[13] This came out much later and is of historical interest. It didn't have any impact then, but it is a very curious incident in a very tragic involvement that perhaps we could learn something from for the future.

In any case, I am very interested in it.

Did you have anything to do in your capacity there with what was called the 34A operation, covert operations? Is that within your knowledge or was that entirely intelligence?

MR. ELLSBERG: That was within my knowledge although I didn't —I didn't play a real role in it.[14]

THE CHAIRMAN: It wasn't too important, but it was one of the incidents. The question arose whether the ships were manned by South Vietnamese and whether we were involved in the operation.

MR. ELLSBERG: I'm sorry . . .

THE CHAIRMAN: Did you know about that? Were the ships that carried on the 34A operations the ones harassing the shoreline of North Vietnam, which in the context of the whole operation

[13] See Austin, *The President's War*, pages 339-40.
[14] One of my regular tasks in the fall of 1964 was to carry—accompanied by a JCS briefing officer—the schedule of planned covert operations against the North (34A operations), to be approved by Llewellyn Thompson in State and McGeorge Bundy in the White House. (See *PP*, III, 571; also, pages 106-81.)

clearly had made the North Vietnamese apprehensive about our objectives?

I think that may be too involved. Rather than go into it now, I would like to ask you to supply for us at your leisure, if you would, your comments upon that which we could make a part of the record. Have you seen the report of the Committee on the whole incident?

MR. ELLSBERG: Yes, some time ago; yes, sir.

THE CHAIRMAN: You could perhaps fill in some gaps in it for the purpose of studying how our Government operates in crises such as this.

MR. ELLSBERG: There was an interesting contrast between that situation and the present one. For some months [in 1964] they had been thinking of trying to get a resolution out of Congress—I suppose you are aware of this part of it as it bears on your own role—and in fact had really given up at a certain point trying to get one. In fact, a matter of days or weeks before the incident they had decided not to press the draft resolution upon Congress, that it just wouldn't go down, particularly in the middle of the election campaign.

The Tonkin Gulf incident then presented itself as an occasion for getting quick passage of such a resolution. The effect was that the Administration then at least paid Congress the respect, in effect, of manipulating, or tricking, or misleading Congress in such a way as to get a blank check which it felt it needed from Congress in order later to escalate. The disturbing difference in this situation is that the Cambodian action seems to have been taken without even bothering to get a blank check. Whether they would have had as much success if they had tried, I would like to think not——

THE CHAIRMAN: They don't even deign to deceive us now. (*Laughter.*)

In a sense I think we were [deceived]. We had an executive hearing purportedly to discuss a request by the Cambodian Government for assistance. The decision to invade was already under consideration and preparation had been made. Not having known of that decision, we didn't ask specific questions, but I think under the circumstances if the Administration had any respect for the Congress' views or its participation, they would have volunteered the information that they were considering it or had made the decision. While it wasn't an overt and obvious deception such as the testimony of the Secretary of Defense on the Tonkin Gulf incident, it was a failure to say what they had in mind and their intentions under circumstances, where if there were any respect for the Committee and the Senate they would have volunteered the information. I think it is fair to say that because the hearing on the Cambodian request for aid took place only two days before the first move into Cambodia. It is inconceivable that that kind of an operation can be made without at least two days of preparation.

This is an endlessly interesting subject. All I can say is that you gentlemen have made a great contribution to the enlightenment of the Committee and to some extent, I hope, the people. We all have a great interest in how our Government operates. We all have a great interest in seeing it play a proper role and a role of which we can be proud.

I wanted to recommend to you one passage in testimony that we had a few days ago, about the moral problem of justifying the deaths of 40,000 Americans in this war. I think Rabbi Greenberg offered one of the most succinct and persuasive justifications, if I may use that word, that I have seen. He dealt with it in a way that it seemed to me would appeal to all of the mothers and fathers of the men who had been lost or been wounded. Dependent upon the policies of this Government from here on, we could make it very justifiable if we could learn the lesson of this war. The parents of these people and the people as a whole could consider this to have been a very worthwhile contribution if it results in a more humane and a more understanding role on the part of this country. It is possible; it is hopeful; we still hope for it.

I think that was the principal objective of many of my colleagues who were pressing for these various methods to try to bring the war to a close. They are quite varied now. . . .

I thank you both. I know it is a great effort to come and answer questions over a long period and rake these things over. It is a very unpleasant duty to ever raise questions about the wisdom of one's own Government, but I don't know how a democracy is supposed to operate if we don't. It seems to me it is an essential element in trying to make a democratic system function.

Do you wish to say anything further, Mr. Ellsberg?

MR. ELLSBERG: I do think of one thing. You have brought up the Tonkin Gulf incident. I was very startled in reading the record of your last hearings, when you were questioning someone or other and you made the remark, Senator Fulbright, that you felt "shame" for your part in that operation of getting the Congressional resolution.

THE CHAIRMAN: Yes.

MR. ELLSBERG: That word leaped out at me because I had not remembered seeing an American official use such a word or in any way imply a sense of personal responsibility to that degree. It is almost un-American to do so, it would seem. There were many people involved in that incident, but you are the only one I have heard admit responsibility and regret. I think your word seems appropriate for you in your position, and I think you have done a service for the Senate in the eyes of the college students and of the older people of this country, as they look at people who like to think of themselves as the Establishment or the power-holders, the decision-makers, in having the courage and the character to acknowledge that publicly. I think that helps.

I regret, on the other hand, that the people who were involved at that same point in misleading you and getting us deeper into the war have unfortunately not been heard from, not even to say "I was wrong" let alone to say that they feel any degree of shame for their role in this. I think the reason that is vitally needed if we are to get ourselves out of this crisis of national self-confidence is that the voters of the country and the youth of this country, everyone, must hear statements from their leadership that imply that those leaders have a sense of personal values and of personal responsibility and are capable of acknowledging it.

The political consequences of refraining from that, of refraining from the indignities of "mea culpas" and post mortems and so forth, are that the lessons of history remain clouded, remain unreadable, and that the current President is put ever more in the position of bearing the whole responsibility for terminating the involvement.

Now he chose to do that, unfortunately, by not even trying to share the responsibilities with Congress on this occasion, but the less he shares it and the more he feels himself that all humiliation and shame for what happens in Vietnam after we leave will accrue only to him, the more we are condemned to this war so long as he is in office. So I feel that it is really important that other people who shared in that decision-making, as I did in a very minor way, but especially the people like McNamara and Rusk and Bundy and the others, be prepared to say, as I hoped they would say before the President took up the standard of Nixon's war last November: "It is not your war. Don't make it your war. It is our war. We made the decisions and the lies and fatal mistakes that got us into this war and kept us in and made it larger. Don't make the same mistakes. Get us out."

I am afraid it is because they have not yet been willing to say that that we find our President and our Executive branch in fact repeating those mistakes today.

THE CHAIRMAN: Since you mentioned it, I have felt very badly about that. I should have had much greater skepticism, of course, but at the time I had no reason whatever to believe that it wasn't just as they represented it.

The study that the Committee made was long after the fact. What I should have done was delayed and held hearings on the Tonkin Gulf resolution and done what we are trying to do now, which is to examine these actions before the fact if we can. I am bound to say, however, that even now in the hearings two days before the Cambodian invasion, we did not receive any reasonable notice of it. Therefore, we were prevented from having any reasonable opportunity to express an opinion prior to the fact.

As a matter of fact, only incidentally but not because they knew it was impending, a number of Senators, specifically people like Senators Cooper and Church and some of those who had been involved in the previous effort to put a restriction on enlarging the war into Laos, had this very much on their minds. But not having any notice whatever that we were going into Cambodia, they had no opportunity to express themselves. This is what I meant by subverting the democratic process.

I should have been more skeptical simply because, well, I always wish I were wiser than I am and that I could have foreseen that it hadn't happened that way. As I look back I had no reason to do it, but still I think as chairman I should have said, "Well, wait a minute." The Gulf of Tonkin resolution passed the House unanimously and it came over, and their greatest plea was that it must be done immediately in order to deter the North Vietnamese from any further actions. To get the full effect we must show unity of purpose and determination, and it would look unpatriotic not to follow the President's recommendation as conveyed in that resolution. At the time it looked that way.

All I say is that I should have been wiser. I should have said, "No, I will have the hearing; I will not allow it to be voted." It is possible that it would have happened, although there were only two dissenting votes in the Senate. Anyway that is history.

I hope we are doing better. At least we are not falling in line like sitting ducks as we did then and we are trying to make an effort to inform the Senate and the public before we get deeper and deeper into greater difficulties. Whether we have any success or not remains for history to prove, but you gentlemen have made a great contribution in my opinion.

I can't emphasize more the importance of understanding how we became involved. It does relate to the conviction on the part of my colleagues and members of the public as to what we should do now. I think it is very important. If we don't have any feel about the justification of the war, how can we have any feel about ending it? If you accept the rhetoric that this is a holy war, why then there is no excuse for urging the President to end it. We ought to go through with it: If you accept some of the basic assumptions, it ought to be pursued to the end. But I don't know any responsible people who wish it.

The most difficult thing, as Senator Javits said, is that rhetoric is one way and the action is the other, and it is always difficult to come to grips with the essential question. You are always in a position of appearing to think the leaders are not telling the truth. This is a rather objectionable position to be in before the American public.

They resent the suggestion that they are being hornswoggled, as they say in the country. Therefore, it destroys your own credibility when you question it.

It is extremely difficult to come to grips with the essential elements involved in this war.

BOMBING AND
OTHER CRIMES

"The solution in Vietnam is more bombs, more shells, more napalm . . . till the other side cracks and gives up."—Brigadier General William C. DePuy, Commanding General, U.S. 1st Division, Lai Khe, January 13, 1967

In mid-January, 1967, Brigadier General DePuy, who was about to leave command of the U.S. 1st Division to return to Washington, invited me to lunch at his tent headquarters at Lai Khe in III Corps, the Corps area surrounding Saigon. As chief planner for General West-moreland before taking command of the Big Red One, DePuy was one of the most experienced officers in Vietnam, and one of the most responsible for the shape and implementation of our military policies there, including the very presence of U.S. combat units, which he had been instrumental in promoting in 1964-65. Since he was now to become the Special Assistant to the Chairman of the JCS for Special Activities—i.e., counterinsurgency and covert operations—the views he would be taking back from his field experience in III Corps seemed of special interest. I passed them on to my boss, Deputy Ambassador William Porter, then in charge of all civil operations in Vietnam.

My notes began with DePuy's remark above, which he had expressed like a slogan. I went on quoting DePuy, as follows:

We're making life unpleasant for the VC . . . at least I think we are. Finally, they'll say "Ho, we're smarter than they are—" [side comment by DePuy: "I don't have much faith in our brainpower, only in our firepower"]—"our cause is more just . . . but enough is enough. Let's lie low for a few years and get the U.S. to go home."

We're winning the war. We're killing VC, guerrillas, Main Forces, destroying their bases, destroying caches of food and weapons, we're getting more Chieu Hoi [defectors]. If people in Washington want to win fast—if they're in a hurry, because of elections or something—they could move five more divisions over here and get the job done faster. But if they're not in such a hurry, we can do the job with what we've got, i.e., including the 9th Division.

Pacification hasn't worked anywhere. But the 1st Division is doing one thing: killing guerrillas.

We have long-range programs now to destroy the Phu Loi Battalion. In general, to get the VC provincial battalions: keep probing, searching, harassing the areas where they take their leave, training, and rest, their bases. Keep bombing their base areas: we need a sensor that would signal to us when someone had entered that area, so we could bomb it.

You need fast reaction to contact: with air strikes. Even against a squad, or snipers, I'd use an air strike; artillery is no good when they have overhead cover.

DePuy undoubtedly practiced what he preached. As a former small-unit infantry officer, I was especially struck, as I observed in my memo, that:

Even in discussing tactics against small sniper bands in populated areas, he never referred to aggressive, small-unit ground action. A high U.S. official [John Paul Vann], who passed a day recently with DePuy in his command chopper, reported that they spent two hours raking a small grove, which several VC had been seen to enter, with their .50-caliber MG's, returning several times for more ammo, although there was a battalion from the 1st Division in the immediate vicinity with one platoon only a few hundred yards away, never ordered in by DePuy. This official contrasted DePuy's caution (almost "ARVN-like") about risking U.S. casualties in ground action —relying almost entirely upon heavy firepower rather than close combat— with DePuy's *personal* aggressiveness and courage. (He does sack commanders on the spot; and he monitors the radio set in his chopper and heads immediately toward contact: a new way of commanding a division in combat. DePuy invited me to spend a day with him in his chopper, confirming that he likes to fly at fifty feet or under—"you can't see anything at fifteen hundred"—and commenting that he estimates his chopper has been hit "forty or fifty times.")

As I reread these notes in 1972, I am struck by the correspondence of this peculiarly "American way of war" on the tactical level to the grand strategy of the Nixon Doctrine and "Vietnamization." Both are designed to economize on American infantry casualties; the strategy simply goes one step further, using local or hired troops, rather than Americans, as live bait to attract targets for air and artillery. Whether as field tactic or foreign policy, our way of war now relies on the use of indiscriminate American artillery and airpower that generates innumerable My Lai's as a norm, not as a shocking exceptional case.

My memo went on, "If such an approach is used in the Delta"— and strategically speaking, much of Asia, the area of application of the Nixon Doctrine, is one large Delta—"it will be hard to avoid large civilian casualties."

When I wrote this memo, I had just returned from ten days of combat observation with an American unit in the Delta. (See the following account, in "War Crimes and My Lai," of incidents in Rach Kien, Long An Province.) My remarks reflected the concern of Ambassador Lodge and Deputy Ambassador Porter about the prospective effects of American troops and firepower in the most densely populated areas of South Vietnam. As in IV Corps to the south, the southern border region of III Corps from which I had just returned was so thickly settled, except for the flooded rice paddies, that a helicopter could scarcely set down on dry land without literally blowing away sections of thatched roofing of huts. Those huts were filled with women and children; some of them, too, were sure to be "blown away" if the choppers used their rockets or machine guns or called in heavier firepower near those homes, i.e., anywhere in the vicinity of treelines, canals, or dry land.

During one "sweep" operation in this area, Horst Faas and Peter Arnett, the two most experienced combat reporters in Vietnam, walked with me part of the day. Though the battalion we were with was not from the 1st Division, DePuy's name kept coming up. As we took hostile fire, Faas said: "DePuy would be flying over here himself right now: about fifty feet above the ground." When artillery, called in against a squad of snipers, was slow in arriving, Arnett said, "DePuy would have sacked the artillery commander on the spot." And when various reports came in of VC in thickets or hamlets in the area, one of them commented: "DePuy would have blanketed this place with artillery and bombs, Delta or not."

Now I asked DePuy himself, "Would you use the same tactics in the Delta?" He thought for a moment, then answered:

It's true that in the Delta, you have more population in the area than we usually have in our TAOR; even so, I'd use an air strike, but first I'd send over planes with loudspeakers and leaflets telling the people to get out in the middle of the open fields within five minutes (where I'd pick all of them up, for interrogation), then hit the place. If the VC wouldn't let them leave . . . that wouldn't make the VC too popular.

As I said before: what you need is more bombs, more shells, more napalm. . . .

DePuy left Vietnam shortly afterward, but his tactical principles did not. Brigadier General Julian Ewell, commanding the 9th Division in the Delta, so completely freed his helicopter gunners from restraints against firing on sampans in canals lined on both sides with housing that the Division reported body-count ratios of "friendly" to "enemy" dead unmatched in the history of the war, or perhaps in any war. The count of captured enemy weapons accompanying these "enemy kills" was—as at My Lai—strikingly low, in fact negligible, and the provincial hospitals overflowed with civilian wounded, which were never reported in the Division statistics or in the weekly accounting given to the home audiences on TV. Ewell got another star, and was later assigned to the negotiating team in Paris.

THE AMERICAN WAY OF WAR

Rand's contract with the Department of Defense provided that any public statement or writing of an employee that related to his area of government-supported research must be submitted in advance for review by the Department, not only for "security" (i.e., disclosure of classified information) but for "policy" acceptability. (In other words, any speech, article, or book by an official or an employee of a "think-tank" like Rand has been approved as acceptable—line by line—by a Government censor, though this guarantee of "acceptability" is nowhere stamped on the product; it can never be presumed that the text appears as the author originally wrote it, or as he might have written it if it had not been subject to review-censorship. The usual indication of "policy" problems would not be specific complaints or demands for deletion but extremely long delays in "clearance.")

An exception to this requirement for advance approval was spontaneous comments in a seminar discussion, or a transcript of such remarks. The following comment is from such a discussion, a seminar on "Lessons of Vietnam" at the Adlai Stevenson Institute, Chicago, Illinois, in early June, 1968; the transcript of the seminar was subsequently edited by Richard M. Pfeffer and published under the title *No More Vietnams* (New York, 1968). I was responding to a point made by Theodore Draper at the conference; footnotes have been added.

This particular comment of mine was not widely admired back at Rand, which had always derived most of its research funds from the U.S. Air Force. It was made shortly after the U.S. Air Force had destroyed large parts of Hué and Saigon, and the Delta towns of Can Tho and Ben Tre. Ben Tre was the province capital of Kien Hoa Province, of which my friend Tran Ngoc Chau had been the province chief when I first met him in 1965, and which he represented at this time in the National Assembly. It was the town that "had to be destroyed in order to be saved."

Theodore Draper commented as follows:

"Massive retaliation," that monstrous doctrine of the 1950's, saved us from large-scale intervention in Vietnam in 1954. But its successor, variously known as "limited war," "graduated response," or "flexible response," did not save us from increasingly large-scale intervention in Vietnam since 1961 and especially since 1965. In fact, I think the doctrine of "limited war" as it was worked out in the latter half of the 1950's outside the Government and taken over by the Government in the 1960's must be held partially responsible for pulling us in.

I do not really agree that it was the theory of limited war that encouraged Americans to favor our Vietnam decisions in the 1960's.[1] I think it was something else, some attitudes and expectations associated with the American way of war.

Specifically, there has been in the U.S. since the Second World War a widespread belief in the efficacy and acceptability of aerial bombing, and in particular of bombing of a strategic nature, aimed at the will of the opponent via his industrial and population resources. This belief played a critical, if not decisive, role in getting us into Vietnam, in reassuring us, in giving us confidence to stay in, and then in stimulating escalation while keeping us reassured as to ultimate success.

In 1961, the group of men most in favor of an enlarged intervention, including the sending of ground troops, was headed by Maxwell Taylor and Walt Rostow. These two pointed, as early as 1961, to the essential problem of stopping infiltration. They took the point of view, rightly or wrongly, that the problem in the South would be insoluble until we were able to stop infiltration from the North, not as it was then but as it could become.

It was clearly stated by them that we must go in with the recognition, especially if we were successful in the early stages, that we could anticipate a high level of infiltration, which some-

[1] I have changed my mind on Draper's point; I now think it has a good deal of substance, though the influence of limited-war doctrines on the decisions of civilian policy-makers was not simple—it involved, to a large extent, their battle with military advisers over the need to rely on nuclear weapons. This subject is not discussed in this book, except for some comments in the final essay, pages 292-93.

how would have to be stopped. These people, both privately and publicly, indicated there was only one effective way to stop infiltration—that, of course, was through bombing.

Thus, their recommendation for expanded U.S. involvement in Vietnam rested on the implicit assumptions that bombing would be used against the North when—as was likely—it became necessary, and that it would be effective.[2] Kennedy may or may not have accepted this reasoning or conclusion; the record is not clear. However, given attitudes within the defense bureaucracy and the larger American public, it would have been difficult, even for the President, explicitly to reject this "solution" in advance. Really, no other proposal was ever seriously made for dealing with that essential problem.

In 1965—when we felt ourselves in trouble in Vietnam in a number of ways, especially with regard to the need to demonstrate our commitment—Johnson was not prepared immediately to send troops; but one thing that came easy to an American President was a demonstration by bombing. In other ways as well, bombing was the natural solution to our problems; it was the key ingredient in our policy that was going, one way or another, to make everything turn out all right. And in 1966 and 1967, despite disappointments, these same hopes persisted and sustained our continued and expanded involvement.

Recently, a former Ambassador to the United States from Vietnam [Vu Van Thai] has expressed a plea that, despite his deep pessimism about the prospects today in Vietnam, we should not precipitously withdraw. He said he was against our immediate withdrawal even though he believed life under the Communists would be better than the continuation of this war: which since 1965—not since 1961 or 1964, but since the bombings of 1965 in South Vietnam and since we came in there with our troops—has begun to demolish his society, to turn it into "a vast zoo," a vast refugee camp. Despite this belief, the Ambassador could not be for ending the war at the cost of a quick and total Communist victory, because he felt that would encourage the North Vietnamese to be doing things in Thailand within five years which *would cause us then to destroy Vietnam totally.*

[2] See *PP*, II, 73-120, especially 97-98.

The calling in of Americans and our subsequent bombing in North and South Vietnam has not brought success; hence the bombing and shelling in the South has gone on long enough to disrupt the society of South Vietnam enormously, and probably permanently. In general, if local governments who call for American aid are in other respects acting effectively, then any bombing we may do need not last very long, and the resulting damage will not be permanent. But if these governments face a strong enemy who can frustrate them and the U.S. and prolong the war, then the damage done by American bombs and artillery can be irrevocable.

We are talking here about lessons for us to learn about ourselves, and lessons for *others*—including those who might ask our aid in the future—to learn about us, from our experience in Vietnam and elsewhere.

The lesson which can be drawn here is one the rest of the world, I am sure, has drawn more quickly than Americans have: that, to paraphrase H. Rap Brown, *bombing is as American as cherry pie.* If you invite us in to do your hard fighting for you, then you get bombing and heavy shelling along with our troops.

Many of us in Vietnam believed that we were there because we should win, and that we could win, though not by the methods we had been using. "Of course, I am against the kind of bombing we are doing"—I can hear myself, with others, saying this hundreds and hundreds of times.

I protected myself, I am afraid, from perceiving what should have been easily foreseeable—especially easy were I not American and terribly reluctant to realize it—namely, that if you bring in Americans like me, as part of a heavy U.S. *combat* involvement, you are going to get both strategic and widespread tactical bombing and heavy use of artillery[3] along with us, no matter how critical these particular individuals may be of it.

If you ask what will happen in Thailand if we go in militarily and have to face prolonged opposition, the answer is bombing and shelling.

[3] Along with the six million tons of bombs we have dropped on Indochina, we have expended six million tons of artillery shells since 1965 (aside from the shells we supplied to the ARVN and the Koreans, who use unobserved, indiscriminate "Harassment and Interdiction" shelling lavishly).

If you ask what would have happened if the Dominican Republic had chosen to oppose us, the answer is that the Dominican Republic probably would have been heavily bombed.[4]

Indeed, a most ominous lesson is there to be drawn by the people of nations whose leaders might call for U.S. military support: that such a plea—if the national leader knew that the conflict would be long and the U.S. military commitment great—could amount to an act of treachery against his society.

[4] One senior Rand colleague—who has done research in South Vietnam, Laos, Thailand, and the Dominican Republic—recalled these propositions two years later. At the time they were made, he had told me he thought them overdrawn and unwarranted; after watching what happened in the months after our invasion of Cambodia, he called me to say he had had to change his position.

WAR CRIMES AND MY LAI

The Congressional Conference on War and National Responsibility convened in Washington early in 1970. The ten Congressional sponsors and, at their invitation, a group of leading American scholars, jurists, and public figures assembled at the Capitol for two days of intensive deliberation. The following excerpts from the edited transcript of the proceedings have been published under the title *War Crimes and the American Conscience*.[5] These were my oral comments in the discussion and reflected, of course, remarks of other participants; footnotes have been added.

The doctrine that certain military activities [may be criminal only] when they are carried out by only one side has very interesting implications.[6] In Vietnam we have unique possession of air weapons and such measures as defoliation and herbicides, as well as almost exclusive use of many kinds of arms, vehicles, helicopters, and so forth.

Actually, however, the guiding practice of past war crimes prosecutions has been that crime is something that can only be charged against a loser. Perhaps this explains why successive Presidents have felt so intensely anxious not to lose their war in Vietnam. But whatever happens in Vietnam and whatever it is called—defeat or victory—does not change many important realities in the world. It does not change the power of the United States and it does not change the ability of our American President to avoid being put in the dock by any other nation.

It is also a reality, I think, that no American President will look upon himself as a possible perpetrator of war crimes. It could not occur to him, it could not occur to the American people—

[5] *War Crimes and the American Conscience,* ed. Erwin Knoll and Judith Nies McFadden (New York, 1970).
[6] This comment responds to a point by Telford Taylor that presumptively illegal activities that had been carried out by *both* sides in World War II—in particular, strategic bombing—were not prosecuted by the Allies at Nuremberg.

except to the young—that war crimes are something that can be charged to Americans.

I have misgivings about the use of the word "genocide" in the context of the Vietnam war as it has been conducted up to this point.[7] It may, indeed, be applicable, in a strict sense, to some of our activities in Vietnam, in particular the designation of large, semi-permanent, free-fire zones. Other activities, such as the massive generation of refugees, both deliberate and inadvertent, might warrant the term "sociocide," the violent destruction of a patterned society; still others, the term "ecocide" that has just been introduced [by Arthur Galston].

Nevertheless, an indiscriminate use of such terms can blur potentially important distinctions about levels of destructiveness. An escalation of rhetoric can blind us to the fact that Vietnam is not only no more brutal than other wars in the past—and it is absurdly unhistorical to insist that it is—but that the Vietnam War is not as bad as other wars that we may have in the near future. And it is not as bad as it could still become. We must remain able to recognize the possibility of the occurrence of such increases in violence and risk, if we are to act to deter them or reverse them.

Thus, I suspect that because critics of the war in 1966 and 1967 tended to exaggerate the effect of the war on the population of Vietnam—as bad as it was then—they failed to discover that in 1968, even after the Tet and May crises, the war became enormously more destructive than it had ever been before. This increase, described to me by participating officials, was a result of changes in our policies that went almost totally unnoticed.

[7] Since these remarks were made, much more has become known about the impact of our bombing in Laos and Cambodia, especially through the efforts of Fred Branfman (for data and reprints, write Project Air War, 1322 18th Street N.W., Washington, D.C. 20036) and of the Air War Study Project of the Center for International Studies, Cornell University, along with the investigations by the Kennedy Subcommittee on Refugees and by Congressman Paul McCloskey in Laos (Truth and Untruth [New York, 1972]). The "generation" of refugees and destruction of rural society by bombing appears to have been more deliberate, and more abrupt and socially devastating in Laos and Cambodia than in Vietnam; see Fred Branfman, "The Era of the Blue Machine, Laos: 1969—," Washington Monthly, July, 1971. Reservations about the strict application of the term "genocide"—as defined by the U.N.—no longer seem justified.

At the time of Tet, with the Vietcong entering the cities for the first time, we dropped the restraints we had previously imposed on the use of helicopter gunships and artillery in populated areas. For a period of several months, almost all of Vietnam became a free-fire zone. Subsequently, the designation of free-fire zones became much more widespread than it had been before. A new generation of helicopter pilots and artillery men came into rural Vietnam beginning in the late spring of 1968, found these new practices that had been instituted because of the back-to-the-wall conditions that surrounded the Tet offensive, and regarded them as normal.

Though the verbal orders have changed somewhat since then, the practices, I am told, have not. Since 1968, the citizens of Vietnam have been under fire in a way that did not apply in 1966 and 1967, although given their flight to the towns and the reduced level of combat, actual casualties are probably less than in 1968. Interrogations of Vietcong prisoners reveal that their greatest miscalculation in launching the Tet offensive was their failure to anticipate the enormous casualties they would sustain. It simply did not occur to them that the United States would be willing to launch firepower as freely as it did in populated areas. The Vietcong felt they would be shielded and protected by the population, but they were not.

In March, 1968, we also came perilously close to a decision that would probably have led to the invasion of North Vietnam. This would have been the likely indirect and ultimate consequence if we had granted the troop increase requested by General William C. Westmoreland. We would then have entered a war incomparably more destructive than anything we have witnessed so far in Vietnam.

The population of South Vietnam has almost surely increased each year in the last five, and the use of the word "genocide" can, therefore, be misleading, even if it is strictly warranted. But if we had invaded North Vietnam and totally unleashed our bombing, the population of neither North Vietnam nor South Vietnam would have increased. In that case, the word "genocide" in its most ominous sense would have come closer to reality.

Finally, if nuclear weapons had been used, as I have been told was contemplated at high levels in connection with the defense of Khe Sanh, a degree of destructiveness incomparably surpassing anything we have yet seen in Vietnam would have come into play.

Without compromising our protest against the Vietnam War as it has actually evolved, we need to maintain reserves of outrage and resistance, and words and perceptions to trigger them, if we are to prevent tragedies still worse.

I see difficulties, too, in the distinctions we draw between the use of high and low technology. My Lai, after all, was not a question of unrestrained use of advanced technology. It was a use of World War I—if not Civil War—weaponry against people. The use of guns, rifles, small arms, stray bullets, the use of grenades, face-to-face killing—that certainly does not rely upon very advanced technology.

There is a tendency to confine the applicability of the war crimes concept just to such crimes of low technology. The concept, after all, dates from a period of low technology, around the time of World War I, and weaponry that has come into use since then has tended to be excluded.

This legal emphasis on low-technology war crimes tends to absolve our use of high-technology weapons—such as B-52's, carrier aircraft, helicopter gunships, CBU bombs—which are our main implements of death, in the Vietnam War specifically. These products are, in fact, regarded very highly by our culture—Western culture in general but, above all, American culture. To condemn the unrestrained use of complex, highly developed technologies is to defy some of our proudest national values. It will be difficult, politically, to extend the notion of "crimes against humanity" to include Anglo-American wartime triumphs of firepower against civilians, as in Dresden, Tokyo, Hiroshima, and now the free-fire zones of South Vietnam. Yet it would be shocking and perverse to condemn only rape and murder in wartime while continuing to tolerate the strategic bombing of noncombatants.

Furthermore, to define atrocities in terms of perpetrators who "looked upon the faces of their victims"—another aspect of current usage—is to say that only those who can see the faces of their victims are, in fact, war criminals. One aspect of such a definition—not, I suspect, a coincidental one—is that it excludes almost everyone above the rank of captain. Only the lowest-ranking soldiers in a war, and not too many of them, ever see the faces of their victims. To depart from that rule—to hold accountable, for instance, the majors who fly in airplanes, let alone the people who command them or who plan their missions—is to lead, of course, to the highest ranks of the military and above that to the highest civilians in the Government. But that, too, is a direction in which we must go. . . .

Who is it that we're talking to? Who is it that we want to hear us? Whose behavior would we like to change? We have raised questions of obedience and responsibility—whose sense of these matters would we like most to affect? Could it be that of soldiers in the field, in the chaos of battle, whose moral choices are made under enormous pressures and under fear of death? This is a worthwhile aim, but it cannot be our main objective, I would think.

The attitudes and behavior I would most like to change are those of my former colleagues in the U.S. Government. I speak not as a researcher but from experience as a former official of the Defense Department and the State Department in Washington and Vietnam—experience that makes me a possible defendant in a future war crimes trial. Some ten years ago I read the transcript of the Nuremberg trials, and that left me with the sense of what an exhibit in a war crimes trial looks like. As I was working in the Department of Defense, I did in some cases have a feeling while reading documents late at night that I was looking at future exhibits. Indeed, if we are to believe published accounts of contingency plans that have been prepared, for example, for war in Central Europe (such as might arise over Berlin), there even exist in locked safes in Washington right now documents that could very aptly be described as plans for escalatory genocide.

Such alleged plans reflect decisions by civilian officials which, I suggest, should be subjected in the future to more conscientious review. It is not unusual for officials to ask, as they draw up such plans: Are these prudent? Are these mistaken? But it is most unusual—almost unknown—for them to ask as well: Does the United States have a right to do such things? And if not, do these officials have a duty to participate or a duty to resist?

A way of causing such questions to be asked in the future is to recognize, protect, reward, and encourage those individuals who might indeed apply such judgments, discuss them with their colleagues, and act on them.

Notice that in the massacre at My Lai and in other such military incidents there were individuals who, despite apparent risk to their lives, did resist the atrocities or at least fail to cooperate. It is a terrible shame—one that I share as a former official—that I know of no civilian official in the Government who has acted comparably in any area of the Vietnam involvement.

Individual acts of initiative and courage cannot, of course, bear the burden of preventing catastrophes like Vietnam. Institutional and political changes are essential. Yet even if these changes do occur, I believe that we cannot avoid much, much worse crimes and horrors than we have seen in the past unless many individuals within the Government do assume greater risks and a greater sense of responsibility than has been shown in the past decade.

Congress should reduce its tolerance of secrecy by the Executive, if only to protect its own need to know the facts. It should act to protect the right of dissent in general and, above all, the right of newspapermen to comment and to report truthfully.

Finally, I would strongly endorse the suggestion that selective conscientious objection be recognized in the draft law. The absence of such legislation has resulted in the imprisonment of young people who have chosen to act more responsibly, more conscientiously, than any other Americans I know.

My Lai

As a peacetime Marine in the 1950's, I was spared the need to confront the possibility that the enemies I was being trained to kill for my country might turn out to be women, children, and babies. I was surrounded then by people who had been in World War II and Korea, and I was trained on war stories of jungle fighting on isolated Pacific islands. These are the myths that have affected the attitudes of this generation of Americans toward violence. Vietnam, of course, has raised questions which this mythic history did not force us to confront—questions about who we are and what we are trying to do and what is permissible to us.

The first point I would like to raise about My Lai is this: If there were no My Lai's, no face-to-face killing of women and children by small arms, would the civilians of South Vietnam really know the difference? As you may have noticed, the South Vietnamese civilians, let alone their leadership, did not really raise much protest about My Lai or even show much interest in it. First of all, they are used to such operations in that area—particularly by Koreans, the allies we brought to Vietnam.

Moreover, it is hard for the South Vietnamese to get very excited about killings committed in that particular way, knowing that nearly all of the enormous number of civilian deaths are caused by high explosives from our planes and artillery. They have come to expect these deaths, the killing of women and children from a distance, as a part of the American way of war.

The question remains, how did this particular face-to-face massacre come about? Is it the nature of this war? Is it inevitable in this sort of war? These questions have all been raised. I would suggest that it is in the nature of this war and to be expected. This is a major reason, I have concluded, that the war in which I participated is one we should not have been fighting. But the cause, I would suggest, is not so much strategic or tactical in any objective sense, but psychological, in terms of the pressures that this war puts on those who participate in it. These pressures lead daily to smaller, unrecorded atrocities, but sooner or later they were likely to produce a My Lai.

The first thing to be mentioned is the frustration to both planners and soldiers of fighting in a war where nothing seems to work, where the rules either don't exist or obviously don't apply, and where they are confronted by impotence and failure day after day. My Lai had to be destroyed not because its occupants posed any threat, but because there was a felt need to destroy some village like it.

I saw that kind of frustration and the effects of it very vividly toward the close of my two years in Vietnam. I saw it develop in a short period—only ten days—in a particular battalion which had been fighting for some months in the jungles of War Zone C where there were no villages. Now the same battalion was exposed to the conditions of the Delta, in Rach Kien district of Long An province, surrounded by villages and surrounded by water —in fact immersed in water constantly, which added to the frustration. The men preferred the dry jungle fighting.

As days went on in which the men were fired at by invisible snipers, losing casualties at a considerable rate but never having the satisfaction of a body to add to their statistics or to give them evidence that they were having an effect, they grew increasingly angry. The only body they encountered in this ten-day period was that of an eighteen-year-old girl killed by a stray artillery shell; she had come from Saigon to spend the day with her parents, and she was cooking for them when their house was hit. (Some AID funds I had with me for such occasions went toward her funeral.)

At this point I took a very odd photograph of a soldier furiously bayoneting a canteen. His lieutenant had just asked for permission to burn an empty house that we had come to and were searching. Because it had this canteen in it and a picture of someone in a uniform that was not familiar to our troops, they assumed it was a Vietcong house and asked for permission to burn it. Permission was denied. There was much swearing and stamping around, and the soldiers took the offending canteen and punched it full of holes. Their desire to burn the house was in part the result of frustration and in part reflected the fact that they honestly didn't know what might work. They had the feeling that at least if they burned the houses, something would happen; their presence would have been marked. Perhaps the Vietcong would be discouraged from operating in that area, though there were many houses, thousands in the area, and unless you burned them all, the Vietcong would still have shelter.

A week later I was on a patrol that burned every house it came to. I assumed the orders had been changed. When I returned to the battalion headquarters, I asked the operations officer why he had changed orders, but he denied they had been changed. I said, "You can see the smoke over there, can't you?" Pillars of smoke were rising. He replied, "Sure, I see that smoke. I called the company commander and asked him what the smoke was and he said they were burning the thatch off bunkers." I said, "They were burning every house they came to." He said he would do something about it. Within ten days this battalion had moved to a state of mind where lieutenants and captains were burning houses in violation of higher orders and lying about it.

The understanding of My Lai has been distorted in some accounts I have read by the suggestion that something like this probably happens all the time. This may be true, on a smaller scale, of the Koreans, but is not really quite true of our troops. My Lai was beyond the bounds of permissible behavior, and that is recognizable by virtually every soldier in Vietnam. They know it was wrong: No shots had been fired at the soldiers, no enemy troops were in the village, nobody was armed. The men who were at My Lai knew there were aspects out of the ordinary. That is why they tried to hide the event, talked about it to no one, discussed it very little even among themselves.

But if My Lai was still exceptional, it was separated only by a very fine distinction from incidents that occur regularly and that are regarded as permissible. A few shots from the village, a few uniforms found in a hut, a measure of resistance, would have removed any question about what happened at My Lai. We operate on the principle that any action is permissible against an "enemy"—even if he is a thirteen-year-old boy who is carrying a rifle—or even, when we come to strategic bombing, against anyone whose death might inconvenience a foe.

I am reminded of the occasion of my first sight of an alleged enemy in Vietnam. I was flying over the Plain of Reeds with a pilot who had a deserved reputation for daring and acuity; he could spot foxholes and bunkers and what-not from a great height, long before I would have seen them. At one point in the flight he told me over the intercom, "There is a VC down there." At his suggestion, I had brought a weapon with me, in case we were shot down. As soon as he spoke, I drew my pistol. He pulled out his M-16 rifle and went into a dive. I looked down and saw two men in black pajamas on the ground, apparently running away from a boat nearby. I noticed that they were not armed, and mentioned this to the pilot. He said he assumed they had left their weapons in the boat. He came down again, firing the M-16 from the moving plane at fairly close range, fifty to one hundred feet. This maneuver we repeated for the next twelve or fourteen minutes. While we were coming down at the men, they would lie on the ground; when we moved off, they would get up and run. We would come down again, dive at them, and fire the rifle. Finally he pulled off, without hitting them, and I asked, "Does this happen often?" "All the time," he said. "Do you ever hit anyone in this way?" I asked, and he replied, "Not very often. It's hard to hit anybody from a plane with an M-16, but it scares the shit out of them. They will be pretty scared VC tonight."[8]

I asked him how he knew they were VC, and he answered, "There's nothing but VC in the Plain of Reeds." The Plain of Reeds was a free-fire zone, which meant we had condemned to death all those who might be found in it. I was later told that there were almost two thousand fishermen in the area who continued to fish during our attacks.

This game, this hunt, is something that goes on daily in almost every province of Vietnam. I am sure the Vietcong will come out of this war with great pride in the fact that they confronted American machines and survived. I came out of that plane ride with a strong sense of unease.

[8] As the plane dove and swung about in tight loops centered on the running men below, I relived the feelings of herding stray cattle with a pickup truck on the plains of Wyoming, twenty years earlier. Senator George McGovern brought back both memories, unnervingly, in a conversation we had during the spring of 1971. He told me that he had gone to the White House to raise doubts, as a former bombardier, about our bombing in North Vietnam, soon after it began. Apparently to demonstrate his own skepticism about military claims and values, President Johnson had assured him, irrelevantly, that he controlled all designations of targets himself. Then he said, "Anyway, there's lot of things the military could be doing that they don't even think about. For instance, I tell them how we hunt rabbits in Texas. We take a shotgun up in a little plane. . . . Now, we've got lots of little planes in Vietnam, and those VC's are just like rabbits, they crawl around. . . ."

MURDER IN LAOS

In each of the twenty-five years of this war, Americans who wished to oppose our role or to tell the truth about it to their countrymen have had to contradict their President. This is the main reason, I have come to think, why opposition to the war has not become broad or durable enough to end it.

Each of the last five Presidents has lied to the public about our involvement in Indochina and where it was likely to go, and always in reassuring, credible ways that made active opposition to his policy seem unnecessary or hopeless. This Presidential deceit has gone through three phases. The first, which lasted over three Presidents from 1946 through 1964, emphasized the theme: "It's not our war; and we won't get in." The next phase, under Johnson, was: "We're winning." Then the current one: "The war is being ended." Each of these assurances has been plausible at the time, much more so than interpretations that contradicted it. Each was what most people wanted to believe, and did believe; each, coming from the President, served to allay concern, to defuse and deter resistance. None has ever been true. The war has always been ours; we have never been winning it; it has never been ending.

So it was, at the time of our invasion of Laos, when the following paper was written. So it is now. By the time this book is published, the ability of the American people—on their own, and despite their President—to recognize and to act on these realities will again have been sharply tested. As I write this—April 16, 1972—what Richard Nixon has feared for three years has come upon him: a dramatic North Vietnamese military challenge in an election year to his policy of an indefinitely prolonged U.S. presence in Vietnam. He has responded in the way my informants and I had feared.

The strategy described in "Murder in Laos"—of which I was first informed, by officials in Washington and Saigon, in the fall of 1969— was designed above all to deter or prevent the present offensive from taking place in 1972. In this it has failed, whatever the results may be of the contest in South Vietnam, pitting massive U.S. airpower against North Vietnamese ground troops. It was not in hopes of fighting televised battles this year—even of winning them—in the districts surrounding Saigon or Hue that President Nixon launched his invasions of '70 and '71 and dropped more bombs than any other head-of-state in history.

Even if U.S. bombs should block the offensive and turn it back— just as an escalated commitment of U.S. resources deprived Communist-led forces of imminent success in 1950, 1954, 1961, 1965, and 1968—the war will not end. Nor is our President likely to end it if the North Vietnamese and NLF forces achieve military successes that are less than total. No pattern is demonstrated more clearly throughout the Pentagon Papers than the extreme tenacity of both sides.

No civilian intelligence estimate of the last decade has supported the hopes of President Nixon and Henry Kissinger that threats, demonstrative invasions, raids, or bombing of the sort that they have employed before, or even more brutal measures, could deter or prevent renewed Vietnamese resistance to our presence and influence. On this point, the letter by my colleagues and myself at Rand in October, 1969, spoke with some authority; three of the other co-signers, who drafted the following passages, had worked for years on Rand's "VC Motivation and Morale" project, analyzing interrogation reports of VC and NVA prisoners and defectors.

. . Short of destroying the entire country and its people, we cannot eliminate the enemy forces in Vietnam by military means . . . What should now also be recognized is that the opposing leadership cannot be coerced by the present or by any other available U.S. strategy into making the kinds of concessions currently demanded.

. . . The opponent's morale, leadership, and performance all evidence his continuing resiliency, determination, and effectiveness, even under extremely adverse conditions (in no small part because of his conviction that he fights for a just and vital cause). Estimates that the opponent's will or capacity (in North or South Vietnam) is critically weakening because of internal strains and military pressures are, in our view, erroneous. Even if a new strategy should produce military successes in Vietnam, substantially reduce U.S. costs, and dampen domestic opposition, Hanoi could not be induced to make any concessions (e.g., cease-fire or mutual withdrawals), so long as they implied recognition of the authority of the Saigon government. Thus, to make the end of U.S. involvement contingent upon such concessions is to perpetuate our presence indefinitely. . . .

We do not predict that only good consequences will follow for Southeast Asia or South Vietnam (or even the United States) from our withdrawal. What we do say is that the risks will not be less after another year or more of American involvement, and the human costs will surely be greater.*

As for destroying Haiphong, blockading North Vietnam, and attacking communications with China in the attempt to shut off the flow of support through North Vietnam, every civilian intelligence analysis or estimate has flatly contradicted military hopes that this goal could be physically accomplished by airpower. It has never been clear whether even the advocates of airpower really believed otherwise, in the face of these analyses, or whether their proposed "unrestricted interdiction" programs were simply to be a cover for the inevitable bombing of civilian population, aimed at "breaking the will" of the North Vietnamese—or exterminating them. This last program—behind a screen of secrecy and of military euphemisms to describe the final solution to the North Vietnamese problem—may soon be under way.

---

* *Washington Post,* October 12, 1969; signers were Daniel Ellsberg, Melvin Gurtov, Oleg Hoeffding, Arnold L. Horelick, Konrad Kellen, and Paul F. Langer. The letter began: "Now that the American people are once again debating the issue of Vietnam, we desire to contribute to that discussion by presenting our own views, which reflect both personal judgments and years of professional research on the Vietnam War and related matters. We are expressing here our views as individuals, not speaking for the Rand Corporation, of which we are staff members; there is a considerable diversity of opinion on this subject, as on other issues, among our Rand colleagues.

We believe that the United States should decide now to end its participation in the Vietnam War, completing the total withdrawal of our forces within one year at the most. Such U.S. disengagement should not be conditioned upon agreement or performance by Hanoi or Saigon—i.e., it should not be subject to veto by either side. . . ."

In this crisis, it is not, as Administration spokesmen put it, our "resolution" which is being tested but our humanity.

Sooner or later, Nixon's policy was sure to lead to heavier fighting of the sort we are now seeing, some time after the North Vietnamese concluded that his reductions in U.S. force levels were leveling off. At that point, when his gamble had failed that the intelligence predictions, described above, about the opponent were mistaken, his second gamble, about the U.S. public, would be sharply tested: namely, that despite some controversy, most Americans would basically accept renewed heavy fighting if it were conducted on our side mainly from the air and with few American casualties. The judgment underneath that second gamble is one widely shared, even by some members of the peace movement: that most Americans are simply indifferent to and cannot be brought to care about bombing or Indochina casualties and refugees; that they are not much troubled by what their Government may do to Indochina, so long as it does not bring back high levels of costs, draft calls, or American casualties.

There is no denying some basis for the assessment. But I have acted for some time on a different belief about American values. Confronting this month's events my gamble, too, might be judged to have failed. Yet, public passivity toward our policy in Indochina may well have at least two explanations other than indifference. One is that the public—educated by a generation of Cold War administrations—has come to feel that it cannot and should not expect to exert much democratic control over foreign policy, or even expect Congress to do so.[1] And the other, described above, has been the prolonged, well-calculated deception concerning our involvement by the Executive branch, in which most major institutions in our society have at least passively collaborated. (Presumably, the current deception, that the war is winding down, will now have to be replaced.)

Meanwhile, over the last two and a half years, many Americans have been acting in hopes of changing the President's policy *before* the next half-million tons of bombs had fallen, and before the bloody

---

[1] The broad support for the Stennis-Javits bill in the Senate, limiting the war powers of the Executive, is an extremely encouraging sign that change can occur toward restoring Constitutional principles. For example, Senator Stennis has now stated: "Congress has a responsibility to express what role, if any, it has in committing this nation to war. We have not been living up to this responsibility, and I have been as guilty as any man" (*New York Times*, April 12, 1972, page 16).

confrontation that has now come about. My own efforts went toward making his policy, as I understood it, *visible* to the public and to Congress, despite effective White House screens. In part this meant addressing the question posed by a sympathetic superior at Rand when I first sketched what I had learned from Saigon and Washington about Administration plans: "Well, if the policy really does get our casualties down, and if the American people accept it . . . what's so bad about it?" In response, some comments of mine that circulated privately in various papers and letters in the fall of 1969 and early 1970 help to complement "Murder in Laos." (The latter focused instead, in March, 1971, on the most publicly puzzling, least foreseen aspect of the Nixon/Kissinger strategy, its sequence of American-initiated escalations pointing, "if necessary," directly to the bombing of Haiphong and Hanoi and beyond that to worse.) Although these intentions had been described to me in September, 1969, I found it difficult to believe they would actually be carried out—until the invasion of Cambodia. Together with "Murder in Laos," these comments of one and two years ago, tragically, serve as preface to this month's news from Indochina.

From background "Notes on the President's Speech of November 3, 1969," written the day after at the request of a group of Congressmen:

. . . What we have to look forward to from this policy is a future like the past, of lulls and "Tets," a cycle of VC inactivity and activity, with no clear limit to the deaths we suffer or inflict . . .

. . . Nixon worries, as did his predecessors, about a domestic political hangover from withdrawal: after initial relief, he foresees, "inevitable remorse and decisive recrimination would scar our spirit as a people" as "we saw the consequences of what we had done." His solution remains that of his predecessors: to postpone such painful withdrawal symptoms simply by continuing the war, with its cost in American and Vietnamese lives. That is the course of the addict; it may be the major hidden basis for our Government's addiction to this war over so many years and so many disappointments. It is not, as he presents it, the hard, courageous way to address this real problem, but the politically easy way, for the short run: easier than admitting past mistakes and facing painful consequences. It is *not*, as he calls it, "the right way."

It seems clear that the President believes this to be a just war, one he would feel dishonored to disown. In his speech, he discusses the consequences of disengagement in emotional words—"defeat . . . betrayal . . .

humiliation"—that warn of more years of war. He implies a sense of U.S. responsibility for political developments in South Vietnam that can be discharged only by indefinite combat engagement. His plan for "winning a just peace" is a plan for continuing United States involvement indefinitely, not at all a plan for ending it.

It is a policy that must goad the Hanoi leadership to challenge it by increasing the pressure of United States casualties; to which the President promises to respond by reescalation, against all past evidence (and consistent, reliable intelligence predictions) that this would neither deter nor end such pressure. In fact, we have heard a plan not only for continuing the war but for returning it eventually to levels—in firepower, commitment of prestige, destruction inflicted—that we recently abandoned. It is a plan and a speech we might have heard, without surprise, from Johnson, Rusk, or Rostow: indeed, we have, many times.

The following is from a long background memorandum on Vietnam policy which I wrote at the request of Senator Eugene McCarthy, January 21, 1970, and later circulated:

. . . I . . . believe that Nixon's policy, probably correctly understood by Hanoi, gives the Hanoi leadership strong incentive to press a strong attack in Vietnam when they are ready, causing great loss of life on both sides; both the lives lost in this offensive and the lives to be lost on both sides *before* this occurs are deplorable in the highest degree. . . .

. . . It is, indeed, not for us to choose the form of government for the Vietnamese people. But it is time to end the deception that we have not made that choice for them, when we support with our armed presence and vast material aid a government that is, on the one hand, totally dependent on that support, and on the other hand, which suppresses all opposition and freedom of expression on dictatorial lines . . .

. . . The most intense political interest of most Vietnamese at this time is not for the rule of one personality or party over another, but for peace. That is a desire that receives neither expression nor representation—thus, one that is hard to "prove"—in a state where (as in the North) freedom of speech and political activity on this very subject are forbidden, and candidates who might voice this desire cannot run for office, indeed, face prison. Yet is there a knowledgeable official of our Government, is there an authority with first-hand experience of Vietnamese society and politics who does not believe that a majority of the Vietnamese people would, in a free choice, prefer peace under either of the opposing governments to a continuation of this war? Knowledgeable people who yet support Administration policy find, rather, reasons why our intervention is "necessary" *despite* the fact that it means imposing a regime and a war upon the mass of the Vietnamese people against their desires. But the reasons are inadequate, the "necessity" is spurious, an illusion or a lie, and the policy that denies the import of these Vietnamese desires is ultimately dishonorable.

For twenty years, we have presented our involvement in Vietnam to ourselves in terms of altruism, generosity, common aims with the Vietnamese
people; we have thought of safeguarding our own interests by way of safeguarding those of the Vietnamese, offering them a freer and better life than
they could hope for under Communist domination. Our goals for the Vietnamese people have not been unworthy, but they have amounted to fantasies hiding the reality of what it was we were constructing as a fortress
against Communism: an alternative dictatorship, a succession of governments
that earned the hatred and opposition of many of the most patriotic and
talented Vietnamese, the contempt of most of the rest, regimes that could
not attract the loyalty and support of most Vietnamese even as an alternative
to Communist rule. And the same fantasies hid from us the horrors being
committed daily by us and by those we have upheld.

Our efforts supposedly in the interests of the Vietnamese have, in fact,
delivered them to governments they can scarcely prefer to Communism and
to an endless, devastating war. It is time at last to deliver them from our help;
from our involvement; from our concern. We can help them, at last, only
by leaving them alone.

As though driven by Che's curse, Richard Nixon seems compelled to create "two, three . . . many Vietnams" in Southeast Asia.

The pace of invasion is quickening. On the first evening of the
invasion of Laos, Vice President Ky pointed to what could be
the next invasion. South Vietnamese ground forces, he said, might
have to cross the 17th parallel into North Vietnam to hit supply
bases above the DMZ. It was six years since South Vietnamese
forces had first done that, in the air, with Ky himself leading the
attack. In fact, Ky was speaking at a dinner marking the anniversary, largely unnoticed in the U.S., of those raids of February
7 and 8, 1965, which "retaliated" for the death of eight Americans
in an NLF attack on Pleiku and led to a three-year bombing campaign against the North (*PP*, III, 269-340). Ky's warning, coincid-
ing with the new offensive in Laos, linked the past, present, and future of a fundamentally unchanging U.S. strategy in Indochina.

In the U.S. itself, not even the Orwellian communiqués seem
to have altered. On February 7, 1965, the White House chose the
occasion of its announcement that U.S. bombers were crossing
the borders of North Vietnam to repeat its past assurances to the
American public: "As the U.S. Government has frequently stated,

we seek no wider war" (*PP*, III, 305). On February 9, 1971, as
U.S. bombers and helicopters were for the first time accompanying South Vietnamese forces—paid, equipped, and supported by
the U.S.—into Laos, Secretary Laird told the nation: "We have
not widened the war." He added: "To the contrary, we have
shortened it."

To the contrary—as all can see—we have widened it. Why?
When and why will we do it again? There is, in truth, a coherent
inner logic to the policy that contains answers to these questions.
It is a logic that has pointed for at least the last year to the invasion of Laos—and beyond.

For twenty years—since the "fall of China" and the rise of
McCarthy—Rule 1 of Indochina policy for an American President
has been: Do not lose the rest of Vietnam to Communism before
the next election. But there was also Rule 2, learned shortly thereafter, in Korea: Do not fight a land war in Asia with U.S. ground
combat troops either. Three Presidents, starting with Truman,
managed to satisfy both constraints during their terms and passed
the challenge on to their successors. The problem grew, and
Lyndon Johnson's Presidency was crushed in its first full term by
the impossibility of fulfilling both requirements. But Johnson's
foundering on Rule 2 did not repeal Rule 1 for his successor:
even in 1969, even for a Republican, even for Richard Nixon.

Like Kennedy and Johnson before him, Richard Nixon believes
he cannot hold the White House for a second term unless he holds
Saigon through his first.

His two predecessors had seen the leaders of the previous
Democratic Administration driven from office after they had been
charged with having "lost China." More specifically, they were
accused of losing China without trying, without making full use
of U.S. airpower or advisors, without giving full support to an
anti-Communist Asian ally: omissions pointing to weakness or
treason. Kennedy and Johnson both feared that the accusation
of "losing Vietnam"—or simply "losing a war"—could rally again
the hounds of McCarthyism against their party.

Nixon does not feel immune just because he once was one of
the leaders of that pack. On the contrary, he knows better than
anyone else just what *he* would try to do with such an issue if he

were on the outside seeking power, even against a Republican President. He is determined not to have to suffer from it in 1972, either from Reagan summoning away his supporters in the convention or from Wallace calling to his voters in the election. (Whether the fears shared by Nixon and his predecessors of a threat from the right are based on political reality, or on a specter of their own making, is not the issue here. What matters is that four of the last five Presidents have felt compelled to take such a threat seriously, and Nixon still does.)

No doubt there are other and perhaps even stronger motives that influence Mr. Nixon's choices, but they point in the same direction. There is good evidence that the President is, even more than his predecessors, a "true believer" in the Cold War premises they all shared, including that of the importance of maintaining U.S. power in Asia, showing strength to the Russians and Chinese, containing Communism—monolithic or not—and avoiding the reverberating damage of a U.S. failure or humiliation.

Which of these instincts is the stronger matters little in this case, for they reinforce each other in Vietnam policy: Saigon must not "fall" . . . above all, not too soon or too suddenly. Those who imagine otherwise, who suppose that Nixon's views on domestic politics conflict with his notions of U.S. interests abroad, and that his instincts for political survival inexorably urge him toward total withdrawal "no matter what," are almost surely wrong.

During 1968 Henry Kissinger frequently said in private talks that the appropriate goal of U.S. policy was a "decent interval"— two to three years—between the withdrawal of U.S. troops and a Communist takeover in Vietnam. In that year, an aim so modest had almost a radical ring; no major public figure, in fact, dared openly to endorse it. But in 1969, when Kissinger moved to the White House, his notion took on a sharper meaning and new urgency. It became not a goal but a requirement; and the "interval," it became evident, could not end before November, 1972. In its new, tougher form, the doctrine had practical implications for policy well beyond 1972. In effect, it meant acting immediately and over the next several years to achieve both an indefinite fighting stalemate in Vietnam and support for such a stalemate in the U.S. And that aim had implications for the prospects of renewed escalation of the air war in Indochina.

To begin with, it was evident in Paris by the spring of 1969 that Hanoi and the NLF would not accept terms that would meet the Administration's needs for assuring non-Communist control in Saigon through at least 1972. Nor would the Russians intervene to achieve this, as Nixon had hoped. So the war had to go on.

Total Vietnamization? U.S. military advisors held out no hope whatever that Saigon could be held with any assurance for three years, or even one year, if *no* U.S. military personnel remained in South Vietnam. No foreseeable improvement in ARVN, or amount of U.S. aid, including air support, would prop up Saigon reliably in the face of North Vietnamese forces if all our troops went home. *Both* U.S. troops and airpower were needed, in sizable amounts, for years, perhaps indefinitely.[2]

In fact, through 1969 and, so far as is known, today, the highest military leaders have never judged officially that the job of holding Saigon could be done, with reasonable assurance and with adequate safety for remaining U.S. troops, with fewer than 200,000 military personnel in the country to provide air support, logistics, communications, intelligence, self-defense, and strategic reserve. That figure, Nixon probably thinks, and with reason, is inflated; but there are limits to what the Joint Chiefs of Staff will certify as "militarily acceptable," and the semi-permanent minimum may well turn out to be not much lower than 100,000 for the end of 1972 and after. It is more likely to prove higher; and it will almost certainly not be less than half that figure, long after 1972.

With the military floor somewhere between 50,000 and 150,000 troops, the political ceiling is surely not very much higher. LBJ's strategy, putting half a million U.S. troops in the South, met the goal he defined in his first week in office; he left the White House five years later accused of many things, but not of being the first President to lose a war. Yet his approach was, obviously, only a partial success; it saved Saigon but lost the White House. As would anyone determined to hold both, Nixon drew an immediate lesson: U.S. troop levels and budget costs must go down, and

---

[2] This was the JCS position in their answers to National Security Study Memorandum No. 1 (NSSM-1) in February, 1969, described in the Introduction.

casualties, draft calls, and news space must go down even more sharply. In fact, even 50,000 troops—still twice as many as LBJ had in Vietnam at the onset of the bombing—could be acceptable to the public or, better, ignored by it, only if U.S. casualties were very low indeed and newsworthy North Vietnamese successes anywhere in Indochina almost nonexistent.

Thus Nixon's practical goal—a "Korean solution," as officials began to call it—became clear: to make Indochina safe for an indefinite presence of 50,000 U.S. troops or more in South Vietnam. The key to a solution, Nixon and Kissinger concluded, was to expand the role of airpower, and, in particular, to restore and increase the threat of bombing the North.

How else, they reasoned, could Nixon ever compel successful negotiations? How could he induce the Russians to use their leverage for a settlement, unless the Russians were made to fear— in Laos, say, or in Haiphong—that they would become more directly involved?

How else could Nixon deter the North Vietnamese forces, once they recovered from the 1968 losses, from making embarrassing gains at will in Laos; or worse, from coming south to overpower ARVN; or worst of all, attacking the reduced U.S. units, either destroying them or forcing them home?

"Vietnamization," if confined to the borders of South Vietnam and with the threat of escalation excluded, had no persuasive long-run answer to these threats. In view of that, and of the unpromising prospects in Paris, the best alternative, to some officials in Washington, was a total, prompt U.S. extrication from Vietnam. To Nixon and Kissinger, it meant instead that a credible bombing threat was essential to their program.

The policy they decided on was in many ways a familiar one, especially for Republicans. Its main ingredients were precisely those prescribed twenty years ago by the "Asia-first" right-wing Republicans in Congress for preventing the "fall of China" and, later, by MacArthur and others, for winning "victory" in Korea— the threat and, if necessary, use of U.S. strategic airpower and allied Asian troops under an authoritarian, and anti-Communist, regime, approved, financed, and equipped by the U.S. and using American advisors and logistical and air support. (Vice President

Nixon had been willing to add some U.S. ground combat troops to that package to save North Vietnam in 1954, before the fall of Dien Bien Phu, but this was considered an aberration at the time.)

If one adds the threat of nuclear weapons—a threat used privately, Nixon believes, by Eisenhower to settle the Korean War, and later used publicly by Secretary Dulles to influence the First Indochina War—one has all the elements underlying Dulles' doctrine of "massive retaliation" and the "New Look" defense posture of the Eisenhower Administration. This was the policy that enabled Republicans to combine aggressive rhetoric with a limited defense budget throughout the years when Nixon was Vice President. As an academic strategist during that period, Henry Kissinger dissented from this formula mainly by stressing the role of "tactical" nuclear weapons (in the book *Nuclear Weapons and Foreign Policy*, which made his reputation). But in Nixon's Administration, the threat of nuclear weapons in Indochina is not—as yet, at least—an essential part of the strategy of Kissinger and Nixon (except, as usual, to deter Chinese intervention)—though they have explicitly refused to foreclose their use. The new strategy differs from the old mainly in relying on the strategic threat of non-nuclear bombing.

But how could Nixon and Kissinger believe, after the experience of the sixties, that threats of massive bombing could solve their problems in Indochina? What could new threats promise now, when the *practice* of sustained bombing under Johnson had in fact failed to deter or physically to prevent even the Tet offensive?

Nixon's answer was that the Democrats had moved too gradually and too predictably, and had never threatened or used *heavy enough* bombing. This is what the Joint Chiefs had been saying all along, though Nixon had no need to take instruction from them. He was using a language he shares with the generals when he explained after the Cambodian invasion that, whereas Johnson had moved "step by step,"

This action is a decisive move, and this action also puts the enemy on warning that if it escalates while we are trying to deescalate, we will move decisively and not step by step.

What he was then threatening, as he had done before the election, was "decisive" bombing of targets long proposed by some U.S. military chiefs and their political spokesmen: Haiphong, "military targets" in Hanoi and unrestrictedly throughout the North, and the communications with China.[3]

Nixon believed the threat would be newly credible and effective because he would demonstrate to Hanoi that it could be carried out without destroying his own political base or ability to govern the U.S. Johnson had lost these, in Nixon's view, because he had combined inadequate air attacks with excessive numbers of ground troops, U.S. casualties, and draft calls. Once those numbers were diminished, Nixon believed, the American public and its representatives in Congress would accept even a semi-permanent and geographically extended war, financed by America but with direct American combat action limited primarily to airpower.

That was a bold judgment to make in 1969. Yet the North Vietnamese had to be forced to accept this judgment if Nixon's threat of bombing were to deter them from challenging a protracted American presence, or bring them, ultimately, to accept his terms for a "just peace." Only convincing *demonstrations* of his willingness and ability to escalate could bring that about.

The notion of "warning demonstrations" has thus been central to the tactics of Nixon and Kissinger, and it explains the sequence of political threats and offensive actions they have taken over the last two years. As early as the spring of 1969,[4] our first air attacks on Cambodia—not officially announced and little noticed in the U.S.—were soon followed by a warning to Hanoi which was

[3] See Leslie Gelb and Morton H. Halperin, "Only a Timetable Can Extricate Nixon," *Washington Post* Outlook section, May 24, 1970; and Halperin, "Vietnam: Options," *New York Times*, Op-Ed page, November 7, 1970. Each of these analysts served both Johnson and Nixon in positions dealing with Vietnam policy, Halperin having served until September, 1969, as assistant to Henry Kissinger in the White House.

This discussion owes a great deal to the thinking of these former colleagues—though they are in no way responsible for any of the interpretations presented here—as it does to a number of others with comparable governmental experience who cannot be named.

[4] Since this was written, members of the Vietnam Veterans Against the War have revealed that a major ground operation into Laos—Dewey Canyon I—took place secretly at this time.

inserted in an otherwise moderate speech by Nixon on a Vietnam settlement.

At the same time the bombing expanded in Laos, and a series of bombing raids began on North Vietnam. As these raids continued, Administration officials gradually dismantled Johnson's 1968 "understanding" which had strictly limited the justification for such raids. Finally, in his televised interview with the press on January 5, 1971, the President virtually abandoned this "understanding."[5]

The ground invasion of Cambodia took place in spring, 1970; in the fall, troops landed in North Vietnam; now we are supporting an invasion of Laos. In each case the White House has conveyed unmistakable warnings to Hanoi that more such action was to come.

All of these actions could be, and were, defended as tactics necessary to delay enemy buildups or "spoil" enemy offensives. Indeed, all of them may keep things quieter in South Vietnam, in the short run. They make offensive action difficult and costly for the North Vietnamese, thus delaying a new offensive until Hanoi once again faces the inescapable need to make the necessary sacrifices. They do, in short, buy time, with U.S. airpower and thousands of Asian lives. The airpower, especially the lavish use of armed helicopters, substitutes for U.S. troops. The fewer American troops in Vietnam, the more need for U.S. airpower throughout Indochina, if U.S. losses are to be cut and the North Vietnamese prevented from taking the initiative.

Of course this view can be challenged on tactical grounds as well. By expanding the war, the U.S. commanders are multiplying their risks and committing themselves to protracted war in three countries, for only limited gains. In Laos, for example, U.S. helicopter losses and South Vietnamese casualties may turn out to be sizable. A right-wing coup may follow our interventions—revers-

[5] Nixon claimed that the North Vietnamese had violated another understanding that our "unarmed reconnaissance planes could fly over North Vietnam with impunity," although former high officials in the Johnson Administration have denied that there was any such understanding. Nixon went on to state that "'if they say there is no understanding in that respect"—as Hanoi leaders do say—"then there are no restraints whatever on us."

(Even before the current offensive [April, 1972] there had been as many raids over the North in three months in 1972 as in all of 1971.)

ing the order of events in Cambodia—with complex repercussions, possibly including an increased Chinese combat presence, which would automatically cause U.S. nuclear contingency plans to be presented for consideration to the Secretary of Defense, if not to the President. And the North Vietnamese have considerable ability, as in Cambodia, to respond to our moves in the border areas by enlarging their control elsewhere.

But, as the White House planners see it, none of this tactical argument really matters. The domestic risks, in their view, are not great ones, even in the worst circumstances. After an unpopular beginning, the operation in Cambodia showed to Nixon's satisfaction that the war can be reduced in visibility while expanding geographically, so long as U.S. ground units are not involved.

In fact, tactical success is not what these initiatives are all about. Their real significance, in every case, is that they are concrete *warnings* to the Hanoi leadership, and to their Soviet and Chinese allies—violent warnings to back up verbal threats.

They warn, first, of what Nixon is willing to do and feels free to do without consulting Congress or feeling limited by Johnson's precedent. Each one of the measures listed above broke a restraint maintained or eventually imposed by Lyndon Johnson in his campaign to bring "pressures on Hanoi." There were, after all, some good reasons for observing those limitations, and many of those reasons are still plausible. Nixon's actions thus serve all the more forcefully as deliberate signals to his opponents that he will not be bound by earlier constraints.

His actions demonstrate, furthermore, how far Nixon thinks he can go by using the rationale of "protecting the lives of American troops" and the formula of "limited-duration interdiction operations, to permit continuation of the withdrawal of U.S. forces." These terms—Hanoi is meant to notice—could be used just as well for the "limited" ground invasion of North Vietnam to destroy depots and bases above the DMZ that has been mentioned by General Ky. The same language could be used to justify the mining and aerial destruction of the port of Haiphong; or full-scale attacks on the land and water links to China and on "military targets" throughout the North, including Hanoi. All of these could be described as "limited in time and space."

In fact, each one of these moves could be presented as a logical progression in a series of "interdictions" running from south to north, just as the present attacks in Laos "logically" followed the closing of the port of Sihanoukville by the Lon Nol government and the invasion of Cambodia. Each step could be explained as "closing" a remaining door in the channel of war materiel to North Vietnamese and NLF forces in South Vietnam.

To be sure, none of these steps could reliably close off that necessary trickle of supplies from the North, even if they were all taken together. But Nixon has been told this; again, that is not what such threatened moves are about. They point, rather, toward the program that the U.S. Joint Chiefs of Staff have urged for over six years[6] in the absence of a permanent and "acceptable" settlement by Hanoi: the final destruction of "the will and capability of North Vietnam to wage war." Or to survive.

Not that Nixon hopes or expects this ultimate escalation will be necessary; his threats and commitments make it contingent on North Vietnamese behavior. Hanoi's leadership is left two options for avoiding this punishment. It can, tacitly but permanently, accept things pretty much as they are in the South, without initiating heavy combat, or with no more than can be handily contained by South Vietnamese ground forces with U.S. air support. The war would continue but military action would taper off and U.S. casualties would virtually cease. Or else, bowing to the conclusion that the American people will support a low-level or airpower war indefinitely, and that the American President will meet any attempt to convert it to a high-cost war by burning North Vietnam to the ground, the Hanoi leaders can seek to conclude a formal settlement on U.S. terms.

U.S. officers choose to call the first possibility a "Korean solution"—though it could mean permanent war and permanent U.S. air operations—because it combines a permanent U.S. presence with very low U.S. casualties. The second possibility, which defines Nixon's aim of "winning a just peace," would more truly be a "Korean solution," especially in view of Nixon's conviction that settlement in Korea was based on the threat of massive

[6] See, for example: *PP*, III, 179 (1964); *PP*, IV, 254-56 (1968).

bombings. Faith in either possibility permits Nixon to deny charges that he has chosen a "no-win" strategy.

So Che's prescription, finally, is turned around to Nixon's ends. Not only did the short-range problem of lowering U.S. casualties during a gradual and limited reduction of strength—the problem of "getting through '72"—invite a broadening of the battleground to include the border bases and supply routes in Laos and Cambodia. Far more important, the symbolism of such widening—the dramatic crossing of frontiers in defiance of domestic protest and contrary expectations—was uniquely suited to making credible Nixon's crucial threat: to extend the battleground to all of North Vietnam. From the moment that Sihanouk's ouster cleared the way, it was almost inevitable that the search for a second "Korea" would lead the President to institute a second and a third "Vietnam"—to warn the North he could create a fourth.

In Laos the Administration is showing that it has learned its "lessons from Cambodia." No American rifle units in action, crossing borders or shooting white college students. No promises, no bulletins, no news at all, in fact. No statement on the operation by the President. Instead, on the afternoon of the day the helicopters and amtracs moved across the border, Nixon went before the TV cameras with a brief message on ecology, beginning (according to the White House press release):

In his Tragedy, *Murder in the Cathedral,* T. S. Elliott [sic] wrote, "Clean the air. Clean the sky. Wash the wind." [sic]
I have proposed to the Congress a sweeping and comprehensive program to do just that, and more—to end the plunder of America's natural heritage.

No TV or news photos of the invasion were permitted; cameramen were barred from recording what we and our allies were doing to the natural heritage of their neighbors. (The Vietnamese were struck, a *New York Times* account reported, by the lushness of the yet undefoliated jungle they were entering.) Instead viewers were offered pictures of the moon and of the staging areas at Khe Sanh: an uncanny juxtaposition, the war-created moonscapes near the DMZ compensating for the lack of live coverage of the lunarization of Laos.

What will this new invasion mean to the people of Laos? War is not new to them, nor are foreign soldiers or American bombers; yet they are now feeling the impact of all these in a new and terrible way. As in Cambodia, the first operations are in relatively unpopulated areas; and as in Cambodia, the North Vietnamese forces will most likely fight back in more heavily populated lowlands, where our bombers and armed helicopters will seek them out. Then the refugees will come—many of them from areas where they have lived for years in the vicinity of Pathet Lao or North Vietnamese troops—to the fetid enclosures on the outskirts of towns that are not being bombed, leaving their dead behind them.

"We have learned one thing in Laos and Cambodia," the counsel for the Kennedy Subcommittee points out. "The mere presence of enemy forces does not lead to refugees. Heavy battles do; U.S. bombing does."

As an essential part of Nixon's "winding down the war" for American troops in South Vietnam, American pilots were sent to inflict the war more heavily on Laos and Cambodia. In the fall of 1969, more than six hundred sorties a day were being flown over Laos; some of the heaviest months of bombing in the war occurred in that year, and again in 1970. The number of refugees in Laos had already risen sharply in 1968, after American bombers were shifted in late March from North Vietnamese targets to areas in both northern and southern Laos.

But in the first twelve months of the Nixon Administration, the number of refugees nearly doubled. The official estimate for the end of 1969—certainly a low one—was at least 240,000 (in a population of under three million). In the first eighteen months there were at least 30,000 civilian casualties, including more than 9,000 killed. The number of refugees continued to rise in 1970; by the fall it was almost three times the estimate for February, 1968.[7]

---

[7] See the Kennedy Subcommittee Staff Report, "Refugee and Civilian War Casualty Problems in Indochina." (Subcommittee to Investigate Problems Connected with Refugees and Escapees of the Committee on the Judiciary, United States Senate, September 28, 1970.) Also see Senator Kennedy's "sanitized" summary of two classified reports on war victims in Laos, released February 7, 1971.

Then in November of last year, U.S. bombing escalated sharply in Laos.

Whatever the impact of recent events on the flight of people within Laos, it is likely soon to be magnified by the effects of operations similar to those in Cambodia, where *well over a million* refugees have been "generated" during the last nine months (in a population of about 6.7 million).[8] There is no available estimate of the number of civilian deaths in Cambodia since last spring's invasion.

How many will die in Laos?

What is Richard Nixon's best estimate of the number of Laotian people—"enemy" and "non-enemy"—that U.S. firepower will kill in the next twelve months?

He does not have an estimate. He has not asked Henry Kissinger for one, and Kissinger has not asked the Pentagon; and none of these officials has ever seen an answer to this or any comparable question on the expected impact of war policy on human life, whether in Laos or Cambodia, or North or South Vietnam. And none of them differs in this from his predecessors. (Systems analysts in the bureaucracy make estimates as best they can of factors judged pertinent to policy: "costs" or "benefits," "inputs" or "outputs." The deaths of "noncombatant people" have never been regarded by officials as being relevant to any of these categories.)

Officials would, however, have an answer of some sort if other parts of the government or the press or the public had ever demanded one. Were it not for the Kennedy Subcommittee there would be no overall official calculations of *past* casualties in Vietnam—not even the underestimated figures that have been made available. But as a result of that questioning and the subcommittee's own surveys and analyses, we now know that at least 300,000 civilians have been killed in South Vietnam—mostly by U.S. firepower—between 1965 and 1970, out of at least one million casualties. Of these, the subcommittee's calculations indicate that about 50,000 civilians were killed in Nixon's first year in office, about 35,000 in his second.

[8] By early 1972, the estimate of the Kennedy Subcommittee was two million.

Though reliable figures for Cambodia and Laos are not available—the Administration still makes no attempt to obtain them—the Kennedy Subcommittee staff estimates that civilian war casualties and deaths throughout Indochina were higher in 1970 than in 1969. Moreover, the refugee rate within South Vietnam began to increase in late 1970, and rose to the highest level in two years for the second quarter of 1971.

So the war is not "winding down" for the people of South Vietnam any more than for their neighbors: as would be apparent to the American public if figures on civilian casualties, refugees, defoliation and bombing tonnages were flashed weekly on the evening TV news along with U.S. and "enemy" casualties.

But even the Kennedy Subcommittee has made no effort to calculate deaths and injuries from American bombing in North Vietnam, or to elicit estimates of future victims throughout Indochina. Nor have the press and television. Nor has there been any public demand for this information.

Given this background of two decades of official and public ignorance of and indifference to our impact upon the people of Indochina, one can understand the ease with which the Nixon Administration has sold the slogan: "The war is trending down." To agree with that proposition—and it is scarcely questioned—is to *define* "the war," very narrowly indeed, as U.S. ground troops, U.S. casualties, budget costs. It is simply to ignore those aspects of the war that are "trending *up*": U.S. air operations and ground fighting outside South Vietnam, and the resulting deaths and casualties we are sponsoring in Laos and Cambodia. It cannot really be said that this narrowed perception is simply a hallucinatory trick played by the Nixon Administration on the public. Americans have always seen the Indochina war this way.

U.S. military officers are sometimes better at perceiving things clearly. "War is killing people," a Rand physicist was once instructed by General Curtis LeMay, one of history's "terrible simplifiers." "When you kill enough people, the other side quits."

But the new Administration is abandoning the previous crude strategy of ground combat "attrition," with its bloody-minded calculus of "body counts" and abstruse models of the birth rate of young "enemy males" to be killed in the future. Most of the victims that the new strategy kills as a result of its "warning demonstrations" have no place in bureaucratic calculations. The same is true of the vast numbers of North Vietnamese people who will be threatened if their leaders, continuing thirty years of armed struggle, decide to fight against a "Korean solution." The plans for air war designed by General LeMay may then be carried out by the Nixon Administration.

Joseph Alsop, whose column noting the "cool courage" of the President in Laos had been distributed widely by the White House, wrote several days after the Laos invasion: "As of now, Richard M. Nixon is beginning to appear as one of our better war presidents."

The passage our war President chose to recall to the American people that Monday afternoon of the invasion does not, in fact, have to do with air pollution, or with any ordinary defilement. As my son pointed out to me: it speaks of murder. It is a chorus of horror chanted as murder is being done, in full view, at the wishes of a ruler, for reasons of state.

> Clear the air! clean the sky! wash the wind! take stone
> from stone and wash them.
> The land is foul, the water is foul, our beasts and our-
> selves defiled with blood.
> A rain of blood has blinded my eyes. . . .
> How how can I ever return, to the soft quiet seasons?
> Night stay with us, stop sun, hold season, let the day
> not come, let the spring not come.
> Can I look again at the day and its common things,
> and see them all smeared with blood, through a
> curtain of falling blood? . . .
>
> In life there is not time to grieve long.
> But this, this is out of life, this is out of time,
> An instant eternity of evil and wrong. . . .

These lines are almost unbearable for an American to read, in the year 1971, after the last six years. If we are ever to return to the soft quiet seasons—and we have not earned an easy passage—

enough Americans must look past options, briefings, pros and cons, to see what is being done in their name, and to refuse to be accomplices. They must recognize, and force the Congress and President to act upon, the *moral* proposition that the U.S. must stop killing people in Indochina: that neither the lives we have lost, nor the lives we have taken, give the U.S. any right to determine by fire and airpower who shall govern or who shall die in Vietnam, Cambodia, or Laos.

THE RESPONSIBILITY OF OFFICIALS IN A CRIMINAL WAR

This is a somewhat expanded version of a lecture originally delivered at the Community Church, Boston, Massachusetts, on May 23, 1971; footnotes, some reflections, and, of course, all direct references to the Pentagon Papers, have been added. The audience was, as I had expected, considerably older than the college audiences I had been facing; it included, though I had not foreseen this, a number of refugees from Nazi Germany. Partly because I felt it would be my last speech for a while—the disclosure of the Pentagon Papers was expected shortly—I chose to talk about some personal aspects that I had not addressed before.

... not to have tried to see through the whole apparatus of mystification—was already criminal. At this initial stage my guilt was as grave as, at the end, my work for Hitler. For *being in a position to know and nevertheless shunning knowledge creates direct responsibility for the consequences—from the very beginning.*

... In the final analysis I myself determined the degree of my isolation, the extremity of my evasions, and the extent of my ignorance ... Whether I knew or did not know, or how much or how little I knew, is totally unimportant when I consider what horrors I ought to have known about and what conclusions would have been natural ones to draw from the little I did know. Those who ask me are fundamentally expecting me to offer justifications. But I have none. No apologies are possible.

The ordinary party member was being taught that grand policy was much too complex for him to judge it. Consequently, one felt one was being represented, never called upon to take personal responsibility. The whole structure of the system was aimed at preventing conflicts of conscience from even arising.

—Albert Speer, *Inside The Third Reich*[1]

"What no one seemed to notice," said a colleague of mine, a philologist, "was the ever widening gap, after 1933, between the government and the people: Just think how very wide this gap was to begin with, here in Germany. And it became always wider. You know, it doesn't make people close to their government to be told that this is a people's government, a true democracy, or to be enrolled in civilian defense, or even to vote. All this has little, really nothing, to do with *knowing* one is governing.

"What happened here was the gradual habituation of the people little by little to being governed by surprise; to receiving decisions deliberated in secret; to believing that the situation was so complicated that the Government has to act on information which the people could not understand or so dangerous that, even if the people could understand it, it could not be released because of national security. And their sense of identification with Hitler, their trust in him made it easier to widen this gap, and reassure those who would otherwise have worried about it.

"This separation of government from the people, this widening of the gap took place so gradually and so insensibly, each step disguised (perhaps not even intentionally) as a temporary emergency measure or associated with true patriotic allegiance or with real social purposes. And all the crises and reforms (real reforms too) so occupied the people they did not see the slow motion underneath, of the whole process of the Government growing remoter and remoter."

—Milton Mayer, *They Thought They Were Free*[2]

Most of you know what it means when 100 corpses lie there, or when 500 corpses lie there, or when 1000 corpses lie there. To have gone through this and—apart from a few exceptions caused by human weakness—to have remained decent, that has made us great. That is a

[1] New York, 1971, pages 19, 113, 33.
[2] Chicago, 1966, page 66.

page of glory in our history which has never been written, and which
is never to be written.

> —Heinrich Himmler
> Address to S.S. commanders, October, 1943[3]

Whoever fights monsters should see to it that in the process he does
not become a monster. And when you look into an abyss, the abyss
also looks into you.

> —Nietzsche, *Beyond Good and Evil*[4]

I find myself, in recent months, thinking a great deal about
Germany in the 1930's and 1940's. I have felt compelled, increasingly, to try to define the responsibilities of the citizens and
officials of our country in terms related to the German experience; and I find myself doing this not as a Jew but as an American.

One of the first times that I felt challenged in just this way
was a little more than a year ago, when I was invited, in the
spring of 1970, to a conference in Washington sponsored by ten
Congressmen on the subject of "War Crimes and the American
Conscience."[5]

On the second day of the conference, I looked around a very
large seminar table of participants—about forty distinguished
people, among them Hannah Arendt and Telford Taylor—and it
came to me that I was the only person present who was a potential defendant in a war crimes trial. This gave me a peculiar
perspective from which to listen to the proceedings, and one
that has been very challenging to me ever since.

The reason that I felt that way should be obvious from my
background—service in the Marines, the Defense Department,
the State Department, service in Vietnam, the Rand Corporation.
In the year since that conference, I've been involved in a great
many teach-ins, especially since the invasion of Cambodia, and
even more since the invasion of Laos. The audiences at these

---

[3] Quoted in Raul Hilberg, *The Destruction of the European Jews* (Chicago,
1967), page 648.

[4] New York, 1966, p. 89.

[5] See *War Crimes and the American Conscience* (New York, 1970). For my
own remarks at the conference, see "War Crimes and My Lai," pages 243-52.

various colleges were made up almost entirely of young people. Which is to say, people who view that list of jobs that I have held as extremely discreditable. They see the war that we are still carrying on as criminal, as well as brutal, inhumane, totally unjustifiable—as I do now—and they nave never seen it any other way.

When I first began to face these audiences, and I would hear the person introducing me begin to run through the whole list of my past associations, one by one, my heart would sink with each sentence, while the atmosphere in the auditorium got colder and colder.

It may seem less difficult to answer the following questions for an audience of older people than for the typical college audience: *How could it be* that our country has for the last ten years —twenty years would be more accurate—remained engaged in the brutality of our policies in Indochina? How could our leaders—honored and respectable men—have involved us so long in this hopeless butchery? How could we have let them, with so little protest?

But even if these questions seem less puzzling to an older audience, to those who have lived through this war and even worse wars in their adult lives, I think they deserve close attention. We are too likely to dismiss them just because they are painful, not because the answers are really obvious.

The Germans face a somewhat different question: "How could we have allowed such an obvious gang of criminals to rule over us for so long and to do the things they did?" They can reply to their own young people: "Well, it was the Nazis' criminal willingness to use terror against us—on their own people—that's the answer. We could do nothing except at the risk of our lives, we were prevented from knowing any of the truth by a totally censored press, etcetera."

But as Americans, we don't have so easy an explanation. To begin with, as Townsend Hoopes has pointed out, "It is well to remember that the advisors [of Presidents Kennedy and Johnson] were widely regarded when they entered government as among the ablest, the best informed, the most humane and liberal men who could be found for public trust. And that was a true assessment."[6]

I must say that I think it's necessary to do what Townsend Hoopes does not do: to reexamine his judgment of these individuals—and of the Eastern Establishment from which they largely were drawn, whose values and perspectives they truly represented—in the light of what we now know they have done over the last decade. But this reexamination will not give us the excuse that their values greatly differed from those of large parts of the population.

So the question remains: How could such respected, "humane, liberal" people—and through them, all of us—have been involved in the burning of villages; herbicides; defoliation; torture; the creation of millions of refugees; air and ground invasions; and the dropping of over six million tons—six megatons, they would say at the Rand Corporation—of explosives from the air, and another six million tons of artillery shells, on the people of Indochina since 1965?

This is not a question I addressed in earlier talks: neither in general nor in specific personal terms. In these speeches I concentrated on what lay ahead in the Vietnam War and what might be done to stop it. I happened to think, and still do, that a lot of war lies ahead; so there was enough to say about that. And I have not talked about personal experiences at all.

But this is the first time I've been invited to give a "sermon" —and it will probably be the last speech I'll be giving for some time—so I felt, as I was thinking about it this morning, that I do want to relate this to personal experiences.

As my background indicates, I cannot view the question of the responsibility of officials from the perspective of someone who has held himself aloof from what the government was doing, much less of one who can say that he had opposed this war or seen through it from the beginning. On the contrary. So, rather than address the question as an outsider, I think it is better for me to do what a few Germans after the war were led to do. That is to think very hard—as Albert Speer put it to himself as

[6] "Legacy of the Cold War in Indochina," *Foreign Affairs*, July, 1970, page 611.

he began his memoirs back in 1945—about how it could have taken me so long to see the wrongness of what we were doing; and to make some guesses about my colleagues and superiors in office.

I know of very few Americans as yet who have really confronted that question closely. And I think it is not too early to do so, even though the war is not over—because some of the officials now in office are as "liberal," as "humane," as any we've had in the past, with assistants as conscientious as I was helping them, and they are still continuing the war. Still keeping secrets well, still lying and killing. And I think they and others like them are likely to continue this for a long time, for many of the same reasons as in the past, unless we develop new standards both for them and for ourselves in our relation to them. So I will not wait for the others to do it; let me begin and ask myself how these things looked to me.

To go back to the question: "How could we . . . ?" I think the answer goes back in part to an event we all remember, in August, 1945. This was the same month when, unknown to me and most Americans, Ho Chi Minh proclaimed the Democratic Republic of Vietnam, with himself as leader: a status recognized by the former Emperor and by the French. We remember August, 1945, instead, because it was the month in which the United States ended a World War with an unprecedented act of genocide, unleashing the power of the sun on the people of Hiroshima.

I remember feeling, at fourteen, some uneasiness about one aspect of that event—the very evident lack of uneasiness in the announcement by our President, Harry Truman. I remember his voice on the radio as he announced in a euphoric tone the great technical achievement of the United States in using this power to save American lives and to end the war. Even then I had a feeling that this was a decision that would better have been made in anguish.

On the other hand, the background to that lack of anguish is known to all of us who lived through that war. Although the atom bomb did begin a new era in the technical capabilities of wiping out mankind, that event was not in itself totally unprecedented by the usual quantitative standards which we used, then as now, to measure such achievements: the body count. As a matter of fact, the atom bomb did not kill as many people as the fire raids on Tokyo, during a period of a day or two earlier that year. Those raids created a firestorm: people who took refuge in the canals were boiled alive; the asphalt in the streets boiled; and the city of Tokyo was destroyed. And that holocaust had been preceded by similar ones: the firestorm in Dresden; the firestorm in Hamburg; and the raids which were comparably destructive on Cologne and Berlin.

These were things that we had been doing for several years. That period was an educational process for the United States: it taught us that there were simply no limits to what was permissible for a United States President to order and carry out —without consulting Congress or the public—once he determined that the stakes were sufficiently high. We emerged from that education potentially a very dangerous nation.

There is an idea that fascinated Dostoevski's Ivan Karamazov: If God does not exist, then everything is permitted. In the four years after 1941, Americans learned: *Hitler exists, therefore everything is permitted.* There was no limit at all—we learned from our own actions—to what one could justifiably do against such an enemy: one who threatened our existence, who used deception and terror, who stopped at nothing—one who carried out actions each more terrible than the last. Even before we learned of the nearly complete destruction of the European Jews, we knew that twenty million Russians were dying in that war, and not in gas chambers. The Japanese, meanwhile, had attacked us directly. So it seemed very clear in fighting such enemies—in fighting for one's life—that secrecy, deception of the public along with the adversary, concentration of power in the Executive, mobilization of all resources, and the use of absolutely unlimited violence were all justified, even required.

Albert Speer tells us he has no doubt that if Hitler had been given the atom bomb, he would have used it against England. But we have no doubt what *we* would have done with the atom bomb, since we did get it, and used it.

All of this created a supreme experience for many Americans, but particularly for officials close to the President. Their role had come to seem absolutely central in the world. Randolph Bourne said during the First World War, of which he was a lonely opponent: "War is the health of the state." But that is not true of all the branches and institutions of the State. The role of Congress, for example, is much diminished, and so is that of the courts and of the press. War is the health of the Presidency, and of the departments and agencies that serve it, the Executive branch. In no other circumstances can the President and his officials wield such unchallenged power, feel such responsibility and such awful freedom.

So what we learned—especially members of the Executive—in those four years from 1941 to 1945 was how exhilarating, in a certain sense, it was to have an opponent like Hitler, if one were to have an opponent at all. And we have not lacked for opponents, in the thirty years since 1941, as our officials took on what they perceived to be the challenge and responsibilities of leading half the world.

But in the last quarter of a century, Hitler has not existed, so it has been necessary to invent him. And we have invented Hitlers again and again. Stalin made a plausible one; Mao, somewhat less so. Even Fidel Castro, Ho Chi Minh, Nasser, and other nationalist leaders of obstreperous former colonies have taken on the guise of Hitler in the eyes of various Western powers seeking to maintain their rule, however exaggerated the image may have seemed to their own allies. Thus, Eisenhower, hoping to keep the French fighting in 1954 by united U.S./U.K. support, suggested to Churchill that the challenge posed by Ho Chi Minh at Dien Bien Phu—for example, to British interests in Malaya— was equivalent to that of Hitler in the Rhineland or at Munich.

If I may refer again to history; we failed to halt Hirohito, Mussolini, and Hitler by not acting in unity and in time. That marked the beginning of many years of stark tragedy and desperate peril. May it not be that our nations have learned something from that lesson? . . .[7]

[7] President Eisenhower, letter to Prime Minister Churchill, April 4, 1954 (PP, I, 99).

Eden and Churchill—men of some authority on the dangers of "appeasement"—refused to rise to this rather blatant appeal to their own past. Eden deprecated Dulles' warnings of Ho's military and expansionist potential and rejected, almost curtly, both the analogy and linkage of the security of French interests in Indochina to those of the British in Malaya: "French cannot lose the war between now and the coming of the rainy season however badly they may conduct it"; Referring to the rest of Southeast Asia, [Eden] said the British were confident that they had the situation in Malaya in hand . . . He said there was no parallel between Indochina and Malaya. . . . Eden said there was obviously a difference in the United States and the United Kingdom estimates and thinking . . ."[8]

John Foster Dulles was so offended by their skepticism that diplomatic relations were strained. But only two years later, Eden convinced himself that the destruction of Port Said from the air and the invasion of the Canal Zone were required and justified because he was fighting an Arab Hitler in Nasser. Surely, from the perspective of the Israelis threatened by Nasser, the analogy was not far-fetched at all. But that was scarcely the perspective of the British, concerned about the loss of imperial control of the Suez Canal, or of the French, concerned about imperial control of Algeria.

This happened to be an event that I watched closely, as a Marine in a Navy troopship that was evacuating Americans from Egypt. I had the opportunity to be bombed by the French—an unusual experience for an American—in the harbor of Alexandria. We were close enough to see the wave of bombers hitting Cairo as a large blob on the radarscope; another wave was hitting Port Said. Later I saw pictures of what had happened to the people and houses of Port Said. I told myself that was something I could not conceive of Americans doing in similar circumstances. At any rate, in that case it was Eisenhower, not Eden, who refused to act—or even to tolerate our allies' acting—on a specious

---

[8] Eden to Ambassador Aldrich, April 6, 1954 (*PP*, I, 477); Eden to Dulles, April 25, 1954 (*PP*, I, 478).

analogy between a local challenger and the global threat posed by Hitler.

I do not want to imply that my own attitude was purely skeptical and critical of these official perceptions in the fifties. I was against the bombing of civilians—whether in World War II or later—or nuclear threats, or pushing around small countries. Still, between 1954 and 1957, I would have been glad to use my Marine training wherever the President directed; and in October of 1956, there was some uncertainty whether that might be against Israel or Egypt. (As our troopship steamed toward the southeastern corner of the Mediterranean at the outset of the crisis, I was assigned—as a battalion operations officer—to draw up an amphibious landing plan for Haifa, while my partner made one for Alexandria. It would have gone much worse for our battalion, we supposed, if we had had to use mine.)

Even earlier, I had come to believe substantially all the Cold War premises, which linked nearly every "crisis" ultimately to our confrontation with the Soviet Union, and identified that with the challenge we had faced before and during World War II. If I accepted then an official American interpretation of events that now seems, at best, ideological and misleading, it was not because I had grown up as a conservative. My ambition, from late high school through most of my college years, had been to be a labor organizer or union economist. Nor had my thinking been influenced by Senator McCarthy. But what McCarthy and his fellow thugs were exploiting, in fact, was in part a credibility gap that had opened on the Left in those same years.

Just as conservatives had lost both credit and confidence in the Depression, and "isolationists" likewise with Pearl Harbor—two developments that weakened Congress in its later relations with the Executive—much of the Left suffered similarly in the late forties from reflexes that led to an implausible and apologetic stand with respect to Stalin's actions. My own political awareness did not begin much before the Truman Doctrine—when I was a junior in high school—and as I read the news in subsequent years of Czechoslovakia, the Berlin blockade, political trials, Korea, and uprisings in East Europe, official U.S. Government interpretations simply came, increasingly, to seem more plausible and reliable than those of "radical" critics who defended Soviet foreign policy. (I wish now that the range of available interpretations in those days had been broader—allowing for great skepticism toward both sides—as it is for students today.)

In my first summer at Rand, as a consultant in 1958, I recall hearing a new colleague who later became a close friend say, in a discussion comparing Adlai Stevenson's foreign policies to Eisenhower's, "I'm more of a Truman man, myself." It was a startling remark to hear at that time—Democrats didn't talk much about Truman anymore—and I remember thinking to myself, in recognition: That's what *I* am! It was, in fact, a common attitude among strategic analysts at Rand; we admired Dean Acheson greatly.

The following spring of 1959 was the occasion of my last public lectures in Boston before this one. These were the Lowell Lectures that I gave when I was a Junior Fellow at Harvard, on the subject of *The Art of Coercion*. The first was called "The Theory and Practice of Blackmail."[9] I was an economic theorist, interested in the abstract analysis of bargaining and decision-making. But I happened to have chosen, for my concrete examples, Hitler's blackmail of Austria, Czechoslovakia, and other countries in the 1930's. This had led me to read almost all of the ten volumes or so of the Nuremberg Documents, which formed the basis of the trials of the major Nazi war criminals. They left me with a strong sense of what evidence looks like at a trial for crimes against the peace and crimes against humanity. And what the documentary record of decision-making in an aggressive war looks like. (It looks like the Pentagon Papers.)

But what I was mainly interested in at the time were the specific tactics and techniques that Hitler had used so effectively to take over territories such as the Rhineland, Austria, the Sudetenland, and the rest of Czechoslovakia without firing a shot. As it happened, it was just while I was giving these lectures that Khrushchev, who in many ways looked very different from Hitler,

[9] Rand P-3883, The Rand Corporation, Santa Monica, California, July, 1968. (Lowell Lecture, The Lowell Institute, delivered March 10, 1959.)

and who *was* different, was making threats about our access to Berlin that sounded uncannily similar to the threats I was analyzing that Hitler had made to President Hácha of Czechoslovakia.[10]

The previous summer I had learned at Rand about the supposed plans of the Russians to build up a huge missile force, which would have the capability of wiping out our retaliatory force. It looked very much—especially in the Air Force intelligence estimates supplied to Rand—like a crash effort to acquire a nuclear superiority, either to back up the kind of blackmail strategy that Hitler had used or even to launch a Pearl Harbor-like attack. Now we were hearing Khrushchev say, as on June 23, 1959: "Your generals talk of maintaining your position in Berlin with force. That is bluff. If you send in tanks, they will burn and make no mistake about it. If you want war, you can have it, but remember, it will be your war. Our rockets will fly automatically."

At this point, I was ready to believe that Khrushchev, with all his differences, might eventually be led not only to sound like but to act like Hitler—particularly if he were encouraged by any weakness or irresolution on our part to believe that the United States was, in President Nixon's recent phrase, a "pitiful, helpless giant."[11] That same month, June, 1959, I went to the Rand Corporation as a permanent employee. From 1959 to 1961,[12] along with my colleagues at Rand, I threw myself into the effort to defend the United States against either threats or surprise attack by reducing the vulnerability of our retaliatory forces and of the Presidential command and control system.

Thus, although I had been only seven at the time it occurred, the example of Munich became as lively a symbol for me as it

[10] My account of Hitler's coercion of Hácha, from my Lowell Lecture entitled "The Political Uses of Madness," is reproduced in Herman Kahn's *On Thermonuclear War*, (Princeton, 1960), pages 403-407.

[11] I remember Khrushchev being quoted, on the morning of one of my lectures, to the effect: "Your Western officials keep speaking of Munich. But the difference now from Munich is that I am not Hitler." I cited his remark that afternoon, commenting: "Of course, he's correct. But it's noteworthy that he didn't feel called on to point out that he was not Chamberlain."

[12] The "missile gap" predictions were disproven by intelligence in the fall of 1961—not earlier, as often supposed—and the Berlin threats subsided soon afterwards, to reappear briefly just before the Cuban missile crisis in 1962.

was for older men like Dean Acheson or McGeorge Bundy or Dean Rusk. It was even a subject about which I knew a fair amount from my research. Likewise, the brilliant historical analysis of the U.S. decision process in late 1941 by my Rand colleague Roberta Wohlstetter—which pointed me toward my own later work on crisis decision-making—made Pearl Harbor seem a vivid and relevant memory. Her study, *Pearl Harbor: Warning and Decision*,[13] had great influence on our sense of what could happen without effective warning, as we read those Air Force intelligence estimates and studied the vulnerability of B-52's in their bases.

The prospect that we might ever be in the position of the Germans or the Japanese—say in Norway or Manchuria—rather than that of their opponents, was far from my mind. But another memory from Harvard comes back to me these days. In 1953-54, as I waited in graduate school to become an officer-candidate in the Marines, I had a student who was somewhat older than I, a German who had fought in the German army when he was seventeen. One afternoon, I remember, we got into a discussion of the Nuremberg and Tokyo trials, which he thought had been very unfair. I brought up, among other things, the Nazis' policy of reprisals, the taking and killing of hostages—as at Lidice—and the practice of torture. I said that these were acts for which people were properly punished, in the eyes of most of the world; they were not justified by war; the United States had not resorted to them as a policy, nor would it ever do so. He immediately replied, "That's because you've never fought guerrillas. That's the way you have to fight guerrillas." And I said, "Well, I don't believe that's a justification; there are other ways of fighting guerrillas, as a matter of fact, and I don't believe we would do that."

He came back to see me the next day. He was very serious, and his usual arrogance was gone. He said that he had discussed the subject with a group of other Europeans, and he wanted to

---

[13] Stanford, 1962. This study took years, and high-level intervention, to be cleared for public release by the Defense Department—though it was based mainly on the public testimony of the Pearl Harbor hearings—but it was available earlier at Rand, in manuscript.

tell me that he now thought there was something in what I had said; he suspected there *was* a cultural aspect to military behavior that made it easier for the Germans to use brutal methods than it would be for Americans. And this troubled him very much: he was going to have to think about it.

At that time, the French were fighting in Indochina, using napalm (which we supplied, along with most of their funds for the war) and also torture. But I knew little about that. Later that same year, in May, 1954, I was on a Marine drill field at Quantico when our drill sergeant told us: "Your rifles had better be clean, because Dien Bien Phu just fell." We hadn't seen a newspaper for a month, so that didn't mean much to us; anyway, our rifles were always clean. Vice President Nixon had been calling for the use of American ground troops, if necessary to prevent a French defeat in Indochina; Marines may even have been waiting offshore. I would have been glad to go at that time. But thanks to President Eisenhower, and to Eden, and to Senators like Lyndon Johnson, we missed an invasion of Indochina which, I believe, would almost surely have led in time to the use of nuclear weapons, and to a much, much fiercer war in the North than we have yet experienced in fighting in South Vietnam.

Instead, as I have said, we left the East Coast later for the vicinity of Suez; and the French went on to Algeria. There again they used napalm and artillery, forced relocation, and tortured on a large scale; they even bombed a neighboring country in "retaliation" for infiltration (once: we condemned it sharply). I sympathized with French critics of their own country and its practice of torture. Like the attack on Suez, I was glad that I didn't have to read in the newspapers about my countrymen doing such things.

Like most Americans', my attention in the spring of 1954 was not focused on the fall of Tonkin, but rather on the fall of Joseph McCarthy in the Army-McCarthy hearings nearby in Washington. My more recent research [discussed in "The Quagmire Myth"], on the origins of our involvement in the Indochina war, has led me to see the crucial relevance of McCarthy's career to our present position. For the politics that McCarthy stood for did not die with him. They included the potent charges not only that the Democrats had "lost China" in 1949 and 1950, but that their unwillingness to take such measures as sending advisors or troops, or bombers, to "save" China, or to use nuclear weapons or conventional bombs against Communist China during the Korean War, could only be explained by their willingness, if not desire, to see the Communists win at the peril of America's vital interests.

That inference, too, was in part a heritage of Hiroshima and what went before it. Once it had been established that an American President had the *right* to use American airpower against a civilian population, from then on important factions of the military, Congress, and the public were bound to expect any President to use it—indeed to tell him that he *must* use it—whenever our "vital interests" appeared to require it. And they could claim that a failure to bomb this way if necessary to avert "defeat" could only be understood as weakness or sentimentality, or possibly even as treason.

Vulnerability to this indictment is one of the risks, in fact, of defining a conflict as involving "vital interests": and the Cold War ideology enormously widened the realm of such conflicts. For, after all, it has always served the purposes of the Executive to define the enemy we were facing as a Hitler. Or, if that were too implausible with respect to the immediate enemy, we pointed to the larger enemies behind him that made it more plausible; China behind Ho Chi Minh, for example, or Russia behind Castro.[14] In those circumstances, every President has knowingly faced the threat of being charged with timidity, or incompetence, or treachery, if he allowed this country to "lose" in a confrontation without having done, as McGeorge Bundy once put it, "all that we could have done": i.e., if he allowed a "Communist victory" to take place without his having used the weapons that World War II had placed—physically and morally—under his command.

---

[14] Or, since Nixon's China visit, Russia behind General Giap. Thus, William F. Buckley, Jr., on April 13, 1972, referring to the current offensive: "The blitzkrieg from the North . . . might as well be the Wehrmacht, marching into Poland. . . . The enemy in this instance is quite clearly the Soviet Union, so identified quite explicitly by the Secretary of Defense. . . . Under such circumstances the meeting between Kosygin and Nixon might as well be a meeting between Hitler and Pétain."

That apprehension has had a strong effect on Presidential decision-making ever since. And at the same time it has given each
President a sense of unique responsibility, while it has tested his
character and powers of restraint.

Indeed, it is not often remembered now that the most salient
issue of the Presidential campaign of 1964 was not so much who
should run the war in Indochina, with respect to the decisions
about bombing in North Vietnam or using ground troops, but
more crucially, who should have his finger on the nuclear button.
Senator Goldwater openly believed in the use of nuclear weapons
in a wide variety of situations, including the Indochina war. He
also promised to give greater authority in international crisis to
military advisers, many of whom shared his faith in nuclear
weapons. Faced with this sort of opponent in an election campaign, many officials in the Johnson Administration tacitly believed, in effect, that a certain amount of deception and manipu-
lation of the Congress, the press, and the public were justified
in order to protect the nation from Goldwater's election and its
consequences. And many Congressmen, among others, saw the
situation the same way. Thus the Tonkin Gulf Resolution was
rammed through Congress without real questioning of the specious testimony for it, and the Administration's own plans for
escalating the war were concealed.

In describing some events and interpretations that were widely
influential in the forties and fifties, I have suggested what I suspect were central considerations in the minds specifically of senior
officials like Lyndon Johnson, Dean Rusk, McGeorge Bundy, and
Robert McNamara, which significantly conditioned their view of
their role in history, of what they were permitted to do, and of
what their responsibilities were. As Howard Zinn has put it, one
of the historical legacies of Hitler has been that any depredations
much less awful than his have come to seem almost acceptable.[15]

[15] "What Hitler did was to extend the already approved doctrine of indiscriminate mass murder (ten million dead on the battlefields of World War I)
to its logical end, and thus stretch further than ever before the limits of the
tolerable. By killing one third of the world's Jews, the Nazis diminished the
horror of any atrocity that was separated by two degrees of fiendishness from
theirs." *The Politics of History* (Boston, 1971), page 209.

It's difficult to think of any American use of non-nuclear violence that U.S. leaders are likely to regard as unthinkable when they think of what Hitler did, or of what *we* did in World War II, or of what the future use of thermonuclear weapons would mean, whether by others or by ourselves.

The obvious fact that in any given situation we could annihilate an opponent with nuclear weapons, or even with conventional weapons, produces an almost inevitable feeling among what Richard Barnet calls our "national security managers" that we cannot be doing anything so very wrong as long as we refrain from that. As a former colleague at Rand, Konrad Kellen, has put it to me, this attitude among high officials can go even further: that an opponent like North Vietnam should feel gratitude to us, and at the very least should give us the small concessions that we are demanding at the moment, in simple appreciation of the fact that we have not yet unleashed the full weight of SAC B-52's or of nuclear weapons upon his cities and population. Such a belief may well underlie the persistent faith of our last three Presidents that the settlement terms they were offering Hanoi were "reasonable," and that someday, after enough of our discriminate bombing, the Hanoi leadership would come to recognize this. The moral doubts of the security managers during a war are also reduced by their knowledge that influential military and political members of the Establishment are anxious to use heavier bombing than is currently going on.[16] Having to counter these opponents reinforces their own sense of moderation and restraint. They can even identify their own survival in office with the survival of the population of Indochina, or really, of most of the world.

Having arrived at this conclusion, there are no further moral issues that they can see. It is obviously for the good of everyone that they do what they feel must be done both to avoid defeat

[16] In March, 1968, Secretary of the Air Force Harold Brown proposed an escalation of the air war in which: "The present restrictions on bombing NVN would be lifted so as to permit bombing of military targets without the present scrupulous concern for collateral civilian damage and casualties. . . . The aims of this alternative campaign would be to erode the will of the population by exposing a wider area of NVN to casualties and destruction . . ." [PP, IV, 261]

in Indochina and defeat at the polls, short of employing "ultimate" measures. They do not have to, and they do not, regard themselves as perfect or infallible to be confident that they are better than the other people who would be making these decisions if they were not there.

We might notice that these invidious comparisons are domestic counterparts to the traditional *imperial* comparison, which has the same moral function: "What we want to do in your country is in any case better for you than what those others would do in your country," where "those others" are imperial rivals, or else local Communists, or native forces of "feudalism" or "chaos"— whoever looms as a practical alternative to the hegemony being fostered.

My purpose in listing these beliefs is not to mock the officials who acted on them. In the actual circumstances, such beliefs often led to conscientious and sometimes anguished dedication to their duties. Indeed, no other performance in government so impressed me or inspired so much loyalty in me as Secretary McNamara's tireless and shrewd efforts in the early sixties, largely hidden from the public to this day, gradually to control the forces within the military bureaucracy that pressed for the threat and use of nuclear weapons. It is no deprecation of the seriousness of or need for such efforts to say, with hindsight, that, in a number of ways they may have helped to influence many civilian officials to promote our policies in Vietnam, and to their spells of optimism about our methods there.

Regrettably, these efforts to reduce the chances of our own initiation of nuclear war were not accompanied by a questioning of the premises or aims of Cold War policy—in part because these high officials shared such premises and values themselves, and in part because President Kennedy communicated to them his sensitivity to his own narrow margin of victory and of support in Congress, and the political risks of challenging the accepted axioms of "security." Thus, in their struggle to escape from the near-total reliance on nuclear weapons in military arsenals, plans and psychology that had evolved under the Eisenhower "New Look" defense budgets, New Frontier officials did not challenge the view of tasks and goals prevailing in the Pentagon but only the nuclear means pressed by the military. In the process, they often moved into the position of being advocates of the feasibility and effectiveness of non-nuclear approaches to the traditional Cold War "challenges," and salesmen of non-nuclear hardware, to skeptical and reluctant military planners.

Counterinsurgency and covert warfare, "crisis-management," helicopters and "air cavalry"—all of these have recently been viewed as romantic obsessions of the civilian planners; but they had another side. It is my guess that these and other similar projects of civilians and some military in the Kennedy and Johnson Administrations—including much of our effort in Vietnam— must be understood, in large part, as tactics in an argument and indeed, struggle with much of the military and its conservative support in Congress, the media, corporations, and the public over the issue of basing our defense and our strategy in the Cold War primarily on nuclear weapons. This creditable motive for proposing alternatives to nuclear threats by no means greatly extenuates either the delusions that came to accompany these programs or the "conventional" violence to which they led. For in this hidden debate, there was strong incentive—indeed it seemed necessary— for the civilian leaders to demonstrate that success was possible in Indochina without the need either to compromise Cold War objectives or to threaten or use nuclear weapons. And in large military bureaucracies, necessity is the mother of illusion—and brutality.

Such concerns remained semi-covert (for it was seen as dangerous to lend substance to the active suspicions of military staffs and their Congressional allies that there were high Administration officials who didn't love the Bomb) and joined with those discussed earlier to provide a framework of attitudes that enabled "liberal, humane" individuals to carry out a war like the one in Vietnam. In stark terms: compared to the probable behavior, as they saw it, either of the Communist "enemy" or of their domestic rivals, civil and military, any evil they might be doing seemed surely to be a "lesser evil." Thus, for example, though they have unleashed twelve megatons of firepower on the people and terrain of Indochina, they have done so in such a way as to kill far fewer civilians than those killed by a fraction of that firepower in recent wars, including the Korean War,[17] and far below what would have resulted from the rejected bombing programs preferred and proposed by the Joint Chiefs—which, after all, defines restraint, does it not?

By focusing on this "restraint," it is unnecessary to face the questions: How many, in fact, *are* we killing? Who are they? How old are they? What had they done, for our officials and commanders and soldiers to sentence them to death? What are we doing to that country, to its society and its homes and its lands and its families? And by what right do we do it?

In sum, to look at a war as a fight ultimately for survival against an implacable and evil enemy—and to know, at the same time, that one is inhibiting the levels of violence urged by much of the public and by rivals for power—is to see that war through a dark glass that screens out the moral dimension. And that is how our officials have sought to view Vietnam, and to teach others to see it. But for increasing numbers of Americans, to watch the Vietnam War at home, up close on a TV screen, is to see ourselves in a mirror: to find us doing monstrous things.

We have come a long way since John Quincy Adams could truly say that America "goes not abroad in search of monsters to destroy."[18] We have been in the process of fighting monsters without stop for a generation and a half, looking all that time into the nuclear abyss. And the abyss has looked back into us.

What that has meant for the consciousness of our officials is measured most starkly for me by the following memorandum,

---

[17] In the language of Professor Samuel P. Huntington of Harvard:

In comparison to the Korean War the Vietnamese War has been a relatively limited and undestructive conflict. In one year of fighting almost every major city in North and South Korea was virtually leveled to the ground. Up to mid-1968 the only major Vietnamese city which has received anything like this treatment was Hué. In Korea somewhere between two and three million civilians were killed directly or indirectly by the war. The civilian suffering in Vietnam, however bad it may be, has been little by comparison. (*No More Vietnams?* [New York, 1968], page 39.)

[18] Cited in Arthur Schlesinger, Jr.'s *The Crisis of Confidence* (Boston, 1969), page 118.

which I first read in the Pentagon Papers. It was written by an official who, from the time I first worked for him in 1964 until his death in 1967, privately hated this war and wanted us—totally, precipitately—out of Vietnam:

Strikes at population targets (per se) are likely not only to create a counterproductive wave of revulsion abroad and at home, but greatly to increase the risk of enlarging the war with China and the Soviet Union. Destruction of locks and dams, however—if handled right— might (perhaps after the *next* Pause) offer promise. It should be studied. Such destruction does not kill or drown people. By shallow-flooding the rice, it leads after time to widespread starvation (more than a million?) unless food is provided—which we could offer to do "at the conference table."[19]

I think that the attitudes that I have described can impel our President, even later Presidents, to carry on this war, or other wars like it or worse, for many more years. In fact, I think they will do so unless, somehow, we as citizens demand more of them and find a way to change these attitudes and ways of behaving. And that probably means first changing ourselves and our own sense of responsibility.

Let me turn to my own responsibility: not to be egocentric or pretentious, but simply to begin where each of us should begin. Not to be masochistic either. There is no need to search out my statements in old memos that seem to me now most foolish, the actions or attitudes hardest to face today; it is enough, for a start, to look hard at the incidents of my involvement that are among those least painful to recall—ones I like to remember as most extenuating.

By the spring of 1970, when the Congressional Conference on War Crimes took place, I had already given the information in the Pentagon Papers to the Senate Foreign Relations Committee. I did so out of a sense of responsibility to share with my countrymen and Government the special knowledge I had acquired as

---

[19] John T. McNaughton, in a memo entitled "Some Observations About Bombing North Vietnam," January 8, 1966 (*PP*, IV, 43). Almost surely, McNaughton made these comments for tactical bureaucratic reasons (see the accompanying memo expressing his skepticism of the whole bombing strategy and the possible need to compromise our aims in the war [*PP*, IV, 46-48]). But that does not make this paragraph easier to read.

a former Executive official and a researcher. The policies and deceptions I was revealing to the Legislative branch did seem to me
to be illegal and unconstitutional, as well as both practically and
morally wrong. But to attribute "war crimes" to a participant
like myself would have seemed to me exaggerated. During that
conference, as I reflected on my own experience in Vietnam and
in Washington, I did see that I might be answerable for it, even
in a legal sense. Yet aside from the insignificance of my influence,
so much of my participation had taken the form of reporting
failures honestly, criticizing mistakes, protesting evils, that I felt
little sense of responsibility, let alone guilt, for those failures or
evils.

For example, one of the very few policy memoranda that the
researchers of the McNamara Study found that criticized the prac-
ticality and the legitimacy of Walt Rostow's proposals of coercive
bombing was largely drafted by me for the Defense Department
when I was still formally a consultant. It included my following
remarks cited in the Pentagon Papers:

> Given present attitudes, applications of the Rostow approach risks
> domestic and international opposition ranging from anxiety and pro-
> test to condemnation, efforts to disassociate from U.S. policies or
> alliances, or even strong countermeasures. . . .
> Currently, then, it is the Rostow approach, rather than the measures
> it counters that would be seen generally as an "unstabilizing" change
> in the rules of the game, an escalation of conflict, an increasing of
> shared, international risks, and quite possibly, as an open aggression
> demanding condemnation . . . [*PP*, III, 201]

Strong words, for the Department of Defense; this may be the
only passage by an official in the pages of the Pentagon Papers
that suggests the word "aggression" in connection with a possible
American policy. (Though I notice, on reading it now, how much
its impact is attenuated by the traditional bureaucratic tactic of
ascribing such a "condemnation" to "domestic and international
opposition," rather than to objective judgment or to myself.)

And yet—it was *after* writing that critique that I came on as
a full-time employee of the Defense Department—assigned to
work on Vietnam policy! My motives, to be sure, were initially
those of an observer, a Rand social scientist interested in under-

standing the internal processes of government. But my role was nevertheless that of a participant, even when I acted as an internal critic.

The situation that I entered in mid-1964,—as it looks to me now —amounted to a conspiracy: the officials who became my colleagues were concerting, in secrecy, to plan and ultimately to wage aggressive war against North Vietnam. The people who proposed and were preparing this—foolishly and wrongly, it seemed to me—all cooperated in keeping secret the facts of their proposals and their plans as they awaited final Presidential approval, which they expected, during an election campaign in which the public was encouraged to believe that the only way to protect against such plans being carried out was to vote for the incumbent President. (The various reasons that may explain this *conspiratorial style* of policy-making—revealed by the Pentagon Papers as a persistent Executive pattern over much of the last quarter-century—have been a primary subject of speculation and analysis in this book.)

Nevertheless, like others who opposed some of these plans, I too cooperated in concealing them. Having expressed my objections, I stayed in place, observed, took part, criticized other policies, and helped those along too when told to do so. In short, I did the jobs assigned to me, including, for example, the one of collecting daily and weekly summaries of Vietcong assassinations and kidnappings for public release in the spring of 1965 to explain why our bombing of the North was justified.[20]

---

[20] This followed McGeorge Bundy's Memo of February 7, 1965, recommending a "policy of sustained reprisal against North Vietnam":

. . . Once a program of reprisals is clearly underway, it should not be necessary to connect each specific act against North Vietnam to a particular outrage in the South. It should be possible, for example, to publish weekly lists of outrages in the South and to have it clearly understood that these outrages are the cause of such action against the North as may be occurring in the current periods. [*PP*, III, 312]

By the time I went to Saigon, I probably had more details in my head of recent Vietcong "outrages" than any other person.

Nowadays the Pentagon also collects statistics on our own terrorists. The "Phoenix" program that we instituted in 1967-68 to "neutralize VC infrastructure," using "counterterror teams" trained, equipped, and paid by the CIA, reports killing or kidnapping more Vietnamese in both 1969 and 1970 than the VC are charged with doing.

Meanwhile, during the year I spent in the Department of Defense, the Congress and the American people heard many lies from Executive officials: not only in the election campaign but long after it. The deception of Congress by McNamara concerning the "34A" covert operations against North Vietnam, preceding the incidents in the Tonkin Gulf of August 2 and 4, 1964, are well known by now.[21] But the Pentagon Papers also give the lie to Rusk's statement to the Senate Foreign Relations Committee that the raids were not followed "from Washington in great detail"[22]; they include some of the detailed schedules of raids which I was assigned to carry around regularly in the fall of 1964 to be approved by Llewellyn Thompson in State and McGeorge Bundy in the White House.[23]

Of course, it was precisely the "sensitive" nature of the operations—i.e., their illegality and covertness, which required lying to the Senate if questions were raised—that called for a high-priced courier like myself, let alone such high-level involvement. Within six months, and for three years thereafter, the management of 34A operations was overshadowed by the Cabinet-level "Tuesday lunch" at the White House where President Johnson and his highest advisers picked the next week's bombing targets in North

---

[21] See Anthony Austin, *The President's War*, passim.
[22] *The Pentagon Papers*, Bantam-New York Times edition, page 266.
[23] For example:

The proposed September 34A actions are as follows: . . . (3) *Maritime Operations*
  (a) 1-30 September—Demolition of Route 1 bridge by infiltrated team accompanied by fire support teams, place short-delay charges against spans and caissons, place antipersonnel mines on road approaches. (This bridge previously hit but now repaired.)
  (b) 1-30 September—Bombard Cape Mui Dao observation post with 81 mm. mortars and 40 mm. guns from two PTFs [patrol boats, supplied by CIA].
  . . . (k) 1-30 September—Bombard Cape Mui Ron in conjunction with junk capture mission [the crew of a fishing junk in North Vietnamese waters, for interrogation] . . . [PP, III, 554]

For the procedures on handling these schedules, for which I was Mr. McNaughton's "designee," see Vance memo (PP, III, 571). Some of these operational details, of the placement of antipersonnel weapons and 81 mm. mortar rounds, and the kidnapping of North Vietnamese fishermen, might seem petty to be occupying the attention of these officials—as well as being at odds with Rusk's account to the Senate—but at the time, this was the only war we had.

Vietnam (*PP*, IV, 209-10). Any war is the health of the Executive branch, but secret wars, major crises, and small "limited wars" with large potential are most invigorating of all for the influence of the group closest to the President.

Well, lies are to be expected in the conduct of covert operations—that is what makes them covert—though whether Congress should have been urged by the Executive to issue a "functional equivalent of a declaration of war" on the basis, in part, of an untrue cover story is now rather widely questioned. But what seems even more questionable—or to use a more precise word, seems unconstitutional—is to launch a major military campaign, involving hundreds of thousands of American soldiers, as if it too were a covert operation. Yet that is what was done in the spring and summer of 1965 [as described in "The Quagmire Myth"], when large and eventually open-ended force-level decisions by the President—along with decisive changes in the offensive mission of these forces—were deceptively presented to the public in much more limited terms. And U.S. operations in Laos, including the bombing ever since the spring of 1964, especially the heavy bombing campaign since the spring and fall of 1968, have always had this character of a "secret war."

I was skeptical of this policy of deception. I did not believe these decisions could be kept very long from the American public—in this, I appeared again and again to be mistaken—and I questioned the need or the desirability of taking such gambles with the trust of the public. And yet, it was not only "they" who had kept all these decisions quiet, hidden from the American public. I had kept them quiet. After all, to use phrases I have heard put to me a good deal in recent months, "who had appointed" me to announce these plans to the American public? "Who had elected" me to decide what should be kept secret and what should be openly revealed? No one could have been more responsive to such strictures, or excuses, than I. Indeed, my whole professional background prevented such questions from arising in my mind. Nor did I ask myself then whether I had the right to collaborate in these deceptions and illicit acts, and to conceal them from the public. By the same token I did not ask

whether lying to Congress and the public was among the functions for which Secretaries McNamara and Rusk had been appointed, and their appointments confirmed; nor "who had elected
the President" to do or to order these things?

Moreover, I proceeded to deepen my own involvement in the
war; I volunteered to go to Vietnam in 1965. This, indeed, partly
reflected a sense of personal responsibility. In the limited ways
open to a staff assistant, I had approved of and encouraged the
view that our investment of prestige in Vietnam by the spring
of 1965 should be safeguarded by a limited commitment of our
troops. This involvement in sending Americans to live in harm's
way made me uncomfortable about watching them do so from
Washington. A preference to share their jeopardy, if we were to
be at war, as well as the desire to understand the war at closer
hand, took me to Vietnam—where I learned a number of things;
and failed, perhaps too easily, to learn some others.

For example, a year after my arrival I took part in a far-rang-
ing study of the "roles and missions" of all American personnel
in Vietnam related to the pacification program.[24] The group was
to make recommendations directly to Ambassador Lodge and
General Westmoreland. We made eighty-one recommendations
altogether, but at the end of the summary of the report we
grouped a few of them, with brief discussions, as being especially
important. One of these was the following:

Although we have not studied the matter in depth, we regard it as
important for the USG and GVN to know more about the actual impact
of the current pattern of bombing and artillery on rural attitudes
relevant to RD. It is possible that the negative impact—particularly,
of strikes not in immediate support of ground action—is considerable,
sustaining villagers' tendencies to collaborate with the VC and limiting
the prospects for progress in RD. At the same time, it is possible that
additional constraints on these operations would have serious military
penalties. Thus the issue is important; but adequate data is not now
available, either on the objective consequences of these strikes in terms
of VC and civilians killed and injured, or on the attitudinal conse-

[24] Part of this study appears under the title "Problems of 'Revolutionary Development,' " pages 156-70.

quences. (Rand reports on its prisoner and Chieu Hoi interrogations do not adequately fill this gap.)

RECOMMEND:

That on an urgent basis an adequate research effort be launched to determine the actual physical and attitudinal consequences of present policies and practices concerning air and artillery; by methods including comprehensive sampling of opinions, both in the affected areas and elsewhere, and operations to discover the objective results of sample air and artillery missions.

We made the recommendation in this cautious form although almost everyone in the study group—which included some of the most experienced Americans in Vietnam—believed he had enough evidence from his own personal observations to conclude that the greater proportion of our bombing and artillery—apart from close support of ground combat operations—*was* "counterproductive" in its human and political effects, even when weighed against alleged military benefits, which we believed to be negligible. But since no such survey had ever been made, and since strong military opposition was inevitable to any proposal to reduce the scale of bombing operations, it seemed fruitless to make any recommendations directly on those operations prior to a comprehensive investigation. (Let alone to mention mere "humane" considerations.)

Yet even this proposed investigation was considered too radical or risky by the Mission Council—the term used was "unnecessary." Even the civilian Public Affairs Office (JUSPAO) rejected it, obviously fearing that any leak to the press about civilian damage would have bad effects on public opinion at home. Thus the civilian officials agreed with the military that there was no "need to know"—no need to find out—such information.

This was a striking instance of a phenomenon I was to see often later, and not only in the Government: the "need not to know" certain unpleasant realities. In particular, a need not to gather data at all, if it might leak to the wrong audience: that is, to Congress, or to the American people.[25]

---

[25] Robert S. McNamara's decision to launch his study of U.S. decision-making in Vietnam—giving the task force virtually free rein—was, of course, a spectacular exception.

Two and a half years later, at the outset of a new Administration, I spent some weeks in the Executive Office Building in Washington, reading and helping to summarize for the President more than a thousand pages of answers from various agencies involved in Vietnam policy to a set of questions I had drafted earlier, as described in my Introduction, which had been sent out as National Security Study Memorandum 1. One of these questions was: "How adequate is our information on the overall scale and incidence of damage to civilians by air and artillery, and looting and misbehavior by RVNAF?" Answers varied in honesty and specificity, but it was clear from the overall set of replies, as I had expected, that such information remained inadequate or nonexistent. As my last task on the project, I drafted a set of directives for additional studies on various subjects and some "Decision Memorandums" on others. One of the latter, addressed to the Secretaries of State and Defense and the Director of Central Intelligence, was, once again, on the subject "Reporting and Compensation of Civilian Damage in South Vietnam":

(1)   The President has directed that the Secretary of Defense, with the assistance of the Secretary of State and the Director of Central Intelligence, establish procedures assuring regular reporting on as comprehensive a basis as possible of damage to civilian lives and property caused by U.S., RVNAF, and other allied operations. As a base point for this reporting, a study should establish as realistically as possible the magnitude of past and current damage, using all available sources for this estimate, and establish the nature of current gaps in our knowledge and reporting.

(2) The Secretary of State and the Secretary of Defense will evaluate the adequacy in scale and promptness of current programs for compensating civilian victims, providing medical aid for civilian injured, and handling refugees, and recommend needed improvements, including U.S. support costs.

This draft memorandum, along with my others, went to Henry Kissinger for his approval on March 1, 1969, the day I left Washington. A week later, I was told that all the proposals looked worthwhile, but that the agencies "had been asked enough questions for the moment." That seemed reasonable . . . for the moment; but the list of studies now reaches well over a hundred, and that particular one has never been included. There are some things Executive officials know better than to need to know.

I could, perhaps, reassure myself that I had at least used the major opportunities that had come my way to urge my superiors to inform themselves about the human consequences of their policies. The effort had, indeed, failed, but I had been on the right side of that issue. And yet, I'm forced to remember that the first episode was in the *middle* of my two years in Vietnam; and that it was followed by another year in which, though there were other occasions when I again made such recommendations, I did not by any means do everything I could have done to inform *myself* of the dimensions of the burden imposed upon the people of Indochina by U.S. firepower. Or to inform anyone else. And much the same is true of the second instance.

It is, in fact, my own long *persistence in ignorance*—of the full impact of the American way of war upon the people of Indochina and of the history of the conflict bearing on the nature and legitimacy of our involvement—that I find most to blame in myself. And my own need not to know required the usual amount of self-deception.

Reading plans and cables in the Pentagon in 1964-65 I had learned about some programs which I thought wrong or even criminal—including coercive bombing of the North, the use of "incapacitating gases" and B-52's in the South, and the concurrent invasion of the Dominican Republic. Keeping silent in public about what I had read and heard made me an accomplice even in these programs; I knew that, and accepted it. Yet during my year in the Pentagon—along with my choices, after consideration, *not* to resign over any of the milestones of policy mentioned above —I did define for myself thresholds that I would never allow myself to cross as an official and at which I must resign. These would be signals that the process of wartime violence had corrupted human standards to a point that a man must resist with his whole weight. They included the threat or use of nuclear weapons, or the unrestricted targeting of cities and population, as we had done in World War II; or a deliberate policy of torture, as our enemies had used in World War II and the French in Algeria.

I left the Government in mid-1967 in large part in order to oppose our policy—though still as an insider—but not because I believed that those particular thresholds had been crossed. Not even the third; for although I was aware that our South Vietnamese "allies" did use torture, with the general knowledge of American advisors, I had not heard, despite my asking, of any but isolated instances of comparable behavior by U.S. units. Thus, even my own tour in Vietnam had not prepared me to expect that a day would come when an American officer like Lieutenant Colonel Anthony Herbert would testify about the routine torture and murder of Vietnamese by American officers.

But neither had my year in the Pentagon taught me to read the "contingency plans" and proposals that had passed through my own hands with the same eyes that my wife and children brought to them six years later. Here is some of the language they read in the Pentagon papers about our bombing policy:

"We all accept the will of the DRV as the real target";

"Judging by experience during the last war, the resumption of bombing after a pause would be even more painful to the population of North Vietnam than a fairly steady rate of bombing";

". . . 'water-drip' technique . . .";

"It is important not to 'kill the hostage' by destroying the North Vietnamese assets inside the 'Hanoi donut' ";

"Fast/full squeeze . . . " option versus "Progressive squeeze-and-talk";

" . . . the 'hot-cold' treatment . . . the objective of 'persuading' Hanoi, which would dictate a program of painful surgical strikes separated by fairly long gaps . . .";

" . . . our 'salami-slice' bombing program . . . ";

" . . . ratchet . . . ";

" . . . one more turn of the screw . . ."[26]

These were phrases—written by senior officials I worked with and respected—that I had read and discussed in offices in the Pentagon and State, often in disapproval of their contents yet with-

[26] Respectively: William P. Bundy, (PP, IV, 649); (PP, IV, 35); (PP, III, 650); Robert S. McNamara, (PP, III, 706); John T. McNaughton, (PP, III, 599); (PP, IV, 45-46); (PP, IV, 44); (PP, IV, 33); Richard Helms, (PP, IV, 65).

out ever seeing or hearing them as my wife did when she characterized them, in horror, as *"the language of torturers."*

When I came back from Vietnam in 1967 I did not yet have a sense that our involvement was outrageous or criminal, but I strongly believed that it must be ended. I began to look for allies among other officials who had left Vietnam or left office disillusioned with the war. And I came up against a phenomenon that has challenged me ever since, both to understand and to deal with: the apparent lack of any strong sense of personal responsibility on the part of many of these individuals to take effective steps to help end the war. Despite their own involvement, and despite their disaffection, most of them semed unwilling to take any more active part in antiwar efforts than they had while they were still serving the Government.

Ought they—ought I—to feel such responsibility? How might it be defined, or weighed, for someone like myself and my former colleagues, who had both participated in events and "opposed" some of them from inside; and who had had special knowledge or the power to acquire it? A starting point, it seems to me, lies in some profound comments on these questions by a man who had had twenty years in prison to reflect upon them in relation to his own life. A German, a Nazi—Albert Speer.

I recommend his memoirs, *Inside the Third Reich.* I wish that all of our former high officials, and our present ones, would read it, as I wish they would read the 7,000 pages of the Pentagon Papers, so they could see their own decisions in context. But for anyone with experience as an official, even at lower levels, Speer's is a very chilling book to read.

Speer was one of the most powerful men in the Nazi regime—in charge of war production. Alone among the defendants at the Nuremberg trial, he accepted full responsibility for his actions and for those of the regime—including those acts in which he had taken no part, even those he said he had been ignorant of at the time. This position amazed his fellow defendants, and his own lawyer urged him not to take it. Nevertheless, he did so for a number of reasons, which evidently he has not regretted. He was sentenced to twenty years in Spandau Prison, which he served; he entered in 1945 and came out in 1966.

Inside the Third Reich is an amazing document, one that has no analogue, so far as I know, among the writings of any American associated with our current or past wars. What is most troubling about this book is to discover that the man who wrote it does not seem to be an unfamiliar type at all. The tone, the point of view, even much of the account of his life could be taken for that of any one of a number of our most respected officials.

Speer was, after all, regarded as the most liberal, humane, and intelligent of the Nazis. What is disconcerting is to find that this means that he would not at all have been the least creditable member of recent National Security Councils. Thus his own explanation of his sense of accountability—the standards that led him to take responsibility as broadly as I have described—would seem to be particularly pertinent.

Recently in an interview, Speer was asked, "How could a man of your intelligence and sensibility allow himself to remain part of so evil a system, however gradually it enveloped you?"[27] It is, in effect, the question Townsend Hoopes has addressed, rhetorically, to our recent officials. Hoopes found the answer in their good intentions and their reliance on a misguided sense of history. Speer's answer is: "There is, unfortunately, no necessary correlation between intelligence and decency; the genius and the moron are equally susceptible to corruption."

On his motives for returning to Hitler's intimate circle after he had left it once, Speer says:

. . . the desire to retain the position of power I had achieved was unquestionably a major factor. Even though I was only shining in the reflected light of Hitler's power—and I don't think I ever deceived myself on that score—I still found it worth striving for. I wanted, as part of his following, to gather some of his popularity, his glory, his greatness, around myself. Up to 1942, I still felt that my vocation as an architect allowed me a measure of pride that was independent of

[27] *Playboy,* June 18, 1971.

Hitler. But since then I had been bribed and intoxicated by the desire to wield pure power, to assign people to this and that, to say the final word on important questions, to deal with expenditures in the billions. I thought I was prepared to resign, but I would have sorely missed the heady stimulus that comes with leadership.[28]

Pride, ambition, an attraction toward the center of power, unfailing loyalty to leaders who can assign them great projects to carry out: all human qualities, not lacking in any of the men chosen for high posts by recent American Presidents.

Speer also speaks of the progression of little crimes that blunted conscience:

Things that would have shocked and horrified me in 1934, such as the assassination of opposition leaders, the persecution of the Jews, the incarceration and torture of innocent men in concentration camps, I tolerated as unfortunate excesses in 1935; and things I couldn't have stomached in 1935 were palatable a few years later. This happened in one way or another to all of us in Germany. As the Nazi environment enveloped us, its evils grew invisible—because we were part of them.[29]

In one particular case, Speer relates, an old friend came to tell him, in a faltering voice:

. . . never to accept an invitation to inspect a concentration camp in Upper Silesia. Never, under any circumstances. He had seen something there which he was not permitted to describe and moreover could not describe. I did not query him, I did not query Himmler, I did not query Hitler, I did not speak with personal friends. I did not investigate—for I did not want to know what was happening there. Hanke must have been speaking of Auschwitz. During those few seconds, while Hanke was warning me, the whole responsibility had become a reality again. Those seconds were uppermost in my mind when I stated to the International Court at the Nuremberg Trial that as an important member of the leadership of the Reich, I had to share the total responsibility for all that had happened. For from that moment on, I was inescapably contaminated morally; from fear of discovering something which might have made me turn from my course, I had closed my eyes. This deliberate blindness outweighs whatever good I may have done or tried to do in the last period of the war. Those activities shrink to nothing in the face of it. Because I failed at that time,

28 *Inside the Third Reich,* page 342.
29 *Playboy,* page 72.

I still feel, to this day, responsible for Auschwitz in a wholly personal sense.[30]

In his interview, Speer sums up the moral burden of the "need not to know" in a stunning image:

If I was isolated, I determined the degree of my own isolation. If I was ignorant, I ensured my own ignorance. If I did not see, it was because I did not want to see. . . .

In my own case, there is no way I can avoid responsibility for the extermination of the Jews. I was as much their executioner as Himmler, because they were carried past me to their deaths and I did not see. It is surprisingly easy to blind your moral eyes. I was like a man following a trail of bloodstained footprints through the snow without realizing someone has been injured.[31]

In the end, after twenty years, the "one unforgettable experience" that dominates Speer's impressions of the past remains . . . the Nuremberg trial itself, with its photographs and testimony presenting, inescapably, not "enemies" but individual human beings, victims, who had become, at last, real to the criminal defendants. In particular, Speer recalls:

. . . there was one photograph of a Jewish family going to its death, a husband with his wife and children being led to the gas chamber. I couldn't rid my mind of that photograph; I would see it in my cell at night. I see it still. It has made a desert of my life.[32]

When I began to read these passages aloud to an audience at the Community Church in Boston in late May, 1971, my private mood as I began was, I thought, detached. I was, in fact, imagining that Robert McNamara, McGeorge Bundy, Dean Rusk, or the Presidents they served were listening—until I heard my own voice growing low and halting. I told my hearers, "I am finding this difficult to read." After a moment, I went on, but I brought the talk to an end. I knew that it was myself who was the listener, my eyes, my voice responding to these indictments.

I was there, too, however minor and "innocuous" my role. "My moral failure," Speer says, "is not a matter of this item and

[30] *Inside the Third Reich,* page 113.
[31] *Playboy,* pages 72, 74.
[32] *Playboy,* page 72.

that; it resides in my active association with the whole course of events." That accusation—and the more specific one of willful, irresponsible ignorance and neglect of human consequences— are truths that I must live with. As should any American official known to me who has been associated with Vietnam.

ABOUT THE AUTHOR

Daniel Ellsberg was born in Chicago in 1931 and grew up in Detroit. He was educated at Harvard College and Cambridge University. After serving as an infantry officer in the Marine Corps, Mr. Ellsberg became a member of the Society of Fellows, Harvard University, and later received a Ph.D. in economics.

From 1959 to 1964 he was a strategic analyst at the Rand Corporation and a consultant to the Department of Defense, which he joined in 1964 as Special Assistant to John T. McNaughton. In 1965 he went to Vietnam for the State Department as a member of the team of Major General Edward G. Lansdale. Returning to the Rand Corporation in 1967, Mr. Ellsberg worked on Secretary McNamara's study of U.S. decision-making in Vietnam, now known as the Pentagon Papers. Since April, 1970, he has been a Senior Research Associate in the Center for International Studies at M.I.T

Mr. Ellsberg lives in Cambridge, Massachusetts, with his wife, Patricia; he has two children by a former marriage, Robert and Mary.